Andrew Hussey

Fractured France

A Journey Through a Divided Nation

GRANTA

FRACTURED FRANCE

Also by Andrew Hussey

The Inner Scar: The Mysticism of Georges Bataille

The Game of War: The Life and Death of Guy Debord

The Beast at Heaven's Gate: Georges Bataille
and the Art of Transgression

Paris: The Secret History

The French Intifada: The Long War
Between France and Its Arabs

Speaking East:
The Strange and Enchanted Life of Isidore Isou

To my mum and dad, John and Doreen Hussey, my sister Dawn and especially my wife Carmel who has always been there.

Contents

Map   xi
Introduction: 'Beautiful and Brutal'   1

Part One: Order and Disorder

1. The Road to Roubaix   17
2. The Battle of Angers   45
3. Paris on Edge   57
4. Escaping Reims   73

Part Two: The Unquiet Centre

5. Return to Dijon   93
6. Lyon, 'My Strange City'   123

Part Three: The South

7. Into Provence   161
8. The Enchantment of Manosque   193
9. The 'Wicked City' of Marseille   231

Epilogue

10. The View from Pernety   287

Notes   297
Acknowledgements   305
Image credits   307
Index   309

FRACTURED FRANCE

Introduction

'Beautiful and Brutal'

The first time I caught a glimpse of the new kind of anger that has convulsed France in the past few years was during a street demonstration on the boulevard Raspail. It was the end of October 2018 and I wasn't there to demonstrate, but was simply trying to ride my bike across the road back to my office after lunch. Nor was I expecting any trouble from the demonstrators in this fairly staid part of Paris; they were mainly middle-aged or older and protesting about, among other things, pension reforms.

I was about halfway through the crowd, however, when I noticed gangs of masked youths snaking their way through the demonstration. To me, they looked like white middle-class students. But boys and girls alike, they were all wearing scarves and gas masks, some carrying red and black flags and sporting slingshots. They were obviously primed for a fight with the police. Although I didn't know it then, these were members of the 'Black Bloc'. This is a loose international coalition of anarchists, recognizable by the revolutionary slogans painted on their clothes, who have made their name as experts in urban insurrection during riots in Athens, Hamburg and Genoa. In previous riots, the French press often referred to these youths as *casseurs*, or 'wreckers'.

As I made my way to the crossroads at Denfert-Rochereau, I was alarmed to find the road blocked by armed police with riot shields, who refused to let me pass. Nearby, rubbish bins had been set alight and there was tension in the air. I was now starting to panic slightly, trapped between the police and front-line rioters, who were daring the police to attack. Suddenly, I was battered by a hail of stones and broken paving slabs from the rioters' side; many of them had come with hammers to smash up the pavement and hand out the fragments to their comrades.

The officers responded with flares and tear gas. A canister landed no more than a metre away from me. I had often seen tear gas used in street battles in Algeria and Morocco, as well as France, but I had never been so near to a canister or felt its full effects. The term 'tear gas' makes it sound relatively benign, as if it just makes you cry, but in reality, the canisters contain a toxic chemical that, bizarrely, although banned from war zones by international treaty, can be used on civilians for crowd control in most countries. When the gas first hits, your eyes burn and a searing pain cuts your throat so that you can't breathe. My lungs then tightened and I felt a severe pain in the chest. I truly thought I might die (I am a middle-aged man who already has a heart condition). I kicked the canister back towards the police – not because I wanted revenge but because I had no other choice. A trio of officers lunged towards me, then fell back into line as I spun around on my bike.

I retreated, coughing and spluttering, making my way through the crowd to the relative calm of the corner of the boulevards Raspail and Edgar Quinet. About two hundred metres away, people were sitting at cafe terraces or queuing for ice cream or *crêpes*, oblivious to or just ignoring the fact that a mini-civil war seemed to be happening just down the road. I, however, was in a state of shock, shaking and tearful, sure that I had narrowly missed being seriously injured. But I was equally shocked by what I had seen and one image that lingered in my mind. This was not the youths attacking the law, but a respectable-looking, middle-aged man throwing rocks at the police. He was not alone; other people of roughly the same generation and social class were also hurling stones and insults.

How did it happen that such outwardly ordinary and peaceful people were attacking their own forces of order with such visible hatred? And what did it mean?

In 2014, I published a book called *The French Intifada: The Long War Between France and Its Arabs*. It opened with similar scenes of violence, that time during a riot in March 2007 at the Gare du Nord in Paris. There was, however, one singular difference. The rioters were mainly Black or Arab, dressed in hip-hop fashion: kids from the *banlieues*, the poor suburbs which surround central Paris and which are made up of a largely immigrant population.

The central argument of the book was that the long series of wars between France and its former colonial subjects in North Africa was still unfinished business. The title of the book was deliberately provocative, and many critics, not looking much beyond the title, worried that my argument, especially my description of the rise of antisemitism among the youth of the *banlieues*, was too pessimistic. My French publisher did not dare to use the original title, fearing Islamist reprisals. Horrifyingly, however, the year after publication, my analysis seemed to come true in the most grotesque fashion with the massacres at the *Charlie Hebdo* headquarters and the Bataclan theatre, and the antisemitic nature of much of the Islamist terror in France.

Since that terrible year, French politics and society have veered off in completely new directions. For one thing, although there have been further Islamist attacks, the full-scale confrontation between France and Islamist groups, promised by ISIS among others, never happened. This was no doubt due to the hard-headed police and military response to potential threats and a much-improved intelligence service. Instead of a terrorist insurgency within France – the so-called French intifada – arguably the most important, strangest and most unpredictable phenomenon over the last decade has been the rise of President Emmanuel Macron and the violent opposition to his government from the *gilets jaunes*. This movement started as a peaceful protest against Macron's planned fuel tax rise, with protesters showing their solidarity by wearing the *gilet jaune* (high-visibility yellow jacket) that every French motorist must carry in their car by law in case of breakdown.

What I saw that October afternoon in 2018 did not look like a peaceful protest, however, but more like a violent rebellion. Before long, the violence and protests had intensified, with Paris and other big cities in flames and a level of civil unrest unprecedented since 1968. The violence continued through to early 2020, when the first news of the Covid-19 pandemic put an unexpected stop to political action in France: the final demonstrations, which had until then attracted over three million people, took place in March 2020, when protesters acceded to government warnings over the dangers of Covid. The anger never went away, however: during the long months of lockdown, graffiti appeared all over France, calling for insurrection and damning Macron as 'the President of the Rich'.

At its height, like many protest movements, the rebellion of the *gilets jaunes* attracted parasitic interest from other groups – not only the Black Bloc, but also the far right. But the agendas of these extreme groups were not really what the protests were about. The new reality is that France is an increasingly divided country, with class divisions now hardened by geography as well as economics.

One of those who have commented most astutely on this reshaping of French society is the geographer Christophe Guilluy. He has identified sixteen towns and cities, including Lyon, Bordeaux and especially Paris, which have forged ahead into globalized economic success. He calls them the 'new citadels', where wealth and power are guarded from the world outside, as if they were medieval fortresses. These places can also seem 'like panic rooms' when riots take place and real violence seems to threaten their stability, he says.[1]

Before the pandemic, as the violence of the *gilets jaunes* was growing ever more threatening to the government, Guilluy agreed to meet me on the terrace of a distinctly downmarket cafe called Le Déjazet at the junction of the boulevard du Temple and Place de la République.

The meeting started badly. I was late because my taxi had become increasingly lost in the forest of detours and deviations caused by the roadworks which punctuated the route. As I struggled through the Paris traffic, Guilluy had been nursing a black coffee and a packet of full-strength cigarettes, scrolling down on his smartphone. Nonetheless, when I arrived an hour late, sweating with impatience and urgency, he was friendly and relaxed. 'Nobody ever arrives on time in Paris any more if you use the roads,' he said. 'It's quite impossible unless you are just walking to the corner shops.' Guilluy blamed this on the Socialist Mayor of Paris, Anne Hidalgo, whose environmental policies of banning traffic and creating cycle lanes meant endless and unpredictable roadworks across the city. Eventually, she planned to get rid of dozens of parking spaces and, by planting corridors of trees, turn the Champs-Elysées into a 'fantastic garden'. Taxi drivers, car owners and commuters hated her. She was no more popular with sections of the media. When she was campaigning for the presidency, I attended an international press conference where she simply didn't show up, without apology or explanation. The assembled journalists were furious. 'This is typical,' a Polish colleague said to me. 'She thinks she's the Queen of Paris. She simply doesn't care.'[2]

Guilluy lived close by Le Déjazet in the rapidly gentrifying *quartier* of Belleville. 'You have to stay in your own area as much as you can,' he said. Guilluy waved a cigarette at the traffic circling slowly around Place de la République – less a noble monument to the glory of the Republic than a heaving, bellowing and horribly polluted circus of death. I don't normally smoke these days but took a cigarette in self-defence as much as anything else.

As a geographer, Guilluy's speciality is the economics of real estate. In his day job he acts as a consultant to regional French towns and cities on how to develop housing projects. He has therefore seen first-hand how most development has been *'sauvage'* – unplanned and driven by a free market in real estate prices.

The problem, says Guilluy, is that this kind of urban development is subject to its own economic laws, which lie beyond the control and reach of the French government, either at local or national level. Instead, it is governed by global market forces. There has been no great conspiracy to move the working class out of the cities, he says, but it has happened all the same, and it is still happening. Put simply, many ordinary French people have been priced out of their own communities. Instead, they find themselves living in what he calls 'peripheral France' – places outside the affluent city centres whose distance from them is to be measured not by kilometres but by access to jobs, medical services, good schools, basic transport infrastructure and cultural events. The mirror image of the gentrification of the French cities has been the 'desertification' of much of the rest of the country. Not a day goes by without a news story on the main French TV channel TF1 about the lack of doctors or the closure of schools. Intriguingly, this is happening not just in remote rural areas but in larger villages, medium-sized towns and even in the great cities; these are places whose only bad luck is to be cut off from the thriving metropolitan economies which sit alongside them.

Guilluy explained to me how this process was changing the deepest structures of French society in the twenty-first century. 'Until now, France has always been like a family, divided between the Right and the Left, who might have hated each other but everyone knew their place in society because it had a recognizable tradition. But now, as the cities have changed shape, the old structures have disappeared – literally, cafes and markets where local people lived and worked together have gone. Now, it's about those who can afford to live in a city and those who can't. So instead of class structures within the city, you have something which is more like America – a country of winners and losers, or insiders and outsiders.'

Guilluy insists on his own working-class credentials. His father worked in low-level factories or was unemployed. Guilluy went to an ordinary state school in the 20th arrondissement but says that his real education was in the French Communist Party, which he joined when he was twenty.

'I'm talking about old-school Communists,' he said, 'not the cringing leftism of nowadays. These were men and women who were hard nuts and believed in class warfare, and that the working class had to win. In some ways, these are still the values I have now.' He went on: 'What I am saying about France today is what many on the Left, or so-called Left, do not dare to say, often because many of them have never met a real white working-class person in their lives, at least not socially or as equals. They think of them as *ploucs*.'

This is an old Breton word still used by Parisian hipsters to describe gormless outsiders to the city. Guilluy continued: 'This is how most Parisians think of the *gilets jaunes* when they come to Paris. That is why nobody in the Macron government seems to take them seriously. The *gilets jaunes* are just *ploucs* with no ideology or ideas beyond smashing a few heads.'

The larger truth behind the violence of the *gilets jaunes* is, however, that in the past two decades, French politics has stumbled into a vacuum. This is what had finally led to the Macron government, which sold itself as 'neither Right nor Left' but was instead built on an illusion – that the whole of France could suddenly transform itself into an American-style nation of go-getters and start-ups. The result of this philosophy, alien and impossible for most ordinary French people, was that Macron became the representative of an international club, separate from the people he governed. He was wealthy, a former banker, and from the moment he took power, graffiti appeared all over France describing him as the 'President of the Rich' – a leader whose priority was money and prestige rather than the French people.

'This is our version of Brexit,' I was told by a *gilet jaune* supporter at one of the weekly demonstrations in Paris in late 2019. He too described himself as 'neither Right nor Left' but had come to the demonstration in Paris to express his disgust at being left behind and ignored, mired in debt and poverty no matter how hard he worked (he was a dairy farmer). He explained his support for the cause of the *gilets jaunes*: 'We are losing faith in democracy because whichever way we vote, nothing ever changes.'

This is, of course, an echo of the rhetoric of Marine Le Pen's far-right Rassemblement National (National Rally or RN), previously the Front National (National Front or FN). This does not mean that France is inexorably on the way to a far-right government. But it does explain why democracy in present-day France isn't working.

In an interview given in late 2021 for *Le Figaro*, Christophe Guilluy described how the democratic model perpetuates itself by raising the spectre of a Fascist victory, which so far has never arrived but means that people preserve the likes of Macron or similar technocrats in power. He wrote: 'There is no loyalty toward Macronism. Only a vote out of fear.'[3]

This is undoubtedly the case. It is also my view that this political paralysis has been driven by a new kind of class or tribe which has evolved in the new citadels. They are sometimes described as 'Bobos' – an abbreviation of 'bourgeois bohemians' or '*bourgeois bohèmes*'. This term was popularized by the American conservative commentator David Brooks at the turn of the century to describe the urban yuppies who have since mutated into contemporary hipsters.[4] The Bobos are a political caucus encompassing the professional classes – academics, journalists, media workers and so on – who think of themselves as liberal left but who are entitled and superior in manner. They are described by Guilluy as '*la gauche hashtag*'.

Their policies do nothing for the French working class – whose problems are low wages, job insecurity and poor social housing – but they are intent on showing a virtuous face to the wider world. The politics of the Bobos are living proof of George Orwell's criticism of the metropolitan left of his day – that it is perfectly possible to be at the same time a revolutionary and a snob. The protests of the past few years contain a message from the working class: that we are here, and we will not go away; the politics of the new citadels is not our politics and that has to change.

I originally set out to write this book in 2017. This was a particularly significant turning point, as French political life would be reconfigured with the elections that year. I was still travelling, writing and researching when the Covid-19 pandemic began to properly hit France. In February 2020, I was in Marseille, taking notes as I explored the newly renovated areas and the housing estates which stood alongside the old city centre, and talking to people who lived there. This is a city I have always loved, ever since I first went there in the 1980s, when it was seedy, violent and corrupt but also driven by a rebellious energy which expressed itself in football and music as well as crime and politics. Since then, Marseille claims to have cleaned up its act, but there are still areas of the city controlled by armed gangs, where it is foolish to venture alone without a fixer or guide who can steer you through the labyrinth. With its elegant Corniche and views across the Mediterranean, all in full view of the bleak tower blocks of northern Marseille, no other city in France captures quite as neatly the physical contradiction that marks all of the country: that it is at once beautiful and brutal.

It was a black irony that when I heard the news of the pandemic I was staying near the Plage des Catalans, 'the beach of the Catalans', in the 7th arrondissement of Marseille, a short walk from the city centre. This beach is named after a band of opportunistic Catalan fishermen who settled there in 1720, believing that most of the population of Marseille had been wiped out by the Great Plague, which had arrived in the city that year (the plague did, in fact, kill 100,000 people).

When I returned home to Paris, talk of the pandemic had become the soundtrack to everyday life, growing louder and more frightening every week, reaching a crescendo in April 2020, when lockdown came into force. Obviously, I would now have to adapt my plans.

Lockdowns, curfews and travel restrictions inevitably determined my itineraries in the early days of writing the book. My travels and research were necessarily driven by hazard, encounters and digressions, rather than the theories or statistical analyses of a professional geographer like Guilluy and his distinguished predecessors, so-called human geographers such as Fernand Braudel and Jean Brunhes.

France is a large and complicated country, and it is impossible to make sense of it without making journeys through time as well as its territories. This is why, although the book has been written very much in the moment, and shifts according to given circumstances, history is never too far behind. This includes my own personal history, recounted necessarily in fragments. Writing about my own life in France, which started properly in 1984, when I moved to Lyon for full-time study, begs several questions. Why did I come here? Why was I drawn to France? What did I find here and why did I stay? There are no simple or easy answers to these questions. The recent journeys I have made in France between 2015 and 2023 described in this book do not provide a complete account, but they have been a way of interrogating myself about France in the present and the past, about what it means and what it has meant to me over the years. If nothing else, I have also been a witness to forty years of change in the country, years which take in the end of one century and the beginning of another.

This has been a period of massive change, as convulsive and

significant as any in French history. France has always been a divided country – class, politics and history have always been sources of ferocious and sometimes violent argument here – but during this period, it seems to have grown even more divided in a way that is quite unprecedented. More precisely, since the Revolution of 1789, throughout the various tribulations of war, defeat and occupation, France has always been held together, sometimes tenuously, by a universalist culture. In the early twenty-first century, it seems to me that this cultural ideal is in danger and that the country is in danger of fracturing or splintering into fragments. This is the second, larger theme which is examined on my journeys in contemporary France, where I am always casting a look backwards, towards my own history here, and to the larger and deeper history of the country.

I do not drive, so my journeys through France – before the pandemic and then as it took hold and sporadically eased – were made using local transport, sometimes walking or cycling, staying in local accommodation, eating and drinking in local cafes, and speaking to the people who live there. Of course, I also spoke to politicians, journalists and cultural commentators. But my aim was to uncover the past and present of the culture of everyday France, which is invisible to most tourists or academics (or academic tourists). This is a culture made by the ordinary people – usually called *les classes populaires* and sometimes *les classes moyennes* – who drink beer, love Johnny Hallyday, holiday in *les campings*, keep pigeons, go line-dancing, watch Saturday night *variété* shows, and enjoy themselves, often against a background of unemployment and poverty. It has always been my view that it is the ordinary people – working or middle class, it makes no difference – who, with their jokes, popular culture and natural sense of disrespect for authority, tell the real story of any nation, despite being generally inaudible to the metropolitan classes.

My travels were inevitably often in the footsteps of many other

English-speaking writers, who down through the centuries have travelled through the country. One of the most forensic of these travellers was Arthur Young – an English agriculturist who from 1788 wrote a book called *Travels through France During the Years 1787, 1788, 1789*, documenting the misery in the French countryside that was invisible to the court at Versailles. Young described France as a nation of 'Landes – landes – landes' ('wastes, wastes, wastes'), 'a country possessing nothing but privilege and poverty'. He saw the coming Revolution before anyone in France did and stayed on during the years of shocking brutality.

Young finally made three long journeys through France, expressing sympathy for but also incomprehension at the simmering violence that he encountered, especially outside the great urban centres. Many British travellers through France have also often expressed fear of what they saw as a lawless country: in the seventeenth century, the diarist Thomas Coryate, travelling from Lyon to the Savoy, noted in his *Coryate's Crudities, Hastily Gobled Up in Five Moneths Travells in France* ... the many corpses hanging from trees along the routes and no sign of the law. Coryate carried a sword at all times.[5]

I have also taken inspiration from those English-speaking visitors to France who have truly loved the place and its history, so much so that they themselves have become part of the story of France as insider-outsiders, invisible spectators to history. Chief among these are the Oxford historian Richard Cobb, a visionary who understood the primacy of every detail in France; M. F. K. Fisher, who is still educating me even now about French food; and the Halifax-born artist Ralph Rumney, who taught me how to understand the art and philosophy of the twentieth-century avant-gardes.

Although I have enjoyed and learned much from their writing and observations, I have also been aware I could never exactly find what these earlier writers had seen in France. But what I could do, following their examples and sometimes their maps, was to seek out the shifting political and cultural atmosphere of the France I have known.

    I began my travels in the north.

Part One
ORDER AND DISORDER

1

The Road to Roubaix

Le musée de la piscine

Although I had never been there, as soon as I got off the train in Roubaix, in the far north-eastern corner of France, I felt at home.

This was in the early spring of 2017, as France was gearing up for the presidential election which would eventually bring Emmanuel Macron to power. I had been spending time in Lille, a city which likes to think of itself as the cultural capital of northern France. With its polished and stylish streets, chic restaurants and bars, and train connections to London and Marseille, and it being only an hour away from Paris, Lille certainly has every reason for its self-confidence. It is very much the kind of 'new citadel' identified by Christophe Guilluy, a fact reflected in its property prices and international atmosphere.

Roubaix is altogether a different proposition. When you get to Roubaix from Lille, after twenty minutes in a run-down, grubby slow train or tramway, it feels like a different, distant place. The train station is scruffy and there is also little sense of the usual Gallic civic pride; the stroll down the main avenue towards the Grand Place is drab and quiet, unlike most French towns. Once a thriving industrial area, the sense of unity that once defined it has splintered as its main industries have declined and withered away.

In the late nineteenth century, at the height of the French Industrial Revolution, in the surrounding Nord-Pas de Calais region the main industry was coal mining, around Valenciennes, Douai and Maubeuge. Roubaix, by contrast, imported wool from Australia, New Zealand, South Africa and South America, and with all the swagger of the age, the town claimed for itself the title of a world capital of the woollen industry, bested only by Bradford and the mills of South Lancashire. Roubaix was known locally as 'the city of a thousand chimneys', with 267 factory chimneys towering over its streets. The Hôtel de Ville in the centre of town, built by no less than Victor Laloux, architect of the Gare d'Orsay in Paris, is a grand monument to this period in the town's history and contains a frieze which depicts all aspects of the wool trade.

From the nineteenth century onwards, Roubaix had been at the heart of an urban conurbation called LRT, after the three interconnected towns of Lille–Roubaix–Tourcoing, whose populations thought of themselves as rivals but also equals, brought together by shared dialects and an industrial sprawl that crisscrossed between France and Belgium. The national border is so serpentine that you can still find yourself drinking in a bar in France and at the end of the same street buying cigarettes in Belgium (the cigarettes are cheaper in Belgium). There are still Flemish-speakers on the French side of the border. LRT is a thin strip of land officially called the Département du Nord

(Department of the North). This tiny area is also the fourth most densely populated part of France after Paris, Lyon and Marseille.

You catch no sight of this density as you leave the station of Roubaix. Instead, you meet the rue de l'Alma, a bleak and empty space littered with shuttered shops, dead warehouses and businesses made out of the small and intricate red-brick patterns typical of the north of France. The streets are punctuated with wasteland and graffiti, and many seem to lead literally nowhere. The place feels abandoned in a way that reminded me immediately of towns like Leigh, Bolton and Wigan in the 1980s, towns I knew well from growing up in the north-west of England. These were places which had effectively been left to rot as Margaret Thatcher reshaped the British economy and moved the source of labour and profit to the south. As I strolled around the area, the soundtrack in my head was not French but rather Joy Division or the Fall, music made out of the shadows and ugliness of the post-industrial landscape.

I had come to Roubaix because it is officially one of the poorest towns in France. It is also, according to most media reports, one of the most troubled. The *quartier de l'Alma*, the area which extends to your left as you follow the rue de l'Alma, has for a long time been a byword across France for drugs and violence. For the past decade, there have been several attempts at urban renewal, none of which have really taken hold. One scheme, set up in March 2018, was to sell off dilapidated *corons* (the French word for the clusters or villages of terraced houses popular in the north of France) for a euro. The idea had been inspired by a similar scheme in my home town of Liverpool. The problem was that, despite generous grants from the local government, and some successes at restoring these formerly handsome properties, nobody wanted to live in an area where – at least according to media reports – the main industry was dealing in drugs, and you could get knifed going to a corner shop.

This plan was followed up in 2019 by the establishment of

a *Brigade de Reconquête Républicaine* (Brigade of Republican Reconquest), a dedicated group of fifteen to thirty police officers whose job was to focus on crime in a designated area (there are about twenty of these groups across France).[1] The word '*Reconquête*' is a loaded one, evoking, at least for the North African population, the Spanish word '*Reconquista*', which describes the long war to drive the Arab and Muslim population out of Spain, and indeed out of Europe, culminating in the fall of the Muslim-held city of Granada in 1492. This word is still used in right-wing discourse in contemporary Spain, and I was to later hear it used in France with the same connotations. It was hard to believe that the choice of this word by the police authorities was innocent.

The presence of the brigade was successful in bringing crime more firmly under control, but the police presence also irritated local residents. Many of the small businesses which dealt illegally in contraband (cigarettes mainly) from across the Belgian border felt especially squeezed. The gangs who controlled the drugs trade were also feeling the pressure. Since then, tensions have been rising fast, and even at the height of the lockdown in 2021, police patrols were attacked by fireworks and there were alleged gunshots.

For all the recent attempts at regeneration, a short stroll down the rue de l'Alma, even in mid-afternoon, can be an eerie experience. Everybody seems to know that you shouldn't be there and suspects that you are either a police officer or perhaps, like me, a snooping writer.

Roubaix has a large immigrant population, with people mainly from North Africa but also from more than sixty other countries. The original North African population of the north of France came from the Rif Mountains of Morocco after the Second World War, when there were severe labour shortages in French heavy industry. The main industry in the Rif, apart from the production of hashish and the cultivation of olives, was phosphate mining, and it was an easy shift for these migrants to work alongside French miners, known as '*les gueules noires*' ('black faces') because their faces were always encrusted with coal dust. The Moroccans and *les gueules noires* were connected by hard work and low pay, and racial tensions were fairly low. This was also due in part to the relative ease with which France relinquished its protectorate in Morocco in 1956 while fighting a cruel and bloody war against insurgents in the neighbouring French-controlled territory of Algeria.

More recently, Roubaix has gained a reputation as a refuge for illegal migrants making for Calais and then the UK, and as a hotbed of Islamist radicalization. In March 2016, in the conservative news weekly *Valeurs actuelles*, a journalist called Rachel Binhas described Roubaix as '*le Molenbeek français*'. She was referring to the suburb of Brussels which had been home to several of the terrorists and sympathizers involved in the November 2015 attacks on Paris, which killed 130 people, including eighty-nine at the Bataclan theatre. Her comparison was based on the high level of Muslim immigration to Roubaix, signified by seven mosques replacing the old mill towers and, even more disturbingly from Binhas's point of view, the fact that seventy per cent of Roubaix's butcher shops were now halal, effectively wiping out the traditional *boucherie et charcuterie*, one of the staples of everyday French life. A few years earlier, the *New York Times* had described Roubaix in glowing terms as a model of multicultural integration. Binhas found the opposite: a town where Frenchness and French values were being replaced by those of Islam, accompanied by rising levels of crime.[2]

My aim in Roubaix in 2017 was to find out how much of this account was true. Later, as I made further trips to the town and grew to know the place and feel at home there, I also wanted to find out what it meant to come from Roubaix in the wider context of French society. Roubaix's bad reputation is not a new phenomenon. The north of France has always been very separate from the rest of the country – poorer, more desperate, and despised as a territory of a backward, angry working class. As the industrial base that was once the mainstay of life and community here has collapsed into ruins in recent decades, the people of Roubaix, and other towns like it in the region, have been abandoned and cast adrift, cut off from the busy, globalized life of the metropolitan centres (including nearby Lille). This was, I thought, as good as any place to start looking at how the French class system was structured and how it worked. Or how it didn't.

The original inhabitants of Roubaix, and indeed the rest of the north of France and French-speaking parts of Belgium, are commonly called *ch'tis* or *chtimis*. The term is an onomatopoeic description of the northern French dialect, in which the soft pronunciation of '*c'est*' is turned into '*ché*', so that a phrase like '*c'est toi*' becomes '*ché ti*', and finally '*ch'ti*'. The term entered popular usage during the First World War, when soldiers from other parts of France came into close contact with their comrades in the north.

Traditionally the *ch'ti* has been a figure of fun in French folklore – good-hearted but a bit primitive, with a taste for chips, beer, *genièvre* (Dutch gin) and *café à la chicorée* (coffee made with chicory). In recent years, there have been attempts to take back the *ch'ti* identity as a source of pride – the name has been given to beers and even a cultural magazine. The *ch'tis* are especially proud of the novelist Maxence Van der Meersch, a native of Roubaix, a lawyer and a novelist, who, in literary terms, never strayed from his native territory and in 1936 won the Prix Goncourt for his novel *L'Empreinte du dieu* (The Footprint of God), a gloomy tale of a young Belgian peasant girl married to a brutish husband and who inexorably and inevitably comes to a tragic end.

At best, the metropolitan view of the *ch'tis* remains patronizing. The most prominent example of this attitude is to be found in the 2008 comedy *Bienvenue chez les Ch'tis* (translated as *Welcome to the Sticks* for the English-speaking world), directed by and starring the comedian Dany Boon. This is one of the most successful French films in French cinema history. It is a simple enough story. A post office manager living in the comfortable south of France is sent by his employer to live and work in the '*nord*'. What follows is a series of goonish misadventures, during which the southerner discovers that his fellow countrymen may be daft but they are loveable too, despite their crude ways.³

At its worst, the metropolitan attitude to the *ch'tis* can amount to a form of contempt akin to racism. In 2008, at a cup final football match between Paris Saint-Germain (PSG) and the northern team Lens, the Parisian supporters who called themselves the Boulogne Boys unfurled a banner which read '*Pédophiles, chômeurs, consanguins: bienvenue chez les ch'tis*' ('Paedophiles, unemployed, inbreds: welcome to the *ch'tis*'). Eventually, five lads from the Boulogne Boys were arrested and put on trial for 'incitement to hatred'.

In my local *quartier* in Paris, with my English accent and fluent French, I have often been taken for a *ch'ti*. As the trial of the Boulogne Boys unfolded, and even the French government began taking an interest in the affair, people in local bars, assuming that I was from northern France and therefore offended, told me that it was just typical Parisian black humour and that *ch'tis* were too dumb to understand it, and not to take it seriously. Nobody I spoke to from the north found this funny. This was when I first heard the newly coined term '*proleophobie*', a new word in French which describes the contempt and even hatred that white working-class people of the north of France feel has been turned towards them.

Probably the most prominent alleged *proleophobe* in France is the novelist Edouard Louis, a young northern writer who rose to fame with his first novel *En finir avec Eddy Bellegueule*, which was an immediate bestseller in France in 2014 (the book was translated into English as *The End of Eddy* in 2018 and was also an international hit). This book gives an account of the adolescence of Eddy Bellegueule (Louis's real name) in the northern town of Hallencourt, near Abbeville. Eddy is gay, bullied at school and brought up in a severely dysfunctional family and society, where nearly everybody is racist, homophobic, alcoholic or obese, or all of these things at once.

The book was highly acclaimed in the metropolitan literary press but there were other, dissenting voices, especially those who knew the north and claimed that he was laying it all on a bit thick and for effect, that the book conformed to every middle-class left-wing prejudice about the northern working classes. Louis's angriest critics came from his home village of Hallencourt. In 2022, after the television channel France 3 broadcast a film about Louis's youth, a reporter from the local newspaper, *Le Journal d'Abbeville*, went back to Hallencourt to speak to those who had known him growing up. They all – including his godmother – fiercely denounced his work as lies and a filthy slur on their poor but hard-working community.

I met up with Louis in Paris on a bone-chilling evening in late January 2024. Our meeting was at the Le Select cafe in Montparnasse, which has been here since 1924 and is one of the most famous literary cafes on the Left Bank in Paris.[4]

'I feel at home here,' Louis said to me, sipping at a *grog au rhum* to warm himself up. I expressed mild surprise, having expected the young iconoclast (he was then thirty-two) to favour the more fashionable drinking dens of the Bastille or Marais districts. 'I know it is old-fashioned,' he went on, 'but that is why I like this cafe. It is like a monument to French literature. Everybody has been here, and writers, publishers and politicians still come, so it is also part of the present. It is a place where I can meet friends easily and connect with the world.'

I told him that I had once seen Patti Smith at a nearby table, wolfing down Le Select's famous (and highly alcoholic) *baba au rhum* all on her own, and he laughed. 'You wouldn't see that in many other places,' he said. Another reason he liked Le Select, he confided, was because he lived nearby in one of the wealthiest and most fashionable *quartiers* of Paris, and there are so many famous customers that he was unlikely to be noticed or bothered by fans. (In 2024, Louis was very much a public figure in France, easily recognizable from his frequent appearances in the French media in publications such as *Les Inrockuptibles*, the bible of French hipsters. He even once guest-edited the magazine and appeared on the cover, confirming his status as a cultural avatar moving in the coolest of Parisian circles.)

Edouard Louis's sense of ease in his surroundings did nothing to counter my suspicion that he was a phoney, no more than a social climber trading on his working-class past to make it big in Paris. This actually made him a stock figure in the French literary canon. I thought of Balzac's Eugène de Rastignac or Flaubert's Frédéric Moreau – smart provincial chancers on the make in the capital. I also thought of Emmanuel Macron, another bright lad from the provincial north making a name for himself in the big city.

The first question I asked him was why should we trust him: how did we know that he was telling the truth about his life and the lives of the people he was writing about? 'I don't think it really matters,' he replied. 'The truth of a text lies in its creation. It doesn't matter how that truth finally appears. We have now in French this genre called 'autofiction', which some use to describe Annie Ernaux's work. Annie is a friend of mine and we have discussed the genre. The emotional truth is more important than names or facts. That is what you set out to find as a writer, and that is where the risk lies because it's frightening what you find out about yourself. But that is what you have to do. There is no choice.'

This was, I thought, a sophisticated but slippery answer, clearly well rehearsed and probably delivered many times before.

But it was also kind of accurate. Truth and fiction are inevitably always blurred in Louis's writing, as in his life. When we met, he had no trace of a northern accent, and he had not only changed his name from Eddy Bellegueule (a kind of comedy name in France) to the more stately Edouard Louis, but along the way he had also changed his clothes, his weight, and even his physical gestures, and had his teeth fixed; he had, in fact, abandoned everything that connected him with the past.

He told the story of how this had happened in another work of autofiction called *Changer: méthode* (translated into English as *Change: A Novel*), published in 2021. I found this book a far more compelling read than *The End of Eddy*, picking up where that left off, following Louis's journey deeper into the French class system. It takes him from his home village of Hallencourt to a *lycée* in Amiens, where he works in a theatre and makes a new friend, Elena, who introduces him to art and literature and middle-class manners. He leaves Amiens for university in Paris, abandoning Elena, who loves him and dreams of a future with him. He takes up with a new best friend, the real-life philosopher and university professor Didier Eribon (an actual close friend of Louis's), who is a former associate of Michel Foucault and a prominent figure on the Left Bank. Eribon, like Louis, grew up alienated and gay in a provincial working-class town. After hearing Eribon give a lecture on his early life, Louis begs him to help him change his life. Eribon becomes a mentor and introduces Louis to the glamorous artistic milieu of Paris and the radical left intelligentsia, who furnish Louis with new political opinions. While he is building this new life, Louis supports himself financially by selling his body to older men, which he finds depressing and degrading.

Ten years on from *The End of Eddy*, in *Change* Louis no longer plays the victim and is unafraid to reveal his own casual nastiness towards his parents and his friends. This was what particularly intrigued me. *Change* is less a misery memoir in the vein of *The*

End of Eddy, but rather more like *The Talented Mr Ripley* as told by Ripley himself. Intriguingly, Louis unabashedly describes himself in this book as a 'class defector', always bent on betrayal. Sharper still, he described himself to me as 'the class enemy' of his parents. What did he mean by this?

'Changing class does not make you happy,' he said. 'That is what this book is about and that is what I have discovered. Instead, it just makes you melancholy. You know that you do not belong to the class you have left and, yes, I feel that I have betrayed my family. But even here [he gestured along the bar of Le Select], I can say that I am at home, but really I know that I do not belong. I am always running to catch up with ideas, books I haven't read. I still don't understand food, or painting. Even if people say that they are left wing, if they do not come from where I come from, they can be sympathetic but that is not the same thing as understanding. Sometimes I feel that I am trapped in exile, and always will be for the rest of my life.'

As he said this, he was less fluent, less composed, but what he was saying was true. He now seemed brittle and fragile. Suddenly, and against all my previous prejudices, I started to sympathize with him. I saw something of myself, thirty-odd years ago, in Louis. At thirty-two, I was not a successful writer or famous or well off, and certainly couldn't have afforded a drink in Le Select. But I did know the loneliness and discomfort that comes from shifting your class position and how, over the years, that never really goes away. I saw in Louis myself: the clumsy working-class autodidact, unsure of how to use or pronounce certain words, and often lost in a labyrinth of cultural references.

This was not helped in my case because I had chosen to leave my working-class life in Liverpool to make another life in a foreign country in a foreign language. I had loved France and French culture from an early age but I came to live here partly because I thought it was a way to sidestep the British class system, which made England feel like a prison to me. I thought I could do this by entering another culture from the outside, as a neutral with no socio-economic baggage. Also, I believed naively that France was as classless as its republican ideals. The longer I stayed here, the more clearly I saw that although the class system in France was different from that in England, and that I was an outsider to it, it was still a hierarchy of castes. The political affiliation to the Left or the Right did not matter: it was about style, manners, background.

The expert on these matters is Pierre Bourdieu, the French social theorist known for his idea that social capital is based as much on cultural background and parental contacts as on what is in your bank account. I was not surprised, therefore, to learn that Louis had edited and published a book of essays on Bourdieu in 2013. He had clearly imbibed Bourdieu's lesson. If nothing else, *Change* is a manual for the would-be social climber following the Bourdieu model – that changing how you appear to the world can actually change your world.

I was at first taken aback, however, by Louis's admiration for Richard Hoggart, the English academic whose classic *The Uses of Literacy*, published in 1957, provided a blueprint for how young British intellectuals from working-class backgrounds – the post-war grammar school generation – could attain social mobility while holding on to their roots and background. Hoggart became fashionable in sociological circles in France after May 1968, when *The Uses of Literacy* was translated into French as *La Culture du Pauvre* (The Culture of the Poor). Although distinctly out of fashion in Anglo-American sociological circles, Hoggart remains an important figure in France for his idea that the key to not being trapped as you move between classes is 'authenticity', to believe in the value of a local, organic working-class culture that is not prey to manipulation from mass media and, ultimately, capitalism.

That is a notion that Louis's mentor Didier Eribon – no doubt the source of Louis's admiration for Hoggart – has written about at length (Annie Ernaux is also a Hoggart fan), and it is an idea that still fires up Edouard Louis. 'I love Hoggart because he does not hide the truth,' Louis said. 'Capitalism is the enemy. But it is not easy to confront. Changing class is never easy either, and does not guarantee happiness. It can lead you away from an authentic life. That is what my book says. There are many marginalized groups in society, but I think class defectors are a kind of hidden minority. Perhaps that will never change. But there is always the sense of living a double exile. You do not and probably will never properly belong in the class you move to, but at the same time you can never go back to the life that you have left behind, and this can make you melancholy, even if you wanted to leave it all behind.'

This is precisely what the narrator feels at the end of *Change*, giving the book its terrible twist. He has risen to a better place in society but feels a painful nostalgia for the abandoned world of his childhood. He feels remorse, too, for all those he has betrayed, especially Elena, whose mother accuses him of 'stealing' a cultural identity from them.

This is all a long way from the life and culture of the north of France, based as it is on tradition and family ties. Louis told me that he never went back there, he didn't want to ever return. He had given a book reading in Lille once and hated it. His audience had given him a hard time because he was writing and speaking about the north but had lost his accent. 'I am not a *ch'ti*,' he said. 'I never wanted to be that. It wasn't just that I didn't belong in the north, but I didn't want to belong either. This was not my world, and I knew that even when I was very young.' Did this make him, then, not just the 'class enemy' but 'a class traitor', someone who had not only turned his back on his family but turned against his own community and culture? He was silent for a while. 'I suppose so, yes,' he responded finally. 'The north made me but I don't know how I feel about that. I want to think that I have no nostalgia, but sometimes I do. I hate myself for these feelings. But traitors don't go back. They can't go back.'

Edouard Louis is right about this, and it is this new cruel, self-lacerating self-knowledge that makes him an increasingly interesting writer as he seems to be moving away from his victimhood. But for all that Louis has left the north and feels ill at ease when he goes back, there is still a real working-class culture which thrives there and needs no metropolitan validation. Louis's problem was that, blinded by the traumas of his childhood and adolescence, real, imagined or exaggerated, he just couldn't see it.

The rest of France also has a problem with how it sees or imagines the north of France. It is true enough that the north has its problems. If you spend any time at all there, whether in the cities, towns or hamlets, you will see a specifically northern variant of poverty – the kind described by Edouard Louis, with families lost to long-term unemployment now that heavy industry has moved on. There is also alcoholism and drug addiction, and there are severe racial and religious tensions between the old, white working class, now abandoned and disenfranchised, and the newly installed communities of immigrants. Added to this, there is plenty of homophobia and racism to go around. But these are not all problems unique to the north of France. Most importantly, alongside these social issues, you will also quickly sense a playful pride in northern identity. 'We are *ch'tis*,' I was told by Bernard, an amiable fifty-something boozer drinking Leffe beer in an *estaminet* (tavern) in the centre of Roubaix. 'It means something to be a *ch'ti*. We've survived wars, occupation, the coal mines, the lot. We are working class, but we are not serfs. We know how to survive. We never give in to anyone. That's our strength.'

Roubaix is mostly pitied or feared by the rest of France. But I quickly found that it is surprisingly easy to have a good time there. The people are open and inviting, often witty and self-deprecating, the food and beer are good, and there is a very working-class commitment to enjoying yourself no matter what. Above all, there is a bracing lack of snobbery, mostly because there is nothing to be snobbish about.

'If you live in Roubaix it is hard to feel connected to the rest of France,' I was told by Hélène Robillard, a junior civil servant who worked at the town council. 'But then again we don't care. We don't need to be connected to the rest of France. We are proud of who we are.'

I ran into Hélène and her friends and comrades one afternoon in the spring of 2017 as I walked down avenue Jean Lebas in Roubaix towards the Grand Place. This avenue had clearly once been the proud entrance to the city and was lined with imposing nineteenth-century buildings, some with creamy baroque facades, others in stolid red brick, once the houses and offices of the merchants who had made the town rich. Now many of them were sporting 'To Rent' signs or just simply lifeless and abandoned. There were a handful of forlorn shops and restaurants – mostly cheap pizza and kebab joints.

Hélène's friends were a group of young women merrily banging tambourines, blowing whistles and chanting slogans outside one of the offices of the local council. They saw me making notes and so they called me over.

They were a friendly and lively bunch. They were taking an extended lunch break to strike against low pay and work conditions (long hours, no promotions) at the council. They were having a laugh, too. I told them that I was in Roubaix to find out what it felt like to live in one of the poorest towns in France.

Hélène was pushed forward by her mates on the grounds that she could speak English, but she was too shy to use her English skills, so she told me in French that she didn't have a bad word to say about Roubaix. The people from the town knew they were poor and were looked down on by those who had done well in Lille or Paris, but she and her pals didn't care.

One of them said, 'That's just propaganda from the well-off people who don't live here or know what we're like.' Others joined in: 'That's it! All northerners are thick and racist. That's just another form of prejudice actually, that we're just *ploucs*, dumb hicks, who don't like outsiders.' I asked what they thought of the high immigrant population of Roubaix and whether there were tensions. 'Of course there are tensions,' one woman said, 'Every single town in France, even the most *bourgeois* places, has difficult *quartiers*, crime and stuff like that. That's just modern life, isn't it? But actually we're proud that we have so many people from all over the world here.'

I asked the women about the film *Chez Nous*. The English-language version of the film is called *This Is Our Land*, but the title really comes from the chant of '*On est chez nous!*' ('We are in our own home!'), then popular with supporters of Marine Le Pen. This had been released only a few weeks earlier and was playing to packed houses across France. Set in a fictionalized town much like Roubaix, it tells the story of a young woman, Pauline Duhez, a nurse who is seduced into joining the FN and standing for a seat on the council. As she learns the party's true positions, she becomes disillusioned and angry. The film ends with Pauline returning to the socialist values of her unemployed father, a former steelworker, culminating in a family trip to watch a game featuring the local football team Lens.

When I was chatting about the film to a young academic in Paris, a self-proclaimed leftist from a privileged background, he remarked sourly that its end was 'problematic' because Pauline had returned to the old-fashioned patriarchal values of the *ch'tis*. The women protesting with Hélène did not see it that way. They were all determinedly anti-FN, and those who had seen the film were full of enthusiasm. 'It is our real life,' said one of them, laughing. 'It shows our true values – not fascism, but football, beer and chips.'

Later, back in Paris, I interviewed Emilie Dequenne, the

actress who plays Pauline in *Chez Nous*, and the film's director, Lucas Belvaux. I had already met and interviewed Emilie a few years earlier just after she had made a film called *A perdre la raison* (*Our Children* in English), a tough film based on the real-life story of a mother who kills her five children. Then we had met in a tatty cafe in a poor part of the north of Paris, where she lives. She liked the neighbourhood because it reminded her of her background – she grew up on the Franco-Belgian border (she is actually Belgian) – and a great deal of our conversation, irrelevant to the interview, was about what a unique place the area was and is: always poor and disconnected from the rest of France (and, for that matter, the well-heeled parts of Belgium). Nonetheless, like her *quartier* in the north of France, she felt at home in the rough and ready atmosphere.

This time we met at the production company's office just off the rue du Faubourg Saint-Honoré in the swish heart of Paris – a corner of the city that couldn't be further removed from the streets of Roubaix. Emilie was unchanged from our last encounter – open and friendly – and I learned that Lucas Belvaux was also intimately connected with the region and the northern working-class life of the Franco-Belgian border. Both of them still have family ties there. I asked them whether the FN really presented a political threat to the region.

'The film is not ambiguous,' Dequenne said. 'It is clearly a warning about being seduced by the far right. But it does have lots of different ambiguities. The main character, Pauline, is a good person and not stupid. She wants to help people. She thinks that this is not the case with the main political parties. So she is attracted by a party that seems to care.'

I told them about my encounter with Hélène Robillard and her pals in Roubaix, and that for all its poverty it was not necessarily a natural home for the far right.

'I agree,' Belvaux said. 'But the film is also a warning. We are not yet a Fascist country, but I do fear that this could happen.

There are big social and cultural divisions in France. Not everybody who will vote for the FN is a bad person, but there are many angry people in this country who feel hurt and damaged. When this is the case, fascism can arrive much more quickly than you think.'

On my next visit to Roubaix in April 2017, I put this to Jean-Pierre Legrand, the then leader of the FN there. He shook his head. 'The problem is with the word "Fascist", and the fact the people do not really know what it means. We are a legitimate, democratic party with views that people either agree or disagree with. But all we want is a stable France, and we don't have that now – there is too much insecurity, crime – whole areas of French towns like Roubaix where you cannot go. What we in the FN want above all is order. So do most other intelligent people in France.'

Our conversation took place in the cafe of the Musée de la Piscine. This is quite an extraordinary place, built in the nineteenth century as a showcase for the textile industry. Since being redesigned and reopened in 2001, it has been the main source of civic pride in Roubaix, an elegant homage to the city and the region past and present. Most striking of all is an elaborate swimming pool that opened for local workers in 1935, which is an elegant mix of art deco and neo-classical architecture.

Legrand was accompanied by Astrid Leplat, a young woman who was a *conseillère municipale*, a town councillor. They had both been at the centre of a controversy in May 2015, accused of having lied or invented stories about crime in Roubaix for the benefit of a visiting Parisian journalist from *Valeurs actuelles*. Their chief accusers were the journalists of *La Voix du Nord*, the best-selling daily newspaper across the north of France. *La Voix* has a long and distinguished history. It began life as an underground journal in April 1941, with a first run of sixty-five issues, dedicated to the support of the French Resistance. These days, its readership is just short of a million people. Its political line has always been roughly centrist but always firmly on the side of the working classes of the region. When the argument blew up with the FN, Marine Le Pen denounced the newspaper as propaganda for the Socialist Party, accusing it of trying to sabotage the FN in the north.

We drank coffee and chatted in the empty but pleasant cafe of the Musée. Legrand and Leplat were easy and agreeable company. I told them that I was not, nor could ever be, a supporter of their party or their opinions, but I did want to see the world as they saw it and understand the reasoning behind their views. They happily accepted this, and neither of them held back or sweetened their opinions for me.

As the conversation moved from pleasantries about the region and grew more political, Legrand became pessimistic. He wished Marine Le Pen well but feared that in the second round, the mainstream parties would gang up and back whoever her opponent was in the coming elections (this was indeed precisely what happened). 'This is what always happens,' he said. 'This is why so-called French democracy is actually a form of dictatorship. You can never really get your hands on power. It belongs to an elite, people like Emmanuel Macron.'

Legrand, who was now sixty-nine years old, had been a supporter of the FN for decades. He smiled a lot and was witty, but he also liked talking tough, like the hard-headed factory boss he used to be. He admired the way that Marine Le Pen had re-invented the party, shedding some of the old-school neo-Nazi trappings. But he was also faithful to, maybe even nostalgic for, the old FN of her father, Jean-Marie Le Pen, who had reached the second round of the 2002 Presidential Election before losing to the centre-right Jacques Chirac. I asked him if he was not really a democrat but, like Le Pen *père*, basically a Fascist. 'I am not afraid of being called a Fascist, or even a Gaullist,' he said.

'But all I really believe in is order and authority. And that is what France needs now.'

Astrid Leplat talked about the charisma of Marine Le Pen. She had only met her once but was obviously flattered and starstruck that Marine had known her name. 'She is impressive,' said Leplat. 'It's hard to describe, but she has a kind of star quality. You can easily see her as a true leader of a new France. Even as a leader of Europe, of France in the world.'

Of course, Astrid Leplat was exactly the kind of candidate that the FN wanted to promote in its new post-toxic era. For one thing, she was quite self-effacing, the very opposite of the pushy media-savvy politician. She said modestly that her only ambition as a politician was to help people, in the same way that she tried to help them in her daily life. There was no reason to disbelieve her.

Her husband, who shared her working-class regional background, was indifferent to politics, but he knew, too, that she was a good person trying to do the right thing. Like Pauline in the film *Chez Nous*, the FN's Astrid Leplat is a nurse. Jean-Pierre Legrand explained to me that this was why she had been hand-picked by Marine Le Pen to stand as a regional councillor. The party has adopted a policy of recruiting *fonctionnaires* (civil servants), especially those who work in the health and support services. This is partly to demonstrate that the FN has left behind its neo-Nazi origins and is now the party of everyday folk, but also to undermine the dominance of public services by the Parti Socialiste (Socialist Party).

I asked Leplat what had drawn her to the FN. She said that she had witnessed the disastrous effects of repeated budget cuts on hospitals, with overstretched departments and increasingly run-down facilities. 'The FN are there to protect us,' she said, and echoing Legrand, 'to give us order where there is none.'

Leplat told me she hadn't seen *Chez Nous* and that she probably wouldn't, because it would upset her. There were also political reasons why she didn't want to see it: it had been partly financed with public money from Hauts-de-France, the northern region that covers Roubaix. When I pointed out that most French cinema relies on public subsidy, she argued that the film's release had been deliberately timed to undermine the February launch of the FN's presidential campaign. 'How else can this be explained? The FN is always persecuted by the establishment elites in culture and politics.'

After coffee, Jean-Pierre Legrand offered to give me a tour of the town in his car to show me the place as he saw it. Straight away, we set off down cobbled streets lined with terraced houses. I liked the centre of Roubaix, which was busier than the area you see when you first get off the train. The town is neatly laid out even if the streets are scruffy. It is also alive with small businesses – Arabic-language bookshops, kebab houses and tea shops, as well as traditional French cafes and bistros. Legrand pointed at the non-French businesses and said, 'That's the problem. This is a town under foreign occupation.' I nodded, not in compliance but in acknowledgement, and said nothing.

Legrand is proud of Roubaix, or at least of what Roubaix used to be, and has chosen to live here rather than in nearby Lille. Having been a blue-collar worker, too, he admires the noble ambitions and graft of the people who built the town. These were the original *indépendants* – the aspiring working class, much cherished by the FN, who believe in the values of hard work and public service. But Legrand told me that when he looks at the streets today, he sees not the cluttered life of twenty-first-century multicultural France but a place that is no longer French. As we drove on, we discussed the real problems facing the town, where forty-five per cent of residents live below the official French poverty line of 977 euros per month. 'These days Roubaix can be a depressing place to live,' said Legrand.

As if to illustrate his point, as we crossed the bridge over a murky canal, we watched two white middle-aged men, both armed with cans of Viking-strength strong lager and obviously pissed nearly to the point of oblivion, lurching about and into each other, in what may or may not have been a mock fight.

'That's a postcard of Roubaix at play,' said Legrand in a sardonic tone. 'Unemployment wrecks lives here. Boredom is literally a killer.' Describing the local poverty, Legrand used the term '*misère*'. This word is sometimes translated as 'spiritual emptiness'. It also translates as 'poverty' or 'wretchedness'. The two meanings certainly came together in this abject scene, which could have easily been pulled from Louis-Ferdinand Céline's 1932 novel *Voyage au bout de la nuit* (*Journey to the End of the Night*), a depiction of life at the bottom end of French society that was praised by George Orwell as 'a book-with-a-purpose, and its purpose is to protest against the horror and meaninglessness of modern life – actually, indeed, of *life*. It is a cry of unbearable disgust, a voice from the cesspool.'[5]

As we drove on through some of the tougher areas, mainly to the north of the town, Legrand pointed out the so-called Salafist mosques, most of them shielded from the streets by the high walls of disused factories. It is these places, unknown and unvisited by outsiders, which have given Roubaix its reputation for radicalism.

It is true that Roubaix has produced extremists in the recent past. The most notorious is Lionel Dumont, who is white, working class and viewed as the leader of radical Islam in the French prison system, where he is serving a twenty-five-year sentence for terrorism offences. Dumont, a former soldier in the French army, was effectively the leader of a jihadist group called Les Ch'tis d'Allah. Their crimes included trying to set off a car bomb during a G7 meeting in Lille in 1996. Dumont had been radicalized in Roubaix. It was also the birthplace of Mehdi Nemmouche, the gunman who fired the shots at the Jewish Museum in Brussels in May 2014 that killed four people.

However, the real reason why Roubaix has produced so many terrorists is not immigration, as the FN would have it, but geography. This part of France is depicted in the media as 'a security black hole', partly because of its proximity to the Belgian border. You can drive into Belgium from Roubaix in ten minutes, as I did with Jean-Pierre Legrand; the border is just an unmonitored roundabout. The French and Belgian intelligence services are minutes away from each other but do not share information or collaborate properly. This allowed some of the terrorists who led the 2015 Paris attacks to escape after the killing spree.

Crossing the border to Belgium, you immediately notice that the roads are lined with gleaming new warehouses belonging to Amazon and other technology companies. By contrast, Roubaix seems like a ruin from the early twentieth century. It must be difficult for its people not to feel trapped and abandoned – by the French elite to the south and the new economy across the border. But caught in this snare, do the working classes of the north necessarily share the views of the NF?

One of the myths of the north in twenty-first-century France is that its white working-class population was becoming increasingly racist. In the run-up to the elections of 2017 and 2022, this was a popular story in the French and international press. But it was not actually supported by the facts.

During the presidential election of 2017, the first round in Roubaix was won by the far-left candidate Jean-Luc Mélenchon, while in the second round, the future President Emmanuel Macron won with almost seventy-five per cent of the vote against twenty-five per cent for Marine Le Pen.[6] Clearly, Roubaix was a town whose long tradition of organized labour and worker solidarity stood stronger than the appeal of the far right. Voting for Macron, an outsider to the traditional tribes of the Left and the Right in France, was a risk, but in Roubaix it was clearly a risk worth taking. In the municipal elections of 2021, the traditional Left reasserted itself by voting for the centre-right Xavier Bertrand, who was well liked across the north of France and won Roubaix with nearly fifty per cent of the vote.

For their part, both Jean-Pierre Legrand and Astrid Leplat had been clear-headed and pessimistic about the real popularity of their party in the north when I met them. I was not at all surprised when, a few months after the 2017 election, they threw their lot in with the newly formed party called Les Patriotes (The Patriots), led by Marine Le Pen's chief of strategy, Florian Philippot. As chief of strategy, Philippot had led the way in 'detoxifying' the FN's public image. He broke away, however, as did Legrand and Leplat, on the grounds that Marine Le Pen had softened her Eurosceptic stance – sometimes called 'Frexit' – and that this had cost her the election. In June 2018, Le Pen renamed her party the RN in yet another rebranding of her version of the far right. When I spoke to Astrid Leplat, she said she felt 'betrayed'.

Although I did not agree for a moment with their politics, I could not bring myself to dislike Jean-Pierre Legrand and Astrid Leplat. Above all, they were honest about their beliefs and their commitment to their region, the place that they called home. As far as I was concerned, they had taken a wrong turn in seeing Roubaix as a place to be defended from outsiders, or 'reconquered' from within. But I could understand how and why they felt displaced and wanted to privilege the local over the international, whether it was protecting themselves against the new globalized hi-tech companies on the other side of the Belgian border, or holding on to a 'French' culture they saw as under threat from the outsiders who now 'occupied' what had once been theirs. Although the threat from the new population of Roubaix was imaginary, there was no doubt that the changes happening around them, which were far beyond their control, were real.

This, I thought, was the key to understanding the siege mentality of the far right in the north of France. In Calais and Dunkirk, ordinary people had armed themselves against the thousands of migrants passing through their territory en route to smuggling themselves into the UK. It was said that all across the north, militias were leading illegal punitive attacks on these migrants, although I never found anybody who could substantiate these rumours.

One of the deeper ironies of the current situation is that this part of France has also been a contested border and often under occupation, most recently by the Germans and then by the British at the end of the Second World War. This was when the historian Richard Cobb had been billeted here. Cobb arrived long-steeped in Parisian culture, having lived and studied there until Hitler intervened. He had a deep love not just of Parisian history but also of Paris itself. In particular, he relished the daily life of the city and its people, conversations overheard in a *tabac* or the metro, the 'unheroic' lives of the working class of Paris as the country hurtled towards the catastrophe of war and occupation. In Roubaix, Cobb was 'sucked in' to the cosy world of *estaminets* and 'the sound of early-morning trams, the crow of cocks or the cooing of pigeons'.[7]

The reference to pigeons fascinated me and is typical of Cobb's keen eye for the telling detail. Like in the north of England, pigeon fancying has long been a working-class hobby here. Raising homing pigeons, or *pigeons voyageurs*, is in fact a popular hobby all over France, but the north is its true capital. It was imported into France from Belgium in the late nineteenth century. It is easy to see why the detailed and skilful care of pigeons is an absorbing pastime, a counterpoint to the noise and dirt of the factory or mine, and a way of connecting with the natural world. More than this, there is a sense of freedom in releasing a bird into the air and watching and waiting for its return, an emotional escape from the claustrophobia of everyday life in a poor industrial town. (Anyone who has seen Ken Loach's 1969 film *Kes*, about a young lad in a poor town in Yorkshire who trains a young kestrel and in doing so finds beauty in the bleak world he lives in, will understand this feeling.) There is even a monument in Lille to the 20,000 *pigeons morts pour la patrie* (who died for the homeland), who were used to carry messages during the First World War. The monument also commemorates the pigeon fanciers who were 'killed by the enemy' for keeping pigeons.

Cobb admired Roubaix's 'harsh geography ... the stark angularity of quaysides and canals ... the blackened brick streets'. Aside from the geography and architecture, there were also deep historical roots which made it easy for English servicemen to feel at home here. This was partly because of Roubaix's former business links to towns like Halifax and Bradford. Added to this, many of the veterans of the First World War had stayed on in Roubaix and married French girls. In an elegiac essay on his time in Roubaix, Cobb reported that there was a friendliness towards the British, reflected in the many photographs in family houses of British regiments stationed there in 1918. In the 1930s, the local football team, then called Excelsior AC Roubaix, had even been coached by a certain Charles Griffiths from Rugby, who had led the team to the *Coupe de France*.

Sport remains a vital part of Roubaix's identity. Most famously, the city is the destination of the annual one-day cycle race from Paris, which was founded in 1896. On 3 October 2021, I watched the televised race in its entirety as the riders covered the 260-kilometre course, notoriously made up of cobbles (known as *setts*) and treacherous unsurfaced roads, which in the past were often no more than compressed cinders. Years ago, the mayors of small towns on the route had been careful to keep the televised race away from their fiefdoms, not wanting them to be thought of as backward by the rest of France. Now they boasted of the *setts*, the difficulty of riding the roads to Roubaix and the importance of the event in the cultural history of France. The race is gruelling, punctuated by mass crashes, and the riders are very quickly covered in mud and soot. For all of these reasons, the Paris–Roubaix race is known as 'the last madness of cycling' or 'the Hell of the North'.

The 2021 Paris–Roubaix competition was won for the first time by the Italian Sonny Colbrelli, who held his *sett* proudly aloft at the prize-giving ceremony in the *vélodrome* of Roubaix. The day before, Elizabeth Deignan, a Yorkshirewoman from Otley, had done the same thing in the first-ever women's race. Fear and pain, said Deignan, had followed her all the way. For his part, Colbrelli, covered in mire and muck, looked like he had survived a war zone, as if he had just emerged from the trenches.

As I watched the riders recover from their battering encounter with the northern terrain, I was reminded of what the beer-drinking Bernard had said: 'We know how to survive. We never give in to anyone. That's our strength.' And perhaps that's the fundamental reason why the town is unlikely to be a breeding ground for fascism. The legacy of organized resistance and not-too-distant memories of the German Occupation is still here. The people of the north are also natural rebels and won't be told what to do by outsiders, which is what the FN are here. They might have local representatives, such as Jean-Pierre Legrand and Astrid Leplat, and at the level of the local town council they might deal with issues that attract working-class support, but the leadership and political ideology of the FN have no roots here. The leadership is based in Paris and the real ideological home ground of the FN, now rebranded as the RN, is the Provence–Alpes–Côte d'Azur (PACA) region, where, for historical reasons, racial tensions are sharper and run deeper.

This is partly because the south is where much of the *pied-noir* population relocated in the aftermath of the Algerian War of Independence (1954–1962). The war, which ended with France handing Algeria back to the Algerians, may seem a long time ago, but in reality, it is within living memory. Part of what fuels the RN is the sense of displacement, bitterness and betrayal within the *pied-noir* population – those who were ethnically

French or European but had been born in Algeria under French rule – who were forced to leave Algeria, a country they believed was theirs. The PACA region is roughly a thousand kilometres from Roubaix and is a distant place which could almost be another country.

Zigzagging in and out of the Belgian border, Roubaix always has been and probably always will be an entirely separate place – a near-perfect example of the urban version of 'peripheral France', forgotten or misunderstood by the rest of the country.

2

The Battle of Angers

A new citadel

Through the first part of 2021, the response to the pandemic in France was one of the bleakest in Europe. Travel was all but impossible. In the meantime, the general sense of anxiety that most people felt, whatever their political beliefs, was heightened by the way that Paris looked and felt in the daytime. The visible changes to my own *quartier* of Pernety in the south of the city were fairly typical. In the space of a few months, a formerly busy working-class district had become forlorn and, in parts, fallen into dilapidation.

The old-style *poissonnerie* (fishmonger) was replaced by yet another pizza delivery shop. Other businesses – including a homely boulangerie, a local hub for gossip and good bread – were boarded up and covered in graffiti. There was an increasing number of homeless people on the streets. Long-time inhabitants swapped stories about rising crime levels, largely muggings and burglaries. My own flat was burgled, for the first time ever in fifteen years of living there. An attempted break-in at my office followed soon afterwards.

One of the police officers who came to check the damage in my flat told me casually that there had been three other burglaries on my street that same afternoon. Rumours of other crimes circulated in the *quartier*. I heard shocking news about a young woman of Algerian origin who had obvious mental health problems and was known to everyone in the district. She had been raped one night by a gang in the local children's playground. I felt then as if the entire city of Paris, indeed the whole of France, was changing shape and character.

In the summer of 2021, government authorities published a report confirming what everyone already knew: that reported crimes in France had reached an all-time high. By that time, however, France had already started opening up again, and it felt like things might begin to go back to normal.

In Paris, there were no more curfews. Most non-essential businesses and cafe *terrasses* reopened in mid-May 2021. You could now eat, drink or shop wherever you liked, and people were no longer required to wear masks in outdoor spaces. Tourism had yet to return, but as you strolled through the city it was clear that a tentative sense of ease had returned.

In October 2021, I travelled to Angers. It was mid-afternoon when my train arrived, and I strolled down through the old town, one of the prettiest medieval towns in the Loire Valley, heading towards a cheap hotel on the banks of the river Maine. These days, Angers is clean, orderly, busy, and visibly wealthy – a perfect counterpoint to somewhere like Roubaix. But the place was not always like this. When Arthur Young passed through Angers in 1788, many decades into the Age of Enlightenment, it remained physically and spiritually a medieval town. This meant that much of its infrastructure was in disrepair, with many buildings rotting away, gutters overflowing, and holes in roofs. Theology and ecclesiastical scholarship, rather than commerce, were the mainstays of its cultural life.[1]

For this reason, Angers was a sharp contrast to the neighbouring city of Nantes, which Young had just visited and was then the principal port of France dealing in sugar, ebony and slavery (no less than Voltaire had five thousand *livres* – a substantial sum – invested in a slave ship which sailed out of Nantes). In Nantes, Young had picked up on a political mood of discontent: he sensed that the newly rich class of merchants seemed to be in a rebellious mood against the local nobility, who earned nothing and produced nothing. There was, he thought, a distinct whiff of mutiny in the air against the old order.

He noticed, too, that both the merchants and aristocrats concentrated their attention on city life, abandoning the countryside and its inhabitants. Between town and country, there was 'no communication – no neighbourhood'. The money made in Nantes never left the town, and the peasantry in the surrounding areas were condemned to poverty and sometimes famine. As he approached Angers from Nantes, Young encountered tensions at the barriers and customs houses along the way.

As an agriculturist, Young admired the quality of the land, which was so different from the 'savage wastes' of Brittany he'd travelled through earlier. Even so, the countryside had a neglected and abandoned air, and the same was true of the town. This was partly because its society had ossified since the medieval period, but it is also true that much of the real life of Angers was hidden away from the eyes of an English traveller: it took place behind walls and closed windows, in priories and chapels. The tolling bells in dead streets were often the only sign that anyone lived in the place. If Young had passed through Angers two years later, he might have detected something of the restive mood he'd found in Nantes. In September 1790, starving quarry workers rioted in protest at the lack of grain, and the wealthy merchant classes accused the clergy of having tolled the bells as an incitement to insurrection. The rebellion was stamped down and sixty workers were killed in the process. The authorities had made their point: there was to be no challenge to the political order in Angers, now controlled by a *bourgeoisie* which, in the wake of the Revolution of 1789, was fiercely pro-Revolutionary and anti-clerical, seeing the church as a threat to their power.

In the twenty-first century, Angers is a gleaming example of provincial charm. The centre of the town is laid out on a gentle incline, which gradually shifts from the neo-classical nineteenth-century main square down to the river through the tangle of streets which made up the original medieval city. Along the way, there are hidden churches and convents as well as elegant cafes and restaurants. This is every foreign visitor's dream version of provincial France. Coralie Mars, a physiotherapist in her twenties (my own physio, in fact), currently resident in Paris but a native of Angers, told me that it was the most perfect place in France and that she could not wait to move back there.

She also told me that there are, like everywhere else in France, 'difficult' areas in Angers – Monplaisir, Saint Léonard, Justices and La Roseraie – but even these places were relatively orderly. The high quality of life and the relatively low cost of real estate make Angers popular with commuters – it is within commuting distance of Nantes and identifies itself as part of the west, the neighbouring *département* of Loire-Atlantique, which has Nantes as its economic capital. Most locals have families who have been here for generations. Unsurprisingly, the political culture of Angers is innately sedate and in recent times has consistently favoured the centre-right.

No extremist politicians, of the Right or the Left, have ever fared well here – they are all too radical and likely to disrupt the delicate balance and harmony. There is also a culture of deference: the natives of the city are notoriously reluctant rebels, preferring to put their faith in the essential goodness of *le bon maître* (the good master) rather than dangerous revolutionary ideas, which are the inventions of volatile Parisian firebrands. For this reason, many French historians have depicted the Angevins, and especially the clergy, as 'bad Frenchmen'; during the time of the Revolution of 1789, they were all counter-revolutionaries, '*mauvais patriotes*', enemies of the people.

This image of Angers as a stolid and reactionary place still lingers in the French imagination. In 1976, François Mitterrand – then still no more than an ambitious politician with an eye on the presidency – famously remarked sarcastically that the day that Angers votes Left, then the whole of France will turn Socialist.

Like most provincial French towns, Angers goes to bed early. After a day of wandering about, I decided to do the same, after finishing off with a few locally brewed beers on the *terrasse* of the Brasserie Le Théâtre. Still, the old town was beguiling in the gathering misty gloom, which was spreading out over the town from the river Maine as I walked back to my hotel at a relaxed pace, admiring the timbered buildings and savouring the melancholy late-autumn atmosphere.

As I reached the rue de la Parcheminerie, the street which would take me to the river, I was accosted by a guy in his late twenties or early thirties, who was either pissed or stoned or most probably both. He was white, reasonably well dressed in a hipsterish fashion, wearing a T-shirt with the slogan 'Khaos' (the name of a rapper from Marseille), and spoke with a slurred but distinctly middle-class accent. He stood squarely in front of me and instead of asking me for money, which was what I was expecting, he pointed to a cluster of young Arab girls drinking sodas in a nearby kebab house and asked me which girl I wanted. When I said that I wasn't interested he offered me drugs instead. Again, I quietly declined the offer. Growing visibly frustrated with this second refusal, he reached towards his flies and asked me if I wanted sex with him. As he began to take his cock out, and I shook my head in refusal, he looked furious, and I realized that I was alone in an ever-darkening street and now in some real danger.

My first instinct was to try to defuse the tension, so in a calm voice I asked his name. This seemed to take him by surprise, and he answered quite politely that it was Sébastien. This is not an unusual name in France, and nor is it particularly posh, but it is also not the usual punkish pseudonym adopted by a vagrant. Suddenly, however, Sébastien's anger flared up again and he tried to throw a punch at me. He was too inebriated to actually hit me, but it was enough to make me stumble. As I tried to steady myself in order to walk around him, he leaned in towards my shoulder, and with a face creased in hatred, he spat at me with as much venom as he could muster. The saliva landed on the collar of my overcoat and started to run down towards my pockets.

Straight away, fearing Covid contamination or God knows what else, I started to wipe myself down and, galvanized by shock and disgust, I pushed him out of the way. Cackling, Sébastien sat down on a bollard in the graffitied rue de la Croix, which I knew already to be a dead-end back alley. He seemed satisfied that he had finally achieved his aim of frightening me and, still laughing to himself, he watched me scurry back to the safety of my hotel. Back in my hotel room, still shaking, I washed my coat and then took a shower. I knew that this would not protect me from disease, but I needed somehow to cleanse myself from this encounter. It didn't work, and, after a late and tasteless dinner in the empty and over-lit restaurant of my cheap hotel, I slept badly and uneasily in my bare room.

The next morning, walking by the river speckled with sunlight, Angers seemed to me as delightful as ever. Drinking a breakfast coffee at a small riverside cafe, shaking off my tiredness, I found it hard to believe that what I had seen last night had actually happened. I started half-wondering whether it had been a sort of nightmare. I shrugged these thoughts away and set about the business of the day.

I had come to Angers to meet David Cayla, a professor of economics at the local university who specialized in globalization and populist politics in France and more generally across Europe. We arranged to have lunch and then talk at a restaurant called Le Bistrot des Ducs which, as it turned out, happened to be only a few minutes away from where I had my run-in with Sébastien. The food and wine were thoroughly excellent (veal, grilled vegetables, a local red wine) and far cheaper than anything of a parallel quality in Paris. As we ate and talked, I decided not to mention the incident which had unsettled me the previous evening. This was partly because I felt ashamed and embarrassed, and in an obscure way slightly soiled, and partly because it was in fact a banality, the kind of unfortunate encounter you could have in a provincial town in France or indeed anywhere. But this was precisely what had disturbed me: in a town like Angers any form of criminality, bad-luck encounter or delinquent behaviour tends to stand out because it is so rare. Despite my restless night, which made me struggle to stay alert, I thought that the abortive assault had no meaning or relevance to what I wanted to discuss.

I was interested to hear more about David's theories on the origins of populism, which in its most authoritarian form became fascism (at least, he said, this was what had happened in Nazi Germany in the 1930s). Most historical explanations for this process, he argued, were political – that disaffected and alienated parts of society thought that democracy had failed them and found a voice instead in anti-democratic movements. This was all true, David said, but it was not the whole story. As an economist, David's analysis was based rather on the contradiction that the democratic ideal of social and financial justice for all could never be achieved in a free market economy, which ultimately determined all social development.²

This was almost exactly the same argument that Christophe Guilluy had made to me in Paris; a great many people in France were angry because they had been marginalized, made 'peripheral', and were beginning to see so-called democracy as a con trick which kept the same old privileged people in power.

I could see how this process worked in a town like Roubaix, which was predominantly working class and cut off from the mainstream Left of the new citadels of Lille and Paris, but was this the same political and cultural fault line at work here in Angers – a town mainly known for its gentle pace of life and long history of moderate social conservatism? More to the point, if it were a given that geography in France influenced politics (as indeed it does in almost all other countries), then what was happening politically in Angers? Could life here really be as fractured and divided as in other poorer parts of France?

David pointed to the cover photograph of his book *Populism and Neoliberalism*, written and published in English, which I had brought with me to our lunch. The photograph, which he had taken himself in Angers just a couple of years earlier in 2019, showed a street packed with a long line of *gilet jaune* demonstrators at the height of the revolts. He told me that the anger and violence here had been just as virulent as elsewhere. How to explain this?

David's analysis seemed obvious and true. The revolt of the *gilets jaunes*, he said, had, of course, been about poverty, fuel prices and the cost of living. But there was an added element which came sharply into relief in a place like Angers. Put simply, the revolt of the *gilets jaunes* was about French identity as much as about the price of petrol.

Angers may have been rich but it was not cosmopolitan. It was a place that prided itself on its 'civilization', which meant both a specific attachment to land and territory and their refinement into art, food, music, thought, literature. This was how Angers had been able, since the medieval period, to easily reconcile religion and the high quality of 'the French way of life'. Globalism and neoliberalism, as found in Paris and all the other new citadels, were the antithesis of this model. Most dangerously, globalism had imported into France values and ways of living that the French could not and would not recognize as their own. It was this fundamental issue which brought together the far left and far right in France, both of whom saw themselves as defending their culture from the outside world.

As French culture in the twenty-first century seemed to be splintering into pieces before the eyes of the French people, for all its violence and rage, the revolt of the *gilets jaunes* was an attempt to hold on to what the French admire and need as the fundamental pillars of the nation, the values of tradition, stability and order, against the forces of chaos.

The confrontation with chaos – the so-called Battle of Angers – arrived here on 19 January 2019. The early demonstrations by the local *gilets jaunes* had been orderly and calm – very much the '*bon enfant*' ('well-behaved child') expected of the working class of Angers, whether they were town-dwellers or from the countryside. But all of this changed when the demonstration turned into the kind of riot which had only been seen until then in the big cities or the well-known poorer parts of France. Even now, several years on, it is hard to piece together why the violence in Angers erupted so swiftly and unexpectedly.

What is certain is that in the week leading up to the demonstration, the civic authorities had already determined to enforce republican order with maximum force. On the morning of 18 January, Matthieu Orphelin, the local representative of the Macron government, decided to 'suspend all dialogue' with the spokespeople of the *gilets jaunes*, in a mood of 'rage' and 'shame' at their 'insults to the Republic'. Banks and shops were accordingly boarded up, heightening the sense of tension.[3]

There were also rumours that the *gilets jaunes* of Angers were to be bolstered by more militant groups from Brittany and other more discontented parts of France. These rumours had prompted the then *Préfet* of Angers, Bernard Gonzalez, to declare martial law. There is no real equivalent to the *Préfet* in the British political system; he or she is officially the regional chief of a *département*, appointed by the government and, among other jobs, responsible for security and policing. In other words, the *Préfet* is a designated officer of the centralized Republic in charge of a local population. From this point, it is easy to see how a stand-off between local demonstrators and central government can feel like a civil war. This is why one of the banners during the demonstration, repeating a slogan now common throughout France, read *'Instaurer une véritable démocratie!'* ('Give us a real democracy!').

The epicentre of the conflict between the heavily armoured police (usually referred to in French news reports as *'les forces de l'ordre'* – 'the forces of order') was in and around the elegant heart of Angers, the Place du Ralliement. Even the Banque de France, a noble and stolid building, the bastion of the *bourgeoisie* who had made Angers so rich, came under attack. The tramways were halted by demonstrators. The air was thick with tear gas, bins had been set alight, and protesters threw stones and were charged by the police.

Such scenes were by now familiar throughout France, in real life or in real time on television, but the civil disorder in Angers was still shocking for ordinary French people for the same reason that my encounter with Sébastien had left me so shaken: neither anti-government riots nor random attacks on strangers were supposed to happen here; both acts made an ordinary, orderly world seem dizzyingly dislocated.

One of the most overused words in the French media and political circles in recent years has been the term *'insécurité'*. This is not a hard word to translate literally – it means 'insecurity' – but it does have a very specific political dimension in France these days. Usually, it refers to criminality or delinquency, both real and perceived forms of disorder, and it is commonly used to describe a wide range of threats to the stability of French life, from drug gangs armed with Kalashnikovs in the lawless suburbs of Marseille or Paris to Islamist terrorism or indeed the spectacular violence which accompanied the demonstrations of the *gilets jaunes* in quiet places like Angers.

By the time I travelled to Angers in October 2021, France seemed temporarily at peace with itself, and in the wake of the pandemic there had been no more riots. And yet my time in Angers, my encounters with Sébastien and David, had put me on edge and alerted me to the feeling that disorder in all its forms was never far away. And all the while, one of the biggest media stories in France was the rumour of a civil war.

3

Paris on Edge

The language of war

It began with a call to arms. In April 2021, the right-wing *Valeurs actuelles* published an open letter from military generals addressed to French President Emmanuel Macron. In the so-called *lettre des généraux*, twenty retired generals and more than a thousand French soldiers condemned what they saw as an attack on French values, emanating everywhere from Islamism to 'the hordes from the *banlieues*', who were all either gangsters, drug dealers or jihadist terrorists.

The letter's signatories targeted 'anti-racists' who 'speak of racialism, indigenism and decolonial theories'. 'But behind these terms,' the letter said, 'these hate-filled, fanatical partisans seek only racial war. They hate our country, its traditions, its culture, and want to smash it into pieces.' The letter concluded that 'a civil war will bring an end to the growing chaos, and the dead, for which you will be responsible, will be in the thousands'.[1]

Général François Lecointre, chief of the defence staff and head of the French army, announced that all those who had signed the letter would face military discipline and would be 'delisted', or forced to retire. Florence Parly, the minister for the armed forces, said the letter was 'a call to insurrection' and 'a naked insult' to thousands of loyal soldiers.

But Marine Le Pen said she understood the mood of the generals and called on them and their supporters to back her in the 2022 Presidential Election. This was, she said, 'a battle for France'. Other commentators on the Left and the Right noted ominously that the letter had been published almost exactly sixty years after France really did come close to an actual civil war. This was on 22 April 1961, when the 1st Foreign Parachute Regiment, led by the retired general Maurice Challe, announced that it had seized all government and military facilities in what was then French Algiers. This was a direct challenge to the presidency of Charles de Gaulle. The *putsch*, however, was quashed when the army declared its loyalty to de Gaulle after the president had appeared on television in military uniform and called on the French people to help him.

In 2021, Macron's party, La République en marche (LREM), which he founded in 2016, could not count on that kind of public support. Indeed, following the publication of the letter, a majority of people – most of whom had never heard of *Valeurs actuelles* – came out in its favour. One poll reported that seventy-three per cent of French people agreed with the soldiers that France was 'disintegrating', effectively collapsing into a state of disorder.

Emboldened, *Valeurs actuelles* published a second provocative letter on 10 May, this one signed anonymously by serving soldiers and addressing the mainstream parties of the Right and the

Left. The tone was bitter and emotive. The authors described themselves as a 'generation of fire' who had fought and lost comrades in action in Afghanistan, Mali and Central African Republic, as well as in counterterrorism operations in France in 2015 – the year of the Paris terrorist attacks at the Bataclan theatre and the *Charlie Hebdo* office. The soldiers wrote about how in foreign combat operations they had been fighting Islamism, which was now gaining more 'concessions' on French soil every day. 'A civil war is brewing,' the letter said. It asked readers to sign a petition in support of its message. By the afternoon of 10 May, according to *Valeurs actuelles*, 145,000 people had signed it.[2]

It seemed fairly obvious that *Valeurs actuelles* was playing a mischievous political game, trying to destabilize the Macron government in the run-up to the French regional elections, which were to be held on 20 and 27 June and were considered a dress rehearsal for the presidential election the following year. But what the support for the letters revealed was the darkening public mood in France, one defined by a lack of faith in politics and in politicians to solve the critical socio-economic challenges undermining the country, and a cynicism about democracy in the nation that claims to have founded it as a modern concept.

To help me make sense of all of this, I went to speak to Elisabeth Lévy, a writer and polemicist, in a small, chic restaurant near the rue de l'Echiquier on the Right Bank of Paris, which is near the office of *Causeur* magazine, which she founded and edits. It is described by its enemies as 'right wing' and even as a media outlet of the extreme right. The magazine is conservative, but, like Lévy herself, it claims no political affiliation. *Causeur*'s defining attitudes are the long-standing French values of scepticism, irony and provocation; these are also its main weapons of resistance to what it calls '*la culture woke*'.

Causeur has a faithful following – its print circulation hovers at around 16,000. Its website attracts 500,000 individual visitors and two million page views per month, and Lévy is well known in France because of her frequent media appearances. According to her enemies on the Left, she is a *crypto-lépeniste* who has helped Le Pen 'normalize' the RN. But Lévy is more of an old-fashioned satirist than an agent of the Right. As I discovered in conversation over our lunch, her sense of humour owes more to the long-standing tradition of *gouaille* – a specifically Parisian form of aggressive wit. When I spilled wine on her skirt, she laughed and said that I was up to something. Seeing that I was embarrassed, she immediately followed up with a joke about Anglo-American puritanism.

Lévy has said many times that France will never give in to the 'demons of fascism'; but beyond that statement, her true political affiliations are a mystery. Lévy sees 'fascism' as emerging from the dogma of the Bobo sections of the French Left. She saw the Bobo Left as a new form of nobility – a self-selected, self-serving elite – adding that they were worse than the older forms of nobility because they were harder to get rid of. She wanted Christophe Guilluy to write about this issue for *Causeur* and wondered if I could help persuade him. Until then, he had always turned her down. She called him '*un salaud!*' ('a bastard!') and smiled again.

Lévy describes herself as a writer and an intellectual. It is no accident that she co-founded *Causeur* with the philosopher Alain Finkielkraut, a figure of hate on the Left for his allegedly anti-Muslim views. Another of Lévy's closest associates is the philosopher Michel Onfray, who is best described as an apolitical contrarian. A Jewish friend of mine, another former Marxist, described Lévy to me as 'brilliant and courageous'. In person, she was astute and quick to pick up on any contradiction in an argument, but always with a rapier wit.

Born in Marseille in 1964 into a family of Algerian Jews, Lévy studied at the prestigious Institut d'Etudes Politiques de Paris and began her career as a self-described socialist thinker. She supported President François Mitterrand in the early 1980s and made her name as a journalist in the 1990s. One of her most important influences was the essayist and arch-ironist Philippe Muray; there were distinct echoes of Muray when she told *Le Monde* in 2013 that her 'only political identity is not to be on the Left'.[3] Most of all, she said to me, she has been disappointed at what she sees as a sharp swerve on the Left to *communautarisme*, which describes a specifically French fear that the needs of individual minority groups (or 'communities') are being given priority over the universal values of France. This fear has indeed been a contributory factor to the decline of working-class support for the Left; the non-metropolitan classes, the 'non-Bobo classes' in particular, feel that their needs are ignored in favour of 'communities', such as LGBTQ+ people and immigrants, and vocal movements such as Black Lives Matter.

I asked Lévy whether the publication of the generals' letter had been a deliberate political manoeuvre by *Valeurs actuelles*. 'I know the people at *Valeurs actuelles* – they do not pay much attention to what other people think. Myself, I think the generals were acting alone, speaking for themselves. There was no precise political agenda. But obviously what they said created a political response.'

What interested Lévy about the whole affair is that so many people agreed with the letter. She emphasized what she called 'the divorce' between the elites in the media and the working and lower-middle classes in France. 'The important word is "disintegration",' she said, 'and that's why there is a fear of civil war.'

Lévy kept returning to this central point: ordinary people could see that France was coming apart. Officially, according to figures provided by the police, overall reported crime went down in 2020. But the perception was that the killing of police officers was part of a larger breakdown in law and order.

It was not just police officers who were under attack. In October 2020, the teacher Samuel Paty was beheaded close to his own school, having been falsely denounced by students for showing images of the Prophet Muhammad during a class.

People were angered not only by the obscene violence but by what was regarded as an attack on the Republic itself. In an emotional tribute at a ceremony held in the Sorbonne, Emmanuel Macron, visibly moved, had described Paty as 'the face' of the values of the Republic.

In the wake of Paty's death, the education pages of *Le Monde* had been full of reports from teachers on the new and dangerous atmosphere in the classroom. But the government barely responded to these complaints. In schools, too, little had changed. Rather, the more vicious students used Paty's death as a way to terrorize and threaten teachers. This was anti-republicanism as a rebel youth subculture, and when another killing came it seemed almost inevitable, at least to teachers who lived with this every day. On 13 October 2023, nearly three years to the day after Samuel Paty's death, a fifty-seven-year-old teacher called Dominique Bernard was killed in an attack by an Islamist in the playground of a school in Arras.

Once again, it was *Le Monde* that voiced the wider political significance of Dominique Bernard's murder in a lengthy editorial, which, referring back to Paty's execution, read: 'Two teachers responsible for training citizens in the exercise of free will, the foundation of democracy, were killed in cold blood, by agents of an ideology that fights precisely the values that bring us together ... If radical Islamists make the French state school a specific target, it's because it's aimed at a project that's unbearable for them.'[4] In response, the Minister of Education announced 16 October as a day of solidarity with teachers.

'That was all very well,' said Alain Poulain as we drank coffee in the sitting room of his small but stylish apartment. Alain is a recently retired teacher of French and my friend and neighbour in the 14th arrondissement. 'The demonstration was supposed to show support for us teachers,' he said. 'But there was no one there who was not a teacher. That made me feel worse, as if nobody cared about what has been happening to us.'

Alain and his wife Laurence (who taught science) had been teachers for thirty years in good and bad schools across the Paris region. Neither of them could ever recall a situation as 'sinister' or 'disastrous' (their words) as this. They had become teachers because they were socialists and believed in making a better world. Their own teachers and mentors had instilled in them the conviction that they were a force for good, the people who could properly catalyse social change in France. 'We thought we were the good guys,' said Laurence. 'So how is it that we became the enemy?'

She recalled a confrontation over the recent banning in French schools of the abaya – a type of all-body covering in Muslim tradition. 'I was asked about this by some girls and I said that as a feminist I thought that girls should not have to hide themselves. I said that I believed in "laicity" because it was the fairest for everybody. Straight away, I was called a white bitch and then a *colon*.' This means 'colonizer' but is specifically loaded as a term referring back to the *pieds-noirs*, the settler population of French Algeria. 'This kind of thing happens all the time. Students want to provoke you, and then insult you, and they say you are destroying their identity. All we want to do is widen their horizons, teach them, and show them the world. But they don't want that. They just want to fight you.'

According to Laurence, the poisoned atmosphere in the classroom had intensified since the summer of 2023, when in the wake of the unlawful police shooting of a young man of Algerian heritage in the Paris suburb of Nanterre, riots had broken out all over France for a week. The main targets of the rioters were specifically public buildings which carried the *imprimatur* of the Republic. 'They burned down libraries and schools. Anything that promoted culture. Why? It is impossible for me to understand. What is at stake here is an attack on all our freedoms – it is "liberticide"!'

Her use of this term surprised me. It is a word that has recently been widely used on the Right and on the Left, in graffiti and in the media, as a rallying cry against Macron's government and his high-handed disregard for the democratic process. But this is not what Laurence meant. 'Liberticide' is not in fact a new word; it dates back to the 1790s, when it was first used by Gracchus Babeuf, a journalist and proto-Communist, who argued that the French Revolution did not go far enough. 'Liberticide' has a long and deep resonance in French political culture. It is a component part of French history and what it means to be French in a country where *liberté*, at all points on the political spectrum, is supposed to be not only a cherished ideal but a lived reality. When Laurence spoke of 'liberticide', she meant that the very concept of '*liberté*', a word that has defined Frenchness, was under threat.

Alain, who had retired a month ago, joined in. 'I'm glad that I retired. Laurence is right. The classroom has become a battlefield. After a while, it wears you out. We are supposed to teach the values of the Republic and discuss ethics and free speech. This is what Samuel Paty did. But students make throat-slitting gestures if they don't agree with you, or denounce you on social media. I'm not ashamed to say that at times I have been frightened.' He said they felt they were '*sans-abri*' ('unsheltered') from the hostility in schools. 'Sometimes it can feel that you're an agent of the Republic on the front lines of a war. But we are teachers, not soldiers.'

Alain and Laurence feared the ascendancy of the far right, but they also felt abandoned by the Left. 'Everybody knows what has been happening in our schools: a war against our values, the Enlightenment if you like,' he said, wearily. 'But what can you do if your own political side is not listening? Do they really not understand it, or are they just pretending to be deaf?'

Alain and Laurence Poulain are on the other side of the political spectrum to Elisabeth Lévy, but in some ways they echo each other. Lévy argued that when the Left claimed that

Islamist attacks were random acts of criminality, it represented a denialism that only hardened public anger. The result of all of this, as Lévy persistently argues in the pages of *Causeur*, is that ordinary people of the Left and the Right now feel a kind of angry despair. More precisely, they no longer trust their political representatives to tell the truth: that a small but significant number of people living in France hated the country so much that they wanted to destroy it. If this truth is denied, how could politicians protect people from the deadly consequences of this denial? If France was not already at war with these people, Lévy has argued further – reinforcing the rhetoric of the rebel generals – then maybe it should be.

Politics aside, imagining a French civil war also makes for potent and lucrative entertainment. In recent years, there has been a whole series of films, most of them box-office hits, which have portrayed the collision between '*les forces de l'ordre*' and the gangs of the worst *banlieues*, unofficially the forces of 'disorder'. This has indeed become a mini-genre of its own, including films such as *Bronx* (*Rogue City* in English), *Banlieusards* (*Street Flow*), *Chouf* (a street Arabic word for 'lookout'), *Les Misérables* and *Bac Nord* (translated by Netflix into *The Stronghold* but really referring to the police division in the *quartiers nord* of Marseille).

These films have been shot all over France but the most popular location is Marseille. This is partly because of the sulphurous reputation of the *quartiers nord* – the 13th, 14th, 15th and 16th arrondissements of the city, which rarely appear on tourist maps and are generally regarded as some of the most dangerous and lawless parts of France (strangely enough, the 3rd arrondissement, the poorest *quartier* in France, is often not included as part of the *quartiers nord*).

The chasm between lawful, mainstream France and its violent, lawless margins, like the *quartiers nord*, is a potent inspiration for the far-right writer Laurent Obertone, who describes a civil war in France in a pair of novels called *Guérilla*. The first of these was published in 2016 with the subtitle *Le jour où tout s'embrasa* (The day that everything exploded). The book begins with a shoot-out between drug dealers and the police in the *cité* of Taubira, a fictional council estate to the north of Paris (and an unsubtle reference to the leftist politician Christiane Taubira, originally from French Guyana, who served as the Minister of Justice in France until 2016). Several dealers are shot and killed by a single policeman, panicked and terrified as he is about to see his young colleague sliced into pieces with a machete. In real-life France, this kind of scenario is usually reported in the media as a '*fait divers*', an everyday news item.

In Obertone's story, the *cité* explodes into violence, which, driven by social media and the mainstream press, soon spreads through the whole of France. Within days, the conflict is out of control and looks exactly like a real civil war. All of this is watched over by Colonel Fourreau, an old-style right-winger and patriot, who is the only person who seems to see what is truly at stake: the importance of order and the very existence of the French Republic under attack from immigrants.

Obertone's novel fits into a long tradition of this kind of writing on the far right. One of the most famous and influential books in this subgenre is *Le Camp des Saints* (*The Camp of the Saints*) by Jean Raspail, which depicts the collapse of Western civilization under the weight of mass immigration from the Global South. Although first published in 1973, *Le Camp des Saints* returned to the French bestseller lists in 2011, a marker of a new distrust and hardening of the attitude towards immigrants in France.

Like Raspail, Obertone takes himself seriously as a literary writer and peppers his text with references to the great and the good of French literature, from Balzac to Camus (as well as the great but not-so-good Louis-Ferdinand Céline, the virulently antisemitic, pro-Nazi novelist). Indeed, Obertone has a vivid turn of phrase and knows how to pace action and cliffhangers. What really appeals to many of Obertone's fans (and there are many in the *Fachosphère* – the term for young and hip hard-right supporters) is how close his caricatures of the Bobo Left are to reality, and how their self-hating, anti-French masochism leads effectively to a form of collective suicide. If *Guérilla* begins well as a standard action-movie page-turner, it soon becomes ludicrous, hysterical and unbelievable. In one of the book's most unpleasant scenes, a weak French president is ripped to pieces by a mob. Unsurprisingly, Obertone quotes approvingly Gustave Le Bon, the nineteenth-century theoretician of crowd violence.

Obertone's follow-up novel, *Le Temps des Barbares* (The Time of the Barbarians) is, if anything, even more melodramatic, and his work has been met with critical silence. It would be easy to dismiss his books, but their high sales figures and Obertone's cult following suggest that he, like the generals, is tapping into a popular willingness to believe in the possibility of a coming war.

The imagined civil war is also the central theme of Michel Houellebecq's 2019 novel *Sérotonine*, which ends with an armed conflict between riot police and disaffected farmers that leaves eleven people dead. *Sérotonine* is convincing where Obertone's fiction is cartoonish, not just because Houellebecq is a more sophisticated writer, but because he widens out the conflicts in French society to encompass many different forms of tension, from the *gilets jaunes* to disaffected and alienated heterosexual males left behind by a world that seems to have abandoned them – in Houellebecq's world, the death of the male libido is another indicator of a civilization that is dying.

The central character of *Sérotonine* is Florent-Claude Labrouste, forty-six, an agricultural scientist. He goes through a mid-life crisis, brooding on his lost loves, and is sent to work in Normandy for the European Union. There, Labrouste sees firsthand how wretched life is in rural France these days. There are compelling descriptions of modern agri-business, nightmarish scenes in poultry farms, and dairy farmers being pushed to redundancy and suicide by EU regulations. The climax of the novel is a bloody confrontation between armed farmers, who have barricaded a road, and riot police. The parallels with the rage of the *gilets jaunes* are easy to see, and it is one of the main reasons the book has been praised, as if Houellebecq were not just a writer but a kind of seer or prophet who when writing his book sensed the tensions in France without knowing what was to come. Perhaps unsurprisingly, in recent times Houellebecq, a declared fan of Obertone, has been frequenting the milieu around *Valeurs actuelles*.

When I first met Michel Houellebecq, I could never have imagined that he would become a literary superstar or the ally of far-right intellectuals. It was 26 June 1996 – a date I remember because we were in his flat watching France and then England get knocked out on penalties in the Euro semi-finals over two or more litres of *rosé* wine accompanied by some sour pink taramasalata, and we talked more about football and music (Leonard Cohen, Neil Young, Brian Wilson) than about literature.

I admired the small amount of poetry Houellebecq had published, which reminded me of early Morrissey (the sadness, the detailed references to places). There were even rhymes, a rarity in most contemporary French poetry. Significantly, Houellebecq had been described to me as a Communist, and it was true that he had started to make his name in Communist circles in Paris.

We barely touched on politics that evening, but when we did I gleaned no Marxist-Leninist optimism or Communist-level love of humanity from Houellebecq, but rather a dark, apocalyptic pessimism, although he was also very witty and sarcastic. ('I am trying to learn English,' he told me, 'so that I can finally speak the language of Donald Duck.') At the time, he was writing a novel called *Les particules elémentaires* (translated as *Atomised*), which was the book that would catapult him from obscurity to an international reputation. He told me about the big themes of the book: the end of Christianity, the death of Western civilization. Cause of death? Suicide.

Houellebecq talked about this dispassionately as if it were a well-known fact. He seriously believed that this had happened, or at least was happening, and as a writer who had lost faith in humanity, as he put it, he was actively willing it on. He came across as an obsessive, if not an out-and-out nihilist. But the serious talk didn't last long. After the dismal football matches, we had a beer and a cigarette out on his balcony. On an opposite balcony, a fattish woman in a Chicago Bears T-shirt was also smoking and drinking beer. 'Look at her, look at us,' he said. He spoke with the slow and deliberate portentousness of someone now quite far gone in drink, but he was lucid. 'This is why France is finished.' We both laughed, but I wasn't sure if I really got the joke. I asked what he meant. 'Look at her,' he said again. 'She is how we live today in France. Our civilization has gone.' He then spoke softly, as if telling me a secret: the fake confidentiality of the drunk. 'We are no longer our own people. Or we do not know who we are,' he said. 'And remember, if France dies, Europe dies.'

In late 2022, Houellebecq provoked severe disquiet in France, not for the first time by now, by taking his ideas out of a novel and into the real world. This was as part of a long discussion with the philosopher Michel Onfray in Onfray's newly founded journal *Front Populaire*.[5] One of Onfray's stated aims for *Front Populaire* is to argue for '*le souverainisme*' ('sovereignty'). This word has had various meanings in the French political lexicon over the past few years, but most recently it has come to stand for opposition to a federal Europe, asserting the uniqueness and independence of France, and opposing the messy, unstructured tolerance of multiculturalism. In the discussion in *Front Populaire*, much to the disgust of his liberal fans, Houellebecq emerged as a declared fan of *le souverainisme*. He went even further, using the language of war to justify his beliefs. 'What we see already,' he said, 'is that people are arming themselves. They're getting hold of guns, taking lessons in shooting ranges. And this is not just the hotheads. When whole territories are under Islamist control, I think that there will be acts of resistance. There will be assassinations and shootings in the mosques and the cafes frequented by Muslims: in other words, the Bataclan in reverse ... What real French people want is not for Muslims to assimilate but for them to stop robbing and attacking the French people. If that doesn't happen, then there will be other solutions.'

These 'other solutions' have also been imagined by some on the Left. Most notably, the 2022 Netflix film *Athena*, directed by Romain Gavras, the son of the veteran leftist film-maker Costa-Gavras and the journalist Michèle Ray-Gavras, sees the French civil war from the point of view of the *banlieue*. The plot of the film hinges on the killing of an Arab child by three police officers in Athena, a fictional *cité* near Paris. The killing ignites riots in *banlieues* all across France, and in Athena itself a roughly assembled 'army' of youths from the housing estate arm themselves and plunge into a violent confrontation with the police with the aim of kidnapping or killing a police officer. Throughout the film, the French media reporting on the events in Athena and elsewhere in France persistently refer to what is happening as 'civil war' (Gavras's working title for the film was the simple and self-explanatory *War*).

The film itself presents the conflict as an epic staged battle, with the *banlieue* as a fortress under attack from the police who, moving in tight phalanxes or on horseback, lay siege to the tower blocks, advancing and attacking like a medieval army. The film is spectacular and technically brilliant – long tracking shots present a poetic and panoramic view of the *banlieue*, all to the accompaniment of a doom-laden soundtrack which melds Benjamin Britten with the music of the late DJ Mehdi (a friend of Romain Gavras).

Cinematically, Gavras is clearly with the rioters. The police exist only as faceless ciphers, apart from one lone young policeman who is trapped behind enemy lines and whose life is in danger. Our sympathy does not last long as the action veers back to the main characters – the three brothers of the dead child, who all have Algerian roots (there are scattered references to the Algerian War of Independence throughout the film).

In interviews, Gavras has avoided coming down too heavily on the side of his fictional rioters. His defence against the accusation that he is anti-police is that at the end of the film, we discover that the killing of the child was a deliberate provocation by a far-right group that wanted to trigger a war. In the same interview, he described the film as 'a tragedy' rather than propaganda (hence the operatic lyrics in Greek, which trace the movement of the film as a Greek chorus). But the film has the feel of propaganda. More precisely, it depicts the rioters as victims whose violence is uncontrollable and frightening but whose rage is justified. It is the French state, by implication, which is at war with the *banlieusards* and not the other way around.

This is not the first time, however, that Romain Gavras has aestheticized violence. In 2008, he directed a music video for the track 'Stress' by the electronic duo Justice. The film caused a mini-controversy in France. It shows a gang from an unnamed *banlieue* on a violent spree through the streets of Paris, where they brutalize random passers-by, attacking an elderly woman, assaulting a girl and beating up a policeman with iron bars. At the end of the video is a frightening slowed-down coda, with the gang of uncivilized savages coming at the cameraman and the audience: mindless, murderous thugs in hoodies.

All of this raw energy makes 'Stress' a powerful video, distinguished by the virtuosity of the camerawork. It is also, however, a clear glorification of violence for its own sake and, as such, a shockingly nasty piece of work. Inevitably it was banned and awards were won. The same aesthetic and effects can be seen in recent 'drill' videos in France, much admired by Romain Gavras, in which rappers threaten to kill the police and ordinary civilians as well as their gang enemies. The biggest names at the moment are Kekra, Gazo and especially Ashe 22, who describes himself as 'Franco-Algérien' and wages a metaphorical war against the French state from his base in Lyon, where he works with a collective called Lyonzon.

For all this cultural noise – in books and films, YouTube videos and rap lyrics – the 'coming civil war' in France is still for now imaginary, a chimera. In the same way, the generals' letter was an expression of frustration at the military's inability to deal with political problems, but there was no serious plan and no real enemy.

Fantasizing about a civil war in France is, however, a dangerous game for both the Right and the Left, for both military and cultural avatars. This is because, as Elisabeth Lévy pointed out to me at our cafe table in the rue de l'Echiquier – now much more serious than at any point in our conversation – there is always a dangerous moment, as all military historians and military professionals know, when, quite suddenly and without warning, the language of war can become the real thing.

4

Escaping Reims

'The jewel-box of France ... defeated, destroyed' Georges Bataille, Notre Dame de Reims, *1917*

The only time I actually came up close to Marine Le Pen was on the bright, sunny afternoon of 11 January 2022 at the Majestic Hotel in Paris, a discreet and elegant address, two streets away from the Arc de Triomphe. The hotel is mostly well known for the '*soirée* of the twentieth century', held on 18 May 1922, when James Joyce, Marcel Proust, Pablo Picasso, Igor Stravinsky and Sergei Diaghilev were brought together by the socialites Sydney and Violet Schiff to celebrate the *première* of Stravinsky's ballet *Le Renard* (*The Fox*). It is also famous as the place where on 25 August 1944, General Jacques Massu, who would later lead the French Paras in the 1956 Battle of Algiers, ordered three hundred officers of the German High Command billeted in the hotel to leave. He was armed with only a revolver and was accompanied by a lone guard. He famously cleared the Germans out with a single word: *'Raus!'* – 'Get out!'

It was in one of the grander side rooms of the Hotel Majestic that Le Pen was to give a private briefing to a handful of invited foreign journalists. I took my place and sat down to wait.

I had been chasing Le Pen for a face-to-face interview for a few months. I had good contacts with her inner circle, people who dined with her frequently, and I was told that Elisabeth Lévy had delivered positive reports of my fair-mindedness to the Le Pen office, but the timing was obviously bad – she was gearing up for what may have been her final shot at the presidency and had already publicly affirmed, 'This time I want to win.' On the advice of friends who knew Le Pen, I contacted her director of communications, a guy from Guadeloupe called Verlaine. He was friendly enough, but also clear that given Marine's busy schedule, there would be no one-to-one meeting.

As I was pursuing Le Pen, there had been some weird moments. At that time I had a small office on the rue Pernety, where I would regularly finish and head home, with boring predictability, around 8.30 in the evening. On the way home was a small bar called Os'Minhotos. I had never been in this bar because it seemed like a private club (Os'Minhotos refers to the inhabitants of northern Portugal, and the bar was populated mainly by elderly working-class Portuguese men). One evening, I was accosted by a tall, blonde middle-aged woman at the entrance to the bar, who asked me if I was the English writer who worked in the *quartier*. She invited me in to have a drink, but I said that I was busy and late (which was true), and I went on my way.

A few days later, the same woman reappeared at the same time in the same place with a dark-haired female companion and a bottle of champagne, already open and now half-empty. She thrust a glass into my hand, and suddenly I was in the bar chatting to them. Within minutes, however, they melted away and were replaced by a guy in his thirties wearing a grey suit and open-necked shirt, who began to ask me who I was and about my work. In passing, he said he was interested in my political views. He knew about the book I had written about France and its Arab population, which had (to my disquiet) been critically well received by *Valeurs actuelles*, and claimed to have read pieces I had written on France for the *New Statesman*. What did I think of Macron? What did I think of Israel? What did I think of Le Pen? We talked for about half an hour, and he said he'd like to speak another time. I never caught his name and never saw him again. Not long afterwards, I was invited to the briefing at the Hotel Majestic. This was as close as I was going to get to her for now.

The room fell silent with anticipation as she strode briskly to the small platform where she was to give a short talk, followed by a question-and-answer session. The small audience and intimate atmosphere made the occasion feel more like a friendly university seminar than a press conference. Smiling beneath an anti-Covid mask, cracking jokes and chatting to familiar faces, she seemed to me to be smaller and softer than the hard-faced figure who appears so regularly on French television. Clearly, this afternoon we were in for a full-on charm offensive as she attempted to quell rumours that her presidential campaign was failing before it had even begun.

In the past weeks, she had seen a wave of defections from her party from senior figures such as Jérôme Rivière, Damien Rieu, Gilbert Collard and Maxette Grisoni-Pirbakas, who all now backed Reconquête! (Reconquest!) – the party that had recently been created by the far-right journalist Eric Zemmour, who for the time being was in the ascendancy and looked to be in serious competition with Le Pen.

I once managed to ask him a few questions at a carefully stage-managed press conference in Paris, where he was theatrically flanked by heavies at a venue dramatically revealed to the press at the last minute. He sneered at me, saying that the English were always the sworn enemies of the French, we had been at war for centuries, and he was glad that Brexit had happened for this reason. He trotted out his familiar line that there was no such thing as the extreme right, repeated his favourite slogans – 'our weakness is our weakness', 'we have to be brutal because reality is brutal' – and made fun of the accents of foreign journalists who asked him questions, cupping his ear in a show of incomprehension. For all the noise around his bid for the presidency, he was a cartoon Fascist who was never going to come to power. The danger for Marine Le Pen, however, was that he was siphoning off a significant proportion of her supporters, especially those who suspected that she was genuinely softening her stance on immigration and *insécurité*.

Marine Le Pen gave an impressive performance at the Hotel Majestic. She began by saying that her priorities were to hold on to a vision of France as the political heart of Europe. She was immediately challenged on this by several journalists. She responded that although Germany seemed to be the most significant economic power in Europe, it was in fact the French who provided the model for European civilization and who had always done so. This was why it was so important for the EU and France to maintain sovereignty over their borders and to properly manage immigration.

She said that she was the candidate of *'les oubliés'* ('the forgotten'), by which she meant the ordinary French people who had been left behind by globalization and were now trapped between the indifference of the globalized elites, as represented by Macron, and the pressures and tensions of mass immigration. So far, this was all familiar Le Pen rhetoric: a conflation of nationalism, protectionism and opposition to a multicultural, non-French, non-European society.

My opening question to Le Pen was, however, about Brexit. To my mind, this issue was particularly significant given that the first major defections from Le Pen's leadership had occurred in September 2017, when, in the wake of her electoral failure that year, her chief of strategy, Florian Philippot, formed the breakaway party called Les Patriotes, arguing that Marine Le Pen's softened Eurosceptic stance had cost her the 2017 election. I asked her, in the light of this, whether she thought Brexit had been an act of folly or, as described by Michel Houellebecq, 'an act of courage'.

'Brexit was neither an act of madness nor an act of courage,' she said. 'It was simply an act of sovereignty, and I am an admirer of sovereignty. I have respect for people who want to have a hand in their own future. After that, they can do what they like with that future.'

She went on to say that the Brexit model would be a good thing for all European nations, including France: 'In fact, it's not Brexit which will determine the future of the British people, but the decisions which will be made with this new, reclaimed freedom. What has really struck me has been the insults thrown at the British people and their leaders, simply because these leaders asked the British people what they wanted to do. These insults from the European elites show you what they really think of the people – how they think the people are just obstacles, and that they can get around them, or just go above their heads. If I understand correctly, according to the recent statements by Emmanuel Macron, you have to even take these people on and fight them.'

This did not seem to me to be a softening of Le Pen's Eurosceptic position; rather, it was the opposite – a straightforward condemnation of the European elite, by which she meant the EU, and its relation to the multiple countries for which it legislates.

Over post-briefing drinks, the journalists I spoke to, of various nationalities from North African to Scandinavian and mainly from left-leaning journals, all agreed that Le Pen had been persuasive and fluent and at this stage was still a serious contender for the presidency. 'That is why it is so hard to interview her,' a Polish colleague remarked. 'Like all politicians, she speaks in a code depending on her audience. The real difficulty is trying to understand what she is really trying to say and which audience she is really speaking to on the political chessboard.'

Someone who has worked long and hard on Le Pen's deliberate ambiguity is Michel Eltchaninoff, a specialist in Russian political thought and editor of the magazine *Philosophie*. In 2017, he published a book called *Dans la tête de Marine Le Pen* (*Inside the Mind of Marine Le Pen*), in which he presents a forensic analysis of her real political ideology.

I managed to catch up with Eltchaninoff at the offices of *Philosophie* in Paris. He began by telling me that Marine Le Pen was the only senior member of what was then the FN who had refused to be interviewed by him, quite probably because she had disliked his book on Putin. When Eltchaninoff's book on her appeared, she was apparently furious. She did not contact him directly, but on the evening of the book's launch he received an angry letter from her then-partner Louis Aliot – now the mayor of Perpignan for the RN. Among other insults, Aliot denounced Eltchaninoff as 'a traitor'. Eltchaninoff shrugged this off. 'Maybe she was unhappy because I had told the truth. After all, I had managed to decipher her code.'

In his book, Eltchaninoff traces Marine Le Pen's life in the FN, from her early engagement with politics in the 1980s under the influence of her father, Jean-Marie Le Pen (whom she expelled from the party in 2015 for his unsavoury views on the Holocaust), charting her ascendancy through the ranks to the presidential candidate for the election of 2012. Now, in the 2022 election, she faced a battle on two new fronts: not only those who had defected to the camp of Eric Zemmour, but, worse than these defectors, a caucus in the RN who openly criticized her electoral tactic of *dédiabolisation*, 'detoxifying' the RN, shedding its hardline neo-Nazi trappings. The latest ploy of Zemmour himself was to attach to her the stigma of 'eternal loser'.

I asked Eltchaninoff about this 'detoxifying' tactic and whether it had paid off. 'I do not think that she "detoxified" the party,' he said. 'It is just a matter of presentation.' Eltchaninoff was also clear that, whatever strategizing had been taking place in her camp, Le Pen's political philosophy had not actually changed. This indeed would be impossible for someone who has spent her life immersed in the history and tradition of the far right in France. The key to unlocking her code was in this history and the language she borrowed from it.

Eltchaninoff is very precise on this language. He notes that one of the most important of the double meanings she deploys is the use of the word *le peuple* ('the people'). This in fact is not, as might be assumed, in terms of a revolutionary proletariat or any other left-wing tradition of dissent. Rather, she is using the language of nationalists such as Charles Péguy and Maurice Barrès, who straddled the late nineteenth century and early twentieth century, with a vision of France and the French as defined by the Catholic religion, those who worked the land, the purity of the French language, the very geography of the country, even its cuisine: everything, in effect, that makes France 'a great civilization'.

This is how Le Pen was able to support the revolt of the *gilets jaunes*. To her, by dint of birth and wealth a patrician, they are peasants, but both she and they are in opposition to the perceived metropolitan elites who have turned the French countryside into a desert. Eltchaninoff also points out that Le Pen has given this nationalism a contemporary twist by quoting (or rather distorting) George Orwell's notion of 'common decency' and citing Michel Houellebecq's novel *The Map and the Territory*, in which he imagines France as a theme park, in which the native French themselves have become tourists in their own country. There was therefore a deeply symbolic reason why Le

Pen launched the greatest push yet in her campaign at a rally in the city of Reims on Saturday 5 February 2022. In the end, I didn't join the press corps. I wandered the city in my own time instead, admiring the architecture and the grandeur of the setting. As ever, I felt something chilled in the air in Reims, a visceral feeling that this place was haunted by sinister ghosts, the dreary phantoms of dead kings of a lost France from the wars not so long ago.

Still, it made sense to me that the RN had invited me to Reims, not Paris, to watch Le Pen perform. The city had not been chosen for the rally by chance, but because it was where the first French kings had been crowned and where, as Le Pen said, France 'had been born'. In her speech, she quoted the nineteenth-century poet Paul Verlaine, who wrote that *L'amour de la Patrie est le premier amour* (The love of the homeland is the first love), and then, using the language of Péguy or Barrès, she eulogized the beauty of the French countryside, the language, the French 'art of living' and so on.

This was the prelude to attacks on globalization, the EU and, above all, Macron's policies on immigration. 'Only the French,' she said, 'have the right to decide who lives here.' This rhetoric was punctuated at regular intervals by the chanting of that old FN slogan '*On est chez nous!*' Immigration was linked to crime, she said, and she made a clumsy pun describing France under Macron as *Orange Macronique* – a reference to the bestselling book by Laurent Obertone called *La France Orange Mécanique*, which, borrowing from Anthony Burgess's *A Clockwork Orange*, is a lurid description of ultraviolence throughout France, explicitly linked to immigrants.

Her speech was interrupted by two activists from the feminist activist group Femen, who, with graffitied bare breasts, approached Le Pen's podium chanting 'Marine is a Fascist! Marine is not a Feminist!' They were soon bundled off in handcuffs by security to a chorus of boos. Le Pen made the most of the moment by quipping that 'you would never see naked women under an Islamist dictatorship'. But this was a sideshow.

The most extraordinary moment of the early evening arrived later in her speech. Entirely out of the blue, and out of character, she stepped down from the podium, the lights were dimmed, and she spoke directly and intimately to her audience about her private life. She explained that she had suffered from growing up in a family that was 'quite particular' and had been persecuted as a child for her father's political views. She recalled the bomb attack on the family home in 1976, the very public divorce of her parents and her life as the mother of three children.

Above all, she said, she had sometimes lost her way, fallen, but had always got up again. In a direct riposte to Eric Zemmour's description of her as a loser, she said that she had 'never lost; she had always either won or learned something' from her experiences. This is how and why she understood the 'suffering' of ordinary French people. The speech was cloying, sentimental, embarrassing and cynical in equal measures. Her obvious intention was to set herself against the vote-winning nastiness of Eric Zemmour by presenting the human face of the far right. Of course, her supporters loved it.

Not far from the conference centre in the business park where Le Pen gave her confessional is the small *commune* of Muizon, roughly ten kilometres from the centre of Reims. It is a fairly nondescript place, neither rich nor conspicuously poor. It is made up of villas, small houses, and apartment blocks and has a distinctly suburban air. By this, I mean that it is in every sense disconnected from big-city life; its population is made up of either commuters or locals.

This may be 'peripheral France', but it does not feel deprived, dangerous or marginal, simply ordinary – a place where people live and work without the grand architecture, fashionable restaurants and all the elegant paraphernalia of Reims. There aren't many cafes in Muizon either. The only one I could find was a place which doubled as a betting shop on the rue de Soissons. The early evening drinkers were not communicative, but I did speak to one guy, middle-aged and slightly drunk, who told me he hated the place but there was nowhere else to go. He was unemployed with no prospect of work. 'I just come here to bet and piss the days away,' he said with a smile.

Muizon is also where the family of the writer and philosopher Didier Eribon settled, having moved there from the housing project in Reims where he grew up. For a long time, he wrote, Muizon was just a name to him and he never visited his parents there. He hated the mediocrity of the place, in the same way and for the same reasons that he hated Reims. This was not what he aspired to – and he knew that he had to be somewhere else, preferably Paris, to be the kind of person he wanted to be, or thought he was meant to be.

When he finally did visit Muizon, after the death of his father, he found a typical example of what he called 'reurbanization': 'a semi-urban space in the middle of fields, where it is difficult to tell if it is still part of the countryside or if, with the passage of time, it has become a suburb'.[1] Contemporary France is littered with such incongruous places. There is no visible trace of racism, or indeed many immigrants who might provoke such a feeling, but there is nonetheless a sense of distance from the outside world.

Eribon recounts his childhood in this part of France in his memoir *Retour à Reims* (*Returning to Reims*). Like Marine Le Pen's speech of February 2022, this book, published in 2009, is also a kind of confessional. Unlike *The End of Eddy* by Eribon's friend Edouard Louis, *Retour à Reims* is not a simplistic misery memoir. Eribon grew up in a working-class family with a violent father, whose hatred of homosexuality became directed at his son as he grew up. He recounts early explorations in the cruising spots of Reims, mostly in the Grand Théâtre de Reims (now called 'Opéra de Reims') and the surrounding streets. He makes tentative forays into the only gay bar in Reims (this is the 1970s) but is ill at ease with the code and manners of the underground life. He is also increasingly distant from his family, whom he looks down upon and despises, a fact which makes him feel as guilty as his taboo sexuality.

He finds comfort in literature and philosophy, first in the writings of Jean-Paul Sartre, which inspire the young Eribon with ideas that the authentic self must be self-made and not made by society. He then moves on to sociology, in particular Pierre Bourdieu and Michel Foucault, who link personal experience to political realities. This helps Eribon move on from the classical Marxism of his family, who are faithful Communists. He comes to realize that traditional working-class communism is, like the Church or any other mass organization, a badge of class identity. In the present day, this is how he explains how his family and so many of the working class, who have abandoned communism, can turn to the far right, in particular the RN, which offers a home to *les oubliés*, whose destiny is never to make it out of their small-town lives.

When Eribon arrives in Paris, he begins a career as a left-wing journalist, and then later as a philosopher. He moves in the rarefied circles around Michel Foucault (about whom he later writes a highly acclaimed book). He is also self-aware and intellectually honest enough to admit to himself that along the way he has become a snob. One day in Paris, by chance he encounters a distant relative, who is working as a window cleaner. They talk for a while, but Eribon is terrified that one of his philosophical pals might see him chatting to a worker – who is, by the way, still an old-school Communist. He is aware of the double bind: like everyone in his circle, he thinks of himself as belonging to the radical far left, but he knows, too, that no one in his new circle has actually met a real-life working-class person, except in a nineteenth-century novel or as the object of literary or philosophical theory.

Retour à Reims is really about the fact that he can no longer go back to Reims. When his father dies, he does not attend the funeral and does not want to see the brothers he has not seen for thirty years. He is still in mourning, not so much for his father, although he discovers a fascination in tracing through his father's life as a factory worker, but as 'a form of confusion and disarray' about who he really is and where he really comes from. Having attained the 'authenticity' of his identity as a gay man, he is still 'inauthentic' as a complete human being.

On finishing the memoir, I was reminded of a lecture I had been to in the mid-1990s given by the great hero of Eribon (and Edouard Louis), Richard Hoggart. It was a brilliant, impassioned lecture (still the best academic lecture I have ever seen), referencing Jean-Paul Sartre and Pierre Bourdieu among others: after his working-class upbringing in Leeds, Hoggart had spent years in Paris and knew his way around what would later become Eribon's world. But after the loud applause when the lecture ended, there was also a silent acknowledgement that the hope Hoggart had once placed in the proles had dissipated, that the social mobility of the 1960s had come to an end and that the English (and European) working classes were not in control of their lives, their culture or their destinies.

Eribon would have read Hoggart's *The Uses of Literacy* under the title *La Culture du Pauvre*, 'The Culture of the Poor'. The French title loses Hoggart's original intention of emphasizing the power of education, but the message was the same: the 'culture of the poor' is a real culture as long as the 'poor', or working classes, hold on to their sense of self. But the problem for Eribon was twofold. Firstly, having grown up in Reims, he could see no culture worth holding on to; he didn't want to be 'working class'. Secondly, his sexuality pushed him even further away from the supposed 'authenticity' of the working class. He was trapped. As a left-wing intellectual in Paris, he was fighting for the liberation of people he really despised and looked down on, except that he was also one of them. Eribon is not alone; very many 'intellectuals' of his generation and background – schoolteachers, journalists, academics – are similarly conflicted, leading to a kind of political paralysis among the Bobos. What makes Eribon different is that he is so self-laceratingly honest about it. This is also what gives his book its real political significance. It is the story of how social mobility always leaves people behind, who are abandoned, 'forgotten'. The experience of these people, who after all are real and as alive as the likes of Eribon, cannot be explained away by theories that mean nothing to them. This, Eribon believes, is what explains the corrosive history of the metropolitan radical Left, which has eradicated the old-fashioned model of class warfare in theory, leaving a vacuum to be filled by the likes of Le Pen. Knowing all this, Eribon sees himself as a defector who cannot return to the people and places he has betrayed, and the result is a feeling of guilt.

Eribon's own writings have been betrayed by oversimplification or misreading. Most significantly, in March 2022 a film version of his book, called *Retour à Reims* (*Fragments*), went on general release in France. The film was directed and the text 'freely' adapted by Jean-Gabriel Périot and narrated by the actress Adèle Haenel, who is as well known for her activism against male violence as for her films. Although the film had Eribon's blessing and received a reasonable critical reception, it seems to me a travesty of the book.

The film depicts the working class as one unthinking bloc, lacking nuance, wit or intellect. Having once all been unthinking Communists, they find it easy to switch to casual racism when the first North African immigrants start to arrive in France as fellow 'workers'. It is then a short leap into the arms of the waiting FN. The final part of the film shows footage of the recent demonstrations by the *gilets jaunes*; glorified images of Black Bloc anarchists smashing up banks; a multiracial group, led by women, charging police lines; speeches peppered with the random abstract nouns beloved of the intellectual French Left – '*Solidarité, Egalité, Ecologie*', and so on. The message is clear: freedom for the working class is possible. But only if they are prepared to be shown the way by university-educated intellectuals. It felt like Eribon's thoughtful, self-interrogating book had been reimagined as a piece of patronizing propaganda.

As I set off on my most recent trip to Reims on a sunny morning in Paris in April 2022, there were posters for the film displayed in cinemas across the city, from the Left Bank to the Gare de l'Est. The poster was a dour photograph of what looked like grim-faced trolls – the working class of Reims – and if you had never visited the city before, you might be more than a little apprehensive about what lay at the journey's end: a tough, grey and abandoned city, not unlike Roubaix.

In fact, when you step foot in the city, you might easily wonder if Eribon had actually been making it all up about his impoverished early life. The cathedral is awe-inspiring and the quarter around it is elegant. Unsurprisingly, Reims is a sophisticated destination for French and foreign visitors. It is the political and economic capital of the Champagne region, and the champagne produced here – Louis Roederer, Taittinger, Lanson, Ruinart and Veuve Clicquot – is acknowledged to be the best in the world. You can sample these wines in specialized cellars by yourself or on guided tours. Reims is not a big place, and since it is dominated by the cathedral, wine cellars and expensive restaurants, at first sight it gives the impression of a self-satisfied museum, untouched by the outside world and its miseries.

Half-drunk on the best of the city's food and drink, it is easy to forget that this was once one of the major battlefields of the European wars of religion. Reims was then also a hotbed of conspiracy and treachery. Indeed, one of the first notable English visitors to Reims was allegedly the English playwright Christopher Marlowe. In 1587, the University of Cambridge hesitated to award him his degree, suspecting that he was planning to go to Reims to be ordained as a Roman Catholic priest, in defiance of a royal edict in defensive Protestant Elizabethan England. Mysteriously, the degree was awarded after intervention from high government offices, who pledged that Marlowe was providing 'good service' for the Crown. No one knows what really happened next, but the speculation persisted that Marlowe was sent to infiltrate the English Catholic seminary in Reims, which was seen by the English as a hotbed of potential sedition, whether military, political, religious or all three at once. Rumours about Marlowe the spy were intensified by his lavish spending of far more than he could normally afford in Cambridge during 1584 and 1585, as well as his unexplained absences from the university at that time.

This evidence may seem flimsy, but many Marlowe scholars are convinced that the playwright was indeed at Reims at some point in the 1580s. Marlowe makes reference to the English seminary in his 1592 play *The Massacre at Paris*, which is about the St Bartholomew's Massacre of 1572 and a nakedly anti-Catholic work of propaganda. Marlowe mentions the transfer of the seminary from 'Douay' (now Douai) to Reims, where 'a sorte of English Priestes: Hatch forth treason against their naturell Queene'.[2] This is not, however, the only reference of the era: indeed the seminary was notorious enough to the English public for Shakespeare to casually mention Reims in *The Taming of the Shrew*. One English spy who was most definitely at Reims around that time was Richard Baines, who planned mass murder in the seminary by injecting poison into the college well or communal baths.

Two centuries later, Arthur Young liked and admired Rheims (the English spelling and medieval spelling in Old French) for its imposing architecture. Having been in Paris the previous month and eagerly anticipating further progress in the Revolution, Young stopped off in Epernay, where he drank a bottle to 'true liberty' in France. The Storming of the Bastille happened less than a week later, and the wine also seems to have temporarily relieved his rheumatism. He entered the city through 'a forest of five miles, on the crown of a hill, which separates the narrow vale of Epernay from the great plain of Rheims'. The forest still exists, and it is possible to approach the city on the same route as Arthur Young. He describes the first view of the city as 'magnificent', continuing, 'The cathedral makes a great view and the church of Saint Rémy terminates the town proudly. Many times I have had such views of towns in France but when you enter them all is a clutter of narrow, crooked, dark and dirty lanes. At Rheims it is very different; the streets are all broad, straight, and well built, equal in that respect to any I have seen.' A few days later, on leaving Reims, he again met rural poverty, 'a sad country . . . a country not France'. His rheumatism returned.[3]

Although Reims today is a wealthy place, poverty sits alongside and sometimes encroaches upon the opulence. As you walk away from the tourist quarter, you easily find broken-down apartments, cheap shopping malls and a scrubby long main street which becomes uglier and more wretched as you progress along it. There are blank and dreary streets which stretch from the centre into industrial suburbs and a business park, and ultimately reach nowhere mini-towns like Muizon.

On a bright early evening in April 2022, not long after listening to Marine Le Pen's speech, I spoke to a group of young people who were hanging out on the *terrasse* of the only McDonald's in Reims, which is in fact only metres away from the majesty of the cathedral. Few of them lived nearby, they just studied here, and as young people often are, they were indifferent to their setting, more interested in flirting, smoking and showing off to each other. They were sulky and funny in the same measure and patient enough to allow themselves to be pestered by my questions.

None of them had heard of Didier Eribon or seen the film of

his memoir. They had no interest in class politics. More important and urgent to them were sexual politics and racism. 'France is behind the rest of the world,' said Claire, a twenty-three-year-old student of fashion, elegantly dressed in a man's suit. She was tall, blonde and androgynous. 'I dress how I feel,' she said. 'France is definitely old-fashioned when it comes to issues like gender fluidity and so on, especially a conservative town like Reims – which is just priests, businessmen and bankers.' Her friend, who was smaller but also blonde and dressed in the same sort of suit, nodded shyly along with her.

When I asked Claire about her class position – did she feel middle class (*bourgeoise*) or working class? – she had nothing to say. Her mother worked in a supermarket and her father was retired. He had worked in an office but she didn't know what he had done. She had no money – 'I buy vintage clothes second-hand,' she said – but she refused to be defined by other people's idea of where she fitted into society.

Her friends, male and female, agreed. I asked the group what it was like to be gay in Reims. 'It's not that hard,' said a young man called 'Oscar', a name he had given himself and who identified as 'asexual'. 'Lots of the older generation don't like it, but we don't like them either. Or they're hypocrites. You see plenty of middle-aged married guys in the gay bars or around here.'

He nodded to the several public toilets in the square around the Opéra de Reims – these 'cottages' are called *salons de thé* (teahouses) in French gay slang. Such places had provoked fear, fascination and desire in Didier Eribon in the closeted 1970s.

The one thing this group of young people did have in common with Eribon was that they were all dying to leave Reims and get to Paris or, better still, London or New York. 'This place is so boring,' they all said. But then again, that's the complaint of young people in small towns across the world.

I hadn't expected that this lively group of young people would have deep or passionate political views, but neither did I expect to meet such indifference to politics. Le Pen and Macron were the same for them, and whoever came next would be just as bad. Even among this mixed-race group, there was no taboo in endorsing some of the things that Le Pen said, even if they didn't really care about her.

'Marine understands the people who are stuck in places like Reims and can't get out,' said Claire. 'I study fashion and I know about the art of fashion, but I am not a student in Paris or Bordeaux. I am a nobody from this town, which is empty of culture, and everybody knows it. At my age, I can already see a long future here, where nothing happens, and this is what I don't want.' Other members of the group now joined in the debate. Those who were eligible to vote said that they couldn't be bothered. What was the point? Nothing ever changed. When I pushed the question about social class, they said they thought of themselves as classless and that this was neither a problem nor a good thing. They were outside of society and that's what mattered. It occurred to me later, drinking a coffee at a cafe *terrasse* near the train station, that this is a generation who are already politically homeless.

Part Two

THE UNQUIET CENTRE

5

Return to Dijon

Parc Darcy, Dijon, where I started to write about France in 1987

The American novelist Henry Miller hated Dijon. Having run out of cash in Paris after spending his limited funds too freely on drink and prostitutes, he came to Dijon in 1932 to make some money teaching English. He later wrote: 'Stepping off the train I knew immediately that I had made a fatal mistake ... silent, empty gloom – that's how it impressed me. A hopeless, jerk-water town where mustard is turned out in carload lots.'[1] Miller's mood did not improve when he turned up at his post at the Lycée Carnot, then, as now, one of the most prestigious schools in Dijon. According to Miller, the school was a freezing hellhole populated by idiots, hunchbacks and other 'pasty-faced' grotesques.

Miller arrived at the beginning of winter, when the pipes froze over and broke, leaking sewage into the corridors of the school, where the air was foul and frozen turds were piled up 'like ant-hills'. The rest of Dijon was no better; a cloud of 'scummy sterility' hung over the town, the result of too much heavy learning and the 'cold, greasy fogs' that permeated every corner of the place. Miller, a tireless satyr, was not at home here: 'I didn't even think of cunt, so dismal, so chill, so barren, so gray was it all.'

Dijon makes few other appearances in English literature. So, when I set off to Dijon in the autumn of 1987 to take up a post teaching English at the local university, Henry Miller had both the first and the last word. Miller's account appears in his 1939 novel *Tropic of Cancer*, which was admired by George Orwell among others for its scabrous, hilarious, snarling prose. I, too, liked the book, but it was most certainly not advised reading for my journey on the boat train to Dijon. Stepping off the train for the first time, I was as full of trepidation as Miller.

In the first few weeks, I wandered the streets looking for accommodation and trying to find my bearings. I discovered that the centre of Dijon is a relatively small place, easily conquered on foot. I stayed in a small hotel on the rue Mariotte near the station. The hotel was bleak and shabby, and it's usually never a good idea to live near a railway station in France – they are places which always attract a floating and usually nocturnal population of beggars, winos and junkies. Dijon is an elegant town but my first impressions were overwhelmingly negative. The nearby streets had a few run-down bars populated by seedy characters, but it was here that I could check ads in the local paper, *Le Bien Public*. I was turned away at every apartment I looked at because I didn't have the right paperwork and a local sponsor and, I guessed, because I was suspiciously foreign.

In the end, the only place I could afford and where I was accepted without a '*dossier*' (bank details, references and so on) was a '*chambre de bonne*' – a small room at the top of a distinguished Renaissance Burgundian townhouse in the Notre-Dame district. In earlier, more prosperous times for the family that owned the house, this would have been the maid's room. Now, money could be made letting it out – this was in fact fairly standard accommodation for down-at-heel students or au pairs in all French towns.

This room was, without doubt, the most wretched place I have ever lived in. It was more like a cave than a room, apparently carved out of the stone interior of the building. There was cold running water and a toilet in the unlit ancient corridor, where you had to constantly watch your step. I got to the room on a rickety, potentially lethal staircase. I was forbidden to enter the main part of the residence by the cleaver-faced lady of the house, who spoke to me with a sort of '*accent pointu*' – a clipped voice which was supposed to sound posh and non-local but sounded mostly like a nasal whine.

From what I could see of the house, the family were still rich – heavy opulent furniture and decor in the *bourgeois* style of the late nineteenth century. A week or so after moving in, I was visited by a female friend, Heather, a fellow teacher at the university. She was appalled at the state of the place and my clothes, which were covered in brick dust. Heather insisted that I move. When she had gone, the gimlet-eyed landlady knocked at my door and told me that under no circumstances was I allowed to receive females, and especially not prostitutes. When I told Heather about this the next day, she laughed and told me again that I needed to move.

The next place wasn't much better. This was a student residence on the rue Jean Baptiste Morlot in the east of Dijon. It was dirty, uncomfortable and noisy, with sporadic heating. I had to give classes at the university at eight in the morning. Although it was a short walk away, there was no bus, and I got soaked several days in a row in heavy downpours while struggling to get there. That autumn, I suffered one heavy cold after another. I missed classes, and the unsmiling and unsympathetic dean of the English department threatened to sack me and send an unfavourable report to my home university in England.

On my occasional walks into the city centre, I passed the Lycée Carnot, where Henry Miller had been so miserable. In my room at the *résidence*, I read more of his attacks on Dijon: 'It is not only winter here but death, misery, especially fog,' Miller confided in a letter to Anaïs Nin, the lover he had left behind in Paris. He went on: 'merely an alley of dead bones, twisted and crawling figures buried in shrouds; effigies or fat little monsters at the front of St Michael's Church. In every crevice of the old gnarled brow, the hollow song of the night wind, and on the lacy rubble of cold and stiff garments, a cloudy slime of absinthe-like fog and frost.'[2]

In my own misery at the *résidence*, I was starting to think Miller had a point. But as I settled into my life there, I began to enjoy the busy energy of the place brought by the students. Dijon was loaded with charm, even beauty if you had eyes to look, and having originally planned to stay for only one year, I stayed on for three more. And although not all of my experiences were positive, even in the worst of circumstances – sick, hungry or hard up for cash – I never quite gave up on the place.

Returning to Dijon in the autumn of 2022, I stepped off the train, this time in anticipation rather than trepidation. But I was wary, too. I didn't know how I would feel revisiting a former, now distant life.

The first thing I noticed was that it was all still there, as solid and unchangeable as ever. The train station was larger and more modern than it had been, and there were now high-speed trains to Zurich, Lausanne and Milan, but the local lines still trundled all across Burgundy. Names on the train route read like a wine menu in a Michelin-starred restaurant, with stops at the noble vineyards of Gevrey-Chambertin, Nuits-Saint-Georges and Meursault, as well as handsome towns like Nevers and Auxerre. Any trip in Burgundy, by train, bus or car, will take you through mild, wooded rolling hills, lush green farmland and some of the richest wine-growing land in the world. Little wonder that Burgundy also claims to be the true gastronomic capital of France, vying eternally with Lyon for this title. Unsurprisingly, as a place that lays claim to such riches, Burgundian culture has always been traditional and inward-looking – a place that has no need of Paris or other big cities. The Burgundian accent still persists across the region, a deep, loamy sound with traces of German and Dutch. Until the nineteenth century, the dialect of Burgundy contained several sub-dialects, and even now you can hear regional differences between the various parishes, villages and towns.

In 1789, Arthur Young spent three days in Dijon, having journeyed through Franche-Comté and most of Burgundy, where he noted 'flat meadows of verdure; commons for great herds of cattle, vastly flooded and the haycocks under water'.[3] He admired Dijon and had contacts to meet there, most notably the scientist Louis-Bernard Guyton de Morveau, who was 'not only the first chymist of France, but one of the greatest that Europe has to boast'. Guyton de Morveau's house still stands at 17 Place Bossuet. Young found him to be 'void of affectation, free from those airs of superiority sometimes found in celebrated characters ... a lively conversable, eloquent man'. Guyton de Morveau's most noted achievement was the discovery of chlorine as a disinfectant. He was also a committed Revolutionary.

'Dijon, on the whole, is a handsome town,' Young also wrote, 'the streets, though old built [are] wide and very well paved, with the addition, uncommon in France, of *trottoirs* [pavements].' Most of what Arthur Young saw in Dijon is still there, notably the Musée des Beaux-Arts, which Young would have known as the Palais des Etats, and the great salon in the Palais called la Salle des Statues, where you can look at the ceiling, which was painted in 1786 by Pierre-Paul Prud'hon, a graduate of the Ecole de Dessin of Dijon. It is a homage to the Prince of Condé, then exiled in Germany and certain to be hanged for treason if he ever returned to Dijon. 'It is a ceiling well executed,' commented Young.

As I exited the station at Dijon, I passed a group of four heavily armed soldiers walking in a phalanx. This is now a familiar sight in Paris and other big cities, and has been since the massacre of 13 November 2015, but in quiet, comfortable Dijon it felt jarring. There was a new tramway system that was smart, quiet and efficient. The avenue Maréchal Foch, which leads the way into the city, was run-down and drab. It had formerly been busy with La Grande Taverne, cinemas, restaurants, but now looked forlorn – a handful of kebab shops and nail bars. Since my absence, the centre of gravity in Dijon had obviously shifted.

Central Dijon is still constructed around squares, parks, monuments and boulevards, and is made up of heavy imposing architecture on the main streets, the cathedral flanked by private houses from pre-Revolution France and the massive and elegant Palais des Ducs. But there was a lot here that was new. There were plenty of non-French shops, which gave the place a more outward, European feeling than the introspective and insular place I had known. The town had a polished look. The historic centre is now pedestrianized and very sleek. As I walked around, I felt that I could have been anywhere in Europe. Money had also been spent on growth and infrastructure in the wider region around the city – unsurprising since Dijon is the political and administrative capital of Burgundy and, as such, a powerful centre of operations throughout the region. With its prosperity and its new, freer, more international identity, Dijon is an almost perfect example of one of Christophe Guilluy's new citadels.

From the avenue Maréchal Foch, I walked to Place Darcy, where there is a small, tidy park and a triumphal arch called La Porte Guillaume, built in 1786 on the site of what had been a gate to Dijon and named after a distinguished abbot from the tenth century.

I remembered an ancient and rather forlorn-looking shop behind the arch which deals in rare stamps called Dijon Philatélique. It was still there. I always used to wonder how this place kept going, given that I had never seen anyone go in or out (where exactly was the door anyway?). But if you glance at the stamps and other documents for sale in the shop – postcards, old letters, call-up papers, coins – the eye-wateringly high prices will reassure you that the proprietor of this dingy shop only has to sell one or two stamps per week to pay the bills.

On the other side of the arch, heading towards the rue de la Liberté, is the Restaurant de la Porte Guillaume. This place has been run by four generations of the Frachot family and specializes in *'cuisine du terroir'* – cooking with ingredients from the rich farmland of Burgundy. The restaurant is not necessarily the best or most fashionable in Dijon, but both the menu and the clientele provide glimpses of the inner life of the city. That evening, I dined in its mildly shabby dining room, crowded with old Dijon families eating the heavy food with characteristic lofty restraint. They were uniformly stony-faced – there was no wine-induced bonhomie here – and they spoke to each other as if they had never met before.

I ate *le véritable jambon persillé de Bourgogne, cigollettes de grenouilles, purée d'ail et jus de persil, le filet de canette rôti, jus au pain d'epices, etuvée de navets boule d'or au miel* and *champignons du hameau de Corcelotte-en-Montagne.* I hate menus in translation, so

I will say no more than this was essentially a feast of ham, then frogs, then duckling and mushrooms – hearty and delicate at the same time, and all local produce. I drank wines which were so good that they made me feel as if I'd never tasted wine before. I was slightly drunk by the end of the meal, which I was aware was considered not to be good form. I left a large tip, which again only underlined my boorish behaviour. I could imagine the stony-faced Dijonnais tutting among themselves as I left. One woman in late middle age, elegantly dressed, was pushing morsels of baby frogs around her plate with a sharp knife as if she was trying to torture them before eating them.

For a few years, I had lived just around the corner from this spot with my girlfriend Sylvie, having escaped the university *résidence*. Sylvie was blonde, wore her hair in a sort of sixties-style bob and was in love with English literature and the idea of the English. She had a sharp tongue and was the first but not the last French person to describe herself unselfconsciously to me as a *bourgeoise*, or, in slang, a *bourge*, which I found confusing. My reading of Marxist texts thus far had always encouraged me to believe that *bourgeois* meant rich, posh and exploiting the workers. She was therefore my class enemy. I didn't let this bother me, as she was beautiful and chic and this would be my first French love affair.

One of the ways that Sylvie defined herself as a *bourgeoise* was by frequently referring to the term *la pudeur* to describe herself; '*je suis très pudique*,' she would often say, using the term in its adjectival form, when she was offended by bad language, bad manners or what she perceived as incorrect behaviour. *La pudeur* is a difficult concept to explain in English. These days, the term is most often understood to refer to a prudishness towards sexual matters, but that is not really what it means. It was certainly first used in the sixteenth and seventeenth centuries to denote mistrust of crudity or immorality with regard to sex, particularly with regard to 'decent Christian women' (this was how it was used by Michel de Montaigne and Corneille). The word has its roots, however, in the Latin *pudor*, meaning a sense of modesty and also honour. This is how it is used in its pure Latin form in other Romance languages. This is also how Sylvie used it: as a moral concept whose only real equivalent in English would be the equally contested word 'decency'. It was *la pudeur* that made her disapprove of my idleness and my vague left-wing politics.

Sylvie dressed in a style that was fashionable for young people in France in the mid-1980s and called BCBG, an abbreviation for '*bon chic, bon genre*' ('good style, good people'). The clothes were basically preppy – boys and girls favoured neat, angular haircuts, smart polo shirts, loafers and multicoloured silk socks or tartan '*chaussettes Burlington*', sometimes slinging an expensive jumper around their necks. Sylvie always sported a Hermès scarf.

The clothes were also a code for a whole philosophy of life which was politically conservative and obsessed with taste and refinement. The natural enemy of BCBG youth was the '*beauf*', a slang word abbreviated from *beau-frère* (brother-in-law), which came into popular usage in the 1970s via the satirical magazines *Charlie Hebdo* and *Le Canard enchaîné*. The *beauf* can take various forms – the bar-room braggart, the football fan, the bingo-going classes – but it always stands for everything indelicate and offensive. The *beauf* is uncultured, ignorant and definitely non-metropolitan, essentially the ordinary working-class French person, and therefore an object of contempt for the classes who want to set themselves up as a new aristocracy. The key word for describing with horror the practices of the *beauf* was '*vulgaire*' – a word which I can never hear in French without imagining it as a sneer. Sylvie used it a lot, usually to chastise me for some transgression or other of the BCBG code (a tie knotted the wrong way, a taste for beer and chips, a liking for reggae or Belgium: it could be anything). If Sylvie had any political leanings, they were to the right. But the contempt for the *beauf* crosses all political lines and has, of course, been inherited by the

Bobos in the twenty-first century, whose politics are left wing but whose distance from the everyday reality of most ordinary French people is just as wide as that of the BCBG.

For a while I felt like a spy in Dijon, connecting codes and meanings and slowly working out the pattern of behaviour and thought in this caste system, where I was still an outsider. Not everyone could be BCBG – this was preserved for the Parisian elites and the old Catholic families of towns like Dijon. But you could buy the clothes and then buy into the lifestyle. With my BCBG clothes and my odd accent, Sylvie's parents had no sense of my true working-class origins (which would have made me unacceptable as a suitor), but nor could they work out quite where I fitted into their world. This is what made them nervous. They were snobs who did not know exactly what they were looking down on. But for a while, love and sex conquered all – at least for Sylvie and me.

The rue Auguste Perdrix, where we had lived, was once quite smart. Our flat thirty years ago was a new build and extremely comfortable and up to date. We had no television but listened to a lot of music. She loved Les Rita Mitsouko and the much-mocked whiny singer Jean-Jacques Goldman, a favourite of teenage girls, and she tolerated my own UK indie tastes. Otherwise, we listened to the news and cultural documentaries on the radio or simply spent our evenings reading.

My main guide then to French society and culture was a book by John Ardagh called *France in the 1980s*, which was a set text in the French department at Manchester University.[4] Ardagh was an *Observer* journalist who had lived in France and Algeria and had a deep and comprehensive knowledge of France, which he was able to present clearly to an apprentice student of the country like me.

As Sylvie and I listened to Europe 1 or France Culture, I would lie on the floor reading Ardagh's book, soaking up stuff about devolution (very boring), nuclear power (slightly less boring), the new consumer society (educational), work structures (useful), how French politics worked (or mainly didn't) and the French media (very interesting: it was all corrupt and biased). It was a map of a society on the move. For all the difficulties it faced, Ardagh's France was a progressive country whose biggest challenges were how to modernize the economy and provide more and better services for its citizens.

But this was not the whole story. Even Dijon had its tough areas, and racial relations could be tense. I had my own experience of this one night when I got beaten up for talking to a girl in a bar on the rue Berbisey, the nearest thing in Dijon then to a multicultural, bohemian quarter. I was out of place in this area; with my BCBG clothes, I looked like the very definition of the enemy to a non-*bourgeois* clientele: a classic young *facho* (Fascist). My attackers were three Algerians. I knew this because before I was punched in the face I was called a racist and a dog and told not to 'fuck with Algerians'. I was knocked to the floor and repeatedly kicked and punched until a police car showed up. My attackers fled, smashing a shop window on the way. The first thing the police asked me in my bloodied and shattered state was whether my attackers were North African. When I said they probably were, they shook their heads. They would be impossible to find, they said. They were all just savages anyway. I limped back to Sylvie and our apartment, leaving a trail of blood from my broken nose along the way. The next day, the neighbours complained about the blood on the stairs of the apartment building.

These days, the flat I shared with Sylvie is slightly dilapidated and faded. The Irish pub on the corner of the street, Le Kilkenny, has been renamed Le Cellier. The small orchard of apple trees, which was our morning view across the street, was still there, now sturdier and stronger than ever in the misty rain.

I didn't linger or feel especially nostalgic or melancholy, just reflective about the passing of time. I walked back to La Porte

Guillaume past the statue of Dijon's most famous son, the sculptor François Rude, born in 1784, who helped provide a passage between the neo-classical style and romanticism in sculpture. The statue depicts Rude at work, with a long beard, a sculptor's apron and a chisel. I always liked this statue, which makes him look like a fierce Russian novelist, which is appropriate since both Leo Tolstoy and Ivan Turgenev had lodged at the old Grand Hôtel La Cloche in March 1857 – this was after Tolstoy, in a fury, had challenged Turgenev to an abortive duel. After my relationship with Sylvie ended, I moved to an apartment at the top of an *hôtel particulier* overlooking the market. I loved the height and panoramic view of the town and drinking *pichets* of cheap but tasty wine in the cafes alongside the marketplace.

The main artery of Dijon is the rue de la Liberté, which spins eastwards from La Porte Guillaume into the older medieval and Renaissance districts. From this road, I took a detour to the Place Grangier. I was not surprised but still a little disappointed to find that the huge and cavernous porno cinema which had once proudly dominated the *angle* of rue du Château and Place Grangier was no longer there. It has been replaced by a three-storey, very smart and very twenty-first-century bookshop with a coffee bar and book clubs. I used to pass this porno cinema most days and wondered how it could keep going given its size and that, as far as I could see, there was only ever a meagre trickle of punters sidling in all day. Sometimes couples would wander in, and after dark a prostitute was usually on duty at the corner of rue du Temple. I vividly remember the poster for a real film called *Fesses de Tonnerre* (Arses of Thunder). This title stuck in my mind, not because of what the film might or might not have been about (easy to guess), but because it struck me as weirdly poetic – as grandiose, monumental and ludicrous as, say, a poem by Victor Hugo.

Opposite the ghost of the porno palace is a mildly sinister building usually called *La Maison Japonaise* (The Japanese House).

It stands out because it looks nothing like anything else in the surrounding streets, or the whole of Dijon for that matter. It is a four-storey triangular building designed in 1907 by the architect Louis Perreau, a native of Dijon, who also built the imposing post office around the corner. The central point of the building's facade juts out into rue du Temple and rue du Château like the prow of a ship, apparently setting sail in the imagination of the architect for the mysteries of the Orient. This much is signalled by the pagoda-like constructions on the roof. The rest of the building is classic art nouveau – sinuous, curved window frames, ornate entrances and highly detailed glasswork. This building would have been at home in Brussels or Barcelona at the end of the nineteenth century, when the art nouveau style in Europe was at its height. In Dijon it is out of place and gloomy, but totally compelling as a piece of street theatre. For this reason, it always seemed to me to sit perfectly in its incongruity alongside its opposite neighbour, the porno cinema.

On a rainy Saturday afternoon in late 2022, I spoke to two students, Justine Mauchamp and Lola Morel, next to La Porte Guillaume. They were second-year medical students collecting for a charity for sick children, and I said that I would give them money if I could just ask them a few questions (I would have given them money anyway). They were happy to answer my questions, even try out a little English. They told me that they were both originally from Dijon and living at home, as is still the norm for many students in France. I asked them if they could tell me a little about their experience of university so far.

Justine began. 'At first, it was hard to understand the administration, where you were supposed to be and what you were supposed to be doing. I think I lost several weeks of the course going to the wrong place at the wrong time,' she said. 'Also, it's hard to make friends at the university unless you already know someone. I have made new friends but there is no proper community of students on campus. You have to really make an effort to meet people, and I think the university doesn't care about our individual experiences.'

Lola jumped in. 'One of the difficulties is that we have such large classes and a huge workload. But we don't have much, hardly any, support from our professors. They usually don't even know our names and just shout at us if we don't know the right answer.'

This reminded me of the week I'd spent in a teaching hospital in Paris with pneumonia. The same hospital had admitted George Orwell, also suffering from respiratory problems, in 1929. The experience inspired his famous essay 'How the Poor Die' – a fact I had bleakly recalled as I lay suffering in intensive care. Happily, the hospital is now a model of twenty-first-century clinical excellence, though the bedside manner of the professors who displayed me as a specimen to their students was as high-handed as ever. As I lay in bed struggling to breathe, I was visited by a professor accompanied by a visibly intimidated gaggle of students.

He didn't acknowledge me but just barked at his students, now gathered around my bed: 'What is the mortality of this man?'

'A few weeks?' suggested one girl tentatively.

I winced.

'*Non!*' he said loudly and angrily. 'I will tell you when I leave this room!'

I'm still wondering now.

When I told this story to Justine and Lola, they laughed in recognition. 'This is the typical French way of teaching,' said Justine. 'It's like they don't want you to learn. I have friends in law, or who study business and modern languages, and they tell the same story. Getting a university diploma in France is a real test, almost like a military test.' They both really wanted to take their studies and expertise abroad, preferably to a British or American university hospital or, failing that, Germany or the Netherlands.

'That is the only way we can really develop our skills,' said Justine. 'In France, the health service is excellent but everyone is underpaid and overworked, exploited in fact. We need another system.' I pointed out that the NHS in Britain was not a good place to work right now, but they were still determined to get out of France.

One of the reasons that students have such a hard time in France is the long-standing division between prestigious *grandes écoles*, which are still the providers of the political and administrative elites, and universities, which are very much the poorer relation. A medical qualification or a law degree will almost certainly propel you towards a career. But a *'licence'* is a mere undergraduate degree, which in too many subjects leads directly to unemployability.

This much was long evident to my friend Eric Pothion, who studied with me in Dijon and graduated with a degree in modern languages in 1989 but struggled to find a decent job in France for the next decade, before striking out and moving to England and then Canada, where he found the kind of work and lifestyle he could never have aspired to in France. During a recent conversation, I asked if he would ever move back.

Eric was born in Chalon-sur-Saône, a small town in eastern Burgundy, to a working-class Socialist family. He was especially proud that his grandfather had played a prominent role in the Popular Front in 1936, campaigning for workers' rights. 'I understand the anger in France right now,' he recently told me. 'I can sense it as soon as I arrive on French soil, back for a holiday. There is a kind of permanent anger, as too many people are disillusioned with their way of life and can't see how to change it. The country is divided, and I come from the part that feels abandoned. This was clear when I was at university and then when I left. Since the 1930s, the working classes have never been properly represented in a French government. Instead, they are despised and have been betrayed. We have not moved forward.'

There is an ambiguity here, which Eric readily admits. Although his sympathies have always been with the Left in France, he sees the Left as divided into two camps: old-school Marxists or Communists, who dream of a revolution led by a proletariat which no longer exists, and the leftist Bobos, who actively despise what shreds remain of the organized French working classes. Both forms of leftism, he says, have paralysed French society and stymied social mobility.

'The French population is "siloed" from the days you begin your education,' said Eric. 'It is a myth that France has no class system. It does not have the same system as Britain but is just as harsh, and you learn this at university, when you are about to enter the world.'

In the 1980s, the French university system was Darwinian, with students kicked out of university for failing fiendishly difficult exams which often bore little relation to what they had studied. When I was teaching in Dijon, the dropout rate after the first year was forty per cent. In Britain or America, this would have led to serious questions being asked of a department, but in Dijon this was regarded by the university management as a satisfying result. People I spoke to in other French universities told me that there was a tacit policy of deliberately giving low grades to second-year students and failing them because otherwise there would be no room to accommodate them in the third.

One of the most difficult jobs I had as a young would-be academic in Dijon was to host literary conversation sessions for students preparing for the *agrégation* examination in English. This is a competitive exam open to students with a master's degree or above. The success rate depends on how many jobs the state decrees to be available in any given year; for example, although 300 students might prepare for the *agrégation* in a rare foreign language like Japanese, there might only be one post available in any given year, so 299 students will spend a year of their lives preparing for an exam that they are doomed to fail. This insane system dates back to 1766, when the Jesuits were banned from educating the elite cadres in France and the *agrégation* was introduced by the state to take over their monopoly. The exam is still seen as the gold standard in the French educational system, and someone who has passed, an *agrégé*, is spoken of in hushed, reverential tones, although this is also partly because it provides a comfy job for life in a *lycée*, a good university or the civil service. The system also produces its fair share of nervous breakdowns and suicides.

My class for the *agrégation* was a tense bunch of determined neurotics who saw failure as the worst thing that could ever happen to them. They were ferociously competitive in class, ruthless in attacking fellow students. This was not a seminar but a bear pit. My job was to act as a referee and try to limit the intellectual violence that they were inflicting on themselves. I remember one student in particular. Edith was always neatly dressed in a *bourgeoise* style, quite small and very correct. When I spoke to her in the corridor or cafeteria, she was perfectly pleasant, if unsmiling. I had to be on my guard as well, in case she slipped in a thorny question about Swinburne or Thomas Percy or someone else whom I hadn't read, or possibly hadn't even heard of, but to the other students, she was a monster.

Her English was extremely refined, sometimes over-refined to the point of incomprehensibility, which was not helped by her strangled neo-Edwardian pronunciation (she did literally speak the dead Queen's English, pronouncing 'gone' as 'gorn' and 'off' as 'orf'). But this suited the nature of the examination, which was not to show that you knew your subject and could teach, but rather that you could use your brilliance to dazzle and destroy. During seminar debates, she would begin a sentence with '*Mais non! Mais non!*' and a raised finger, the classroom equivalent of a bull snorting and pawing the dirt and looking at you dead in the eye.

But this is what it took to succeed (she did pass the exam,

while the rest of the class failed). Even then, as a fledgling teacher myself, I couldn't see the point of an exam in which you produced a seven-hour-long argument deconstructing obscure texts and then showed off to a panel of examiners with your arcane and archaic English. I certainly couldn't see how this would make you a better teacher of English to a bored and restive group of teenagers.

I hated these sessions. Everybody was older and better qualified than me, aggressive and intolerant of any perceived ignorance. It didn't help that the set text that we were reading that year was *The Private Memoirs and Confessions of a Justified Sinner* by James Hogg, a classic of Scots literature from 1824 and as full of traps and snares as *Tristram Shandy*. Worse still, much of the vocabulary was in Scots. After a lot of reading, I had a vague idea of the tricky plot of the book, but when it came to the vocabulary, I could not confess to my group that I was baffled: they would have despised me even more than they did already. I had no option but to lie. So over the weeks that we studied the book, a new version of Hogg's novel emerged, one rewritten with my own invented interpretation of Scots. When asked to explain a sentence like, 'They find ma bits o' gibes come hame to their hearts wi' a kind o' yerk, an' that gars them wince', I stuttered, then adopted a look of supreme confidence to try to reassure the class (not always successfully; there were French mutterings) and said whatever came into my head. I would have felt guilty about my lying ways but, after all our weeks of study, the text never came up in the final examination, so none of this seemed to matter. This was my secret justification for being a fraud. More to the point, it revealed the whole vacuity of the exercise.

Since I was last a very minor component of the French educational system in the 1980s, there have been attempts to improve the system, particularly with regard to admissions. Now there is a system called 'Parcoursup', in which students can see information about departments in advance and can apply to up to ten universities and hold twenty applications in reserve. However, as might have been anticipated, this has generated massive amounts of paperwork for the universities. Students also complain that they have no idea what criteria each university uses to accept or decline their application.

Predictably, the political parties of the Right and the Left have been slogging it out over the rights and wrongs of Parcoursup. Roughly speaking, the Left argues that it gives access to students from poorer and more diverse backgrounds; the Right argues back that there are already too many students and that France is anyway no longer a true meritocracy. And so the stranglehold of the *grandes écoles* is maintained, and instead of embedding the concept of '*egalité*' across universities, the Parcoursup has created social stasis. Although the chaos that followed the introduction of Parcoursup in 2018 has been controlled to a relative extent, for both sides of the political argument, the French educational system still doesn't work.[5]

'We believe in our studies,' said Lola Morel, 'but we have no faith at all in the system or the future.'

When I lived in Dijon, I sometimes used to walk or cycle back into the town from the university through the *banlieue* of Les Grésilles, a jumble of villas and concrete *cités* which housed an immigrant population, mainly from North Africa. Les Grésilles was built in 1955 and was originally supposed to be a new form of urban utopia. This was the period of *les Trente Glorieuses* in France, the thirty years of the post-war period which saw unprecedented economic growth in the country, a boom in new housing and the birth of a new consumerist society. The first inhabitants of Les Grésilles were middle class, reflecting the aspirations of the architects, who designed the suburb to create a new way of living in a revitalized and modernized France.

The architects' dreams began to crumble away during the financial crisis of the mid-1970s. During this period, the middle classes gravitated back to the centre of Dijon, where they could be sure that their money was well invested and where the standard of living was high. Les Grésilles was neglected, buildings fell into a state of disrepair, and some of them were in such an advanced state of dilapidation that they were uninhabitable. Demolition of the grimmest tower blocks, only twenty years old, soon followed. Before long, the dream suburb was abandoned by its original inhabitants and left to an immigrant population, newly arrived in France from its former colonies, who had no connection to Dijon, its culture or its history. The area was soon demonized for its drug crime, violent clashes with the police, and the sense that it was out of control.

Back then, I was drawn to Les Grésilles specifically because it wasn't central Dijon. Women often wore the veil in this area, cafes didn't always sell alcohol, and there were mosques. There was always the distinct sense that you were walking through someone else's culture but I never felt threatened. In fact, the only time I glimpsed something of the fractures between French society and the Islamic world was back in the city centre of Dijon in the *quartier* of Saint-Bénigne, where I was teaching English at a private school for adults to make money on the side. One of those I taught was a medical student from Syria who spoke fluent French and carried a French passport. The one-to-one classes were friendly and good-natured until I casually broached the subject of the recent *fatwa* against Salman Rushdie and the book-burning demonstrations then taking place in the north of England. I remarked on the madness of religious extremism versus artistic freedom, fully expecting my student, a Sunni Muslim, to nod along in acquiescence – he was after all a moderate and highly educated young man who lived in the West. Instead, my student exploded with rage, accusing me of stupidity and ignorance, and stormed out of the classroom. I never saw him again.

In recent times, there have been strange and unpredictable

conflicts in this area. The most dramatic and widely reported example was the battle between Chechen and North African immigrants in Les Grésilles in 2020. On 12 June, a sixteen-year-old Chechen was badly beaten up by North African drug dealers as a 'warning' to the Chechens to stay out of the local drugs trade.

According to Chechen sources, the police took no action, so the community decided to take the law into its own hands. A call to arms went out on social media and, suddenly, on the night of 13 June, Les Grésilles was packed with Chechens, apparently from all over France and Belgium, some armed with iron bars and baseball bats, some of them flaunting Kalashnikovs for selfies and social media, although you couldn't tell whether they were real or fake. Cars were set alight, and any young male who looked North African was set upon.

The chaos deepened when a group of a hundred or so Chechens came into central Dijon to smash up a cafe called Le Black Pearl on the boulevard de La Trémouille, near the busy Place de la République. This was a *shisha* bar known to be the hang-out of the North African gang leaders. Eyewitnesses posted videos of the Chechens storming the cafe. A young Chechen called Lamro, originally from Saint-Etienne, claimed in the pages of *Le Bien Public* to be a member of the group that attacked Le Black Pearl, and testified that the assault was not on Dijon or its inhabitants but specifically targeted the drug dealers. This did not reassure any of the Dijonnais, who saw only wild destructive forces invade their city that night.

The next few days saw a kind of guerrilla warfare between the Chechens and the North Africans, as the North Africans tried to reclaim their ground around Les Grésilles. At one point, a car was driven at top speed into a group of armed Chechens. The car overturned, and its driver, who was badly injured, was dragged out of the car by hooded men, who cried 'Allahu Akbar'. The police struggled to contain the violence; there were blockades, fires, smoke and gunshots. The television channel BFMTV, incredulous at and hypnotized by what was happening, led the news with the headline 'Scenes from the Far West in Dijon!'

On 10 July, Les Grésilles was visited by the Prime Minister, Jean Castex, the Minister of the Interior, Gérald Darmanin, and representatives from the local town council. The television footage shows the stand-off between the politicians and the Chechen population of Les Grésilles. Castex was clearly angry. When a local North African inhabitant called Ayadi tried to plead with him that the fighting was only in self-defence, Castex replied sternly that the police had acted impeccably and upheld republican values. 'The behaviour here cannot be tolerated anywhere in the Republic,' he went on, in a schoolmasterly manner, saying that the authorities knew who was responsible for the violence and that the culprits would 'be sanctioned with greatest severity'. In this exchange, you can see the distance between the two worlds of the *banlieues* and 'official France', which in every sense do not speak the same language.

Returning to Les Grésilles in 2022, I was completely disorientated. In the past three decades, most of the original buildings had been either demolished or renovated, and I could not easily pick out the points of reference which I had formerly used to guide my wanderings. Much of the new building was attractive. Apartment blocks and community housing had been fitted to a human scale. There were green spaces. Money had been invested in sports facilities and community associations.

I walked through the area for several hours, noting the physical improvements. When I stopped for a coffee in a cafe called Le Guim's the atmosphere was relaxed, even convivial. Most of the fellow drinkers were either Turks or East Europeans. Conversation centred on football, as it so often does in such places, and it was easy to fall into the small talk. Mention of the violence of 2020 was waved away with laughter and jokes about the police.

Yet on leaving Le Guim's, I felt a simmering sense of unease that deepened as I headed back to central Dijon – a half-hour walk away. There was no logic to this. I had been met by nothing but smiles and friendly banter in Les Grésilles. My disquiet came rather from the feeling that Les Grésilles was technically France but somehow not quite French. This was nothing to do with the ethnic composition of Les Grésilles, but simply the feeling that lives were being lived here which would never connect with mainstream French society. There seemed to me to be a potentially dangerous *décalage* – a French word which is hard to translate but often means 'lack of concordance'.

Dijon is one of the major capitals of what is often termed '*la France profonde*' ('deep France'). This is a term which has several loaded meanings.

Most often, it has been used in the twentieth century to describe a now-lost France – a traditional, usually rural part of the country whose language, dialects, culture and politics stood apart from the sophisticated ideas and ideologies of Paris. This was an imaginary version of French history but one that was useful for the ideologues of French fascism, most notably the writers Charles Maurras and Maurice Barrès, who in the late nineteenth century and early twentieth century developed a vision of France which was quite literally rooted in its soil – a nationalism of land, peasants and the '*pays réel*', meaning 'real France'. It is easy to see how this vision persists in the culture of the far right in France: Marine Le Pen is only the latest and loudest cheerleader for this version of France which resists immigration, rootlessness, globalization.

At the same time as Fascist intellectuals were theorizing about the *pays réel*, there was a mass migration from *la France profonde* towards Paris. Many of the new arrivals entered lower-middle-class professions such as schoolteaching and clerking. Their first instinct was to assimilate into the city and bury their provincial origins. To do this, they sought to adopt '*le bon ton Parisien*' ('the right Parisian tone') by sneering at life outside Paris. Their guide in this was the left-leaning satirical journal *Le Canard enchaîné*, which in the 1930s constructed an imaginary France of clumsy peasants and provincials who could barely speak French. In Paris, '*la France profonde*' became a byword for backwardness and stupidity – a France of cassocks and priests in shovel hats, with peasants wearing clogs and gormless expressions, a world of superstition and harsh short lives.

In the pages of *Le Canard*, Dijon was what Richard Cobb called one of the 'joke towns', alongside Perpignan (even its name sounded comic to Parisian ears), Limoges and any number of obscure towns and villages in the south or in the wilds of Auvergne.[6]

This reputation stuck, and Michel Houellebecq used Dijon as the setting for a section of his 1998 novel *Les Particules Elémentaires* (*Atomised*). More precisely, one of the main characters, Bruno, moves there from Paris in 1984, at the age of twenty-eight, to take up his first job as a teacher in the Lycée Carnot. His wife is pregnant and Bruno stops having sex with her. Instead, he lusts after the young girls he teaches and, driven by guilt, becomes a devout Catholic. 'I was doomed,' he says, 'I felt dead inside.' Bruno was unhappy in Paris, but he is even more unhappy in Dijon, where 'the only things that mark out your life are visits to the doctor and watching your kids grow up'. Life in deep France, it seems, is only stasis and anomie, especially for a Parisian.[7]

La France profonde also has a third meaning. Most notably, it was reclaimed by the sociologist Michel Dion, who in 1988 published a book called *La France profonde*.[8] Based on interviews with political actors in the *départements* of Lorraine and Mayenne, Dion argued that as the influence of the Communist Party diminished in these regions and the Catholic Church loosened its grip on everyday life, a new form of socialism would emerge and re-energize France. Dion's new socialism never arrived: instead, anger, poverty and alienation created new forms of protest, chief among them the disorderly revolt of the *gilets jaunes*.

Until the past few years, the political life of Dijon had been calm and stable. Dijon, and Burgundy as a whole, has traditionally been a fiefdom shared by the two major mainstream parties in France: the socialists and the conservatives. In 2022, however, the presidential election suggested that unprecedented social changes were taking place. The two 'historic' parties of the centre suffered catastrophic losses, with Emmanuel Macron's LREM faring better. There was a loss of faith in the older order and a sense that the old consensus was breaking up.

What happened? According to Dominique Andolfatto, a political scientist from the Université de Bourgogne and an expert on trade unions and industrial relations, the election results were a symptom of the seismic changes that had been taking place in French political life over the past few years: at the very top of the political establishment, it was now a contest between the far right and Macron's LREM, which was centre-left or centre-right depending on which way you looked at it.

Speaking on the news channel France Info, Andolfatto noted that in the Burgundy region there had been a fragmentation of votes, reflecting the lack of cohesion in French society as a whole. As a result, Dijon remained in the hands of its avuncular mayor, François Rebsamen, a long-standing and high-handed Socialist who had served as a minister under François Hollande. In the wake of Macron's victory in 2022, Rebsamen had thrown his hand in with Macron's new political party, Renaissance, which was launched with its current name in September 2022. Meanwhile, the Parti Socialiste was collapsing into feuds and general disarray. The centre, shared by socialist or conservative parties, had melted away.

'What we are seeing,' said Andolfatto, 'is the end of the mass party where members must follow the party's ideology. We're also seeing the "depoliticization" of society in the sense that nobody is really interested in politics until the presidential election. This is the moment when politics becomes a consumer product.'

All of this is true, but there is also another reality. Dijon and the rest of Burgundy have been changing over the past decades, shifting as a geographical and political space. In this more complex and fast-evolving society, flux and impermanency have replaced old certainties. More to the point, there is not necessarily any link between one issue and another. If you are suspicious of immigration, this doesn't always mean that you are a racist. If you are anti-capitalist, it does not follow that you are against investment in services and employment. In Dijon these days, as in the rest of France, every political thought is fraught with contradictions.

It is not often that you see Henry Miller and Henry James compared to each other but, like Henry Miller, Henry James did not like Dijon. The city was the end point of James's French journey of 1883 and 1884, as described in his book *A Little Tour in France*. James commented with his usual waspish manner: 'Dijon was a good deal of a disappointment ... I will say plumply that the ancient capital of Burgundy is wanting in character; it is not up to the mark. It is old and narrow and crooked, and it has been left pretty well to itself: but it is not high and overhanging; it is not, to the eye, what the Burgundian capital should be. It has some tortuous vistas, some mossy roofs, some bulging fronts, some gray-faced hotels.'[9]

One American writer who did fall in love with Dijon was Mary Frances Kennedy Fisher, better known as M. F. K. Fisher, who came here in 1929. She was then twenty-one years old and freshly married to her first husband, Alfred Fisher, whom she called 'Al' and later divorced on the grounds that he could not meet her sexual needs. Still in the first flush of love, the couple came to Dijon because Al wanted to pursue a doctorate at the university, then well respected for the study of English literature. Dijon proved to be a revelation to Fisher. In spare but sensual prose, in her memoir *Long Ago in France*, she describes Dijon as a mysterious and complex place, dense with meaning and often hard to understand.[10]

As an American, she is a stranger to the Byzantine class system that she encounters and so able to skewer it all the more effectively. Her greatest discovery during her three years in Dijon is, however, the traditions and endless delights of Burgundian cuisine. She describes her meals – *escargots d'or*, ten-year-old *terrines*, *potage Richelieu*, grilled rare steaks, oysters and so on – with a lusty relish and carnal delight. The food, she realizes, is the key to understanding Dijon and its history in the most visceral manner. These experiences led the way to Fisher's later career as a food writer, which was launched with the book *How to Cook a Wolf*, published at the height of the Second World War, when food staples were in short supply. It is a cookbook but an unusual one, offering advice on how to cope with the rigours of wartime (sadly, there is no recipe for cooking wolves: the 'wolf' is a metaphor for hunger).

Fisher's Dijon was deeply provincial and an unlikely setting for one of the most significant events in twentieth-century modernism, but it was here that James Joyce's *Ulysses* was printed at the workshop of Maurice Darantiere in 1922. Darantiere's workshop was at 65 Chabot Charny. It is on one of the main arteries of Dijon and opposite the Fishers' lodging house. This was not lost on Al Fisher, who, as well as working on his doctorate, was sketching a poem which would be called *The Ghosts in the Underblows*, heavily influenced by Joyce and T. S. Eliot.

The Fishers also made friends with another American, Lawrence Clark Powell, who would go on to become a writer, librarian and distinguished bibliophile, but was then working on his doctorate at the university. Powell was a frequent visitor to Darantiere's workshop, fascinated by the lack of English (how did they print *Ulysses*?) and the workings of the place. 'I loved going there to the print shop,' he wrote much later, 'the clanking of the linotype, and the monotype – picking up the galleys, going and sitting on my ass at a cafe and reading the proof, drinking a *vin blanc-cassis*, the Dijon cocktail of white wine and cassis'.[11]

By sheer chance, Powell had the fortune, or misfortune, to encounter Henry Miller during his short sojourn in Dijon. The meeting happened on the staircase of the Faculty of Letters, where they were introduced to each other by Miller's boss at the Lycée Carnot, Jean Matruchot, 'a stocky Burgundian' who had served as a translator for the Franco-American allies at Dijon during the First World War. In time, Powell became friends with Henry Miller, but not in Dijon. For the duration of their brief meeting, Powell expressed his very visible contentment with the delights of provincial France, while Miller, an angry and intimidating malcontent, only wanted to get back to Paris and its wicked and decidedly non-provincial pleasures.

Late in 1987, I too longed to be back in Paris, but reading M. F. K. Fisher was part of what brought me to Dijon. As I settled into the city, with all its discomforts, I found hidden places. One of these was a bookshop called the Librairie du Soleil Noir. This was a ramshackle labyrinth of untidy, unshelved volumes with a singular devotion to all kinds of avant-garde literature. I bought and devoured books on alchemy, obscure Symbolist poets, Marquis de Sade and Georges Bataille. I took an obscure pleasure in the fact that this subversive spot was right in the heart of respectable Dijon, a stone's throw from the thirteenth-century Gothic majesty of Cathédrale Saint-Bénigne.

It was around this time that my friend Heather cracked up in Dijon. One Friday night, while drinking with a group of lecturers and students in a bar called Le Brighton on rue Auguste Comte, she lost control of herself and smashed up the plate-glass windows. She wasn't drunk. It was a psychotic attack. She was stabilized in hospital but continued to feel shaky long after her release. There were many reasons behind her breakdown – some of which I could guess at, some of which I could not – but afterwards she came to see Dijon itself as part of the problem. Dijon was killing her, she said. It was too small, too comfortable; everyone knew their place and seemed to have the secret of a happy, normal life, which was the opposite of the chaos in her head. She left Dijon by the end of the year.

I stayed on for two more years. Even though Dijon was close at hand during the two decades I lived in Paris, I never wanted to go back. I wasn't sure why I had this feeling. It was a reluctance to remember who I'd briefly tried to be during my time there perhaps, or an instinct to preserve the identity I'd formed since leaving. I cannot claim to have seen or understood what my friend saw in Dijon, but I did grasp that somehow the paralysing claustrophobia of French provincial life, where all is order and social masquerade, could do harm. In adopting the BCBG clothes and trying to fit myself into the life of a true Dijonnais, and in becoming part of an examination system so brutalizing, I had come to feel dislocated from myself. An old friend from Dijon days, now a journalist in Paris, said to me that after two consecutive weekends in Dijon, it always felt like a comfy prison. In this environment, Heather's disordered mind felt ever more out of place, and she was alienated and scared.

When I left Dijon in 1989, I was more than ready to go. After spending time there in 2022, I felt that same relief when the train pulled out of the station to take me home.

6

Lyon, 'My Strange City'

Le Vieux Lyon

At about eight o'clock in the morning in late February 2015, I was standing on the esplanade next to Basilique Notre-Dame de Fourvière in Lyon. I was there with a small film crew to shoot the opening section of a short film for Channel Four news which would examine the tensions in France in the wake of the massacre at the office of the satirical magazine *Charlie Hebdo* in Paris. A few weeks earlier, on 7 January, twelve people had been killed and eleven others injured. The two murderers responsible for the attack, Saïd and Chérif Kouachi, were both born in France (in the period leading up to the killings, Saïd Kouachi had settled with his family in an apartment block in Reims). They claimed allegiance to the Islamist terrorist organization al-Qaeda in the Arabian peninsula and declared that the attack was in response to the magazine's so-called blasphemy (it had published satirical cartoons of the Prophet Muhammad).

We had come to Lyon because it is often described as the capital of the French heartlands. This is not just because Lyon is the third city in France but because its culture – not just its art and literature, but also even its food – is very much set against Paris and is therefore perceived to carry an essence of what is meant by 'Frenchness', an identity at some remove from the globalized mishmash of the capital. My task now was to see how much of this 'Frenchness' still remained in a country that, in the wake of the *Charlie Hebdo* atrocity, seemed to be splintering.

We had chosen the esplanade of the Fourvière as the beginning of the film because it is so visually arresting. The esplanade is at the top of a hill and offers a panoramic view of what seems to be all of Lyon at once. The trees of the Jardin du Rosaire partially mask Vieux Lyon, an intricate tangle of alleys, lanes and dark corridors whose origins can be traced back to the Gallo-Roman period, when Lyon was known in Latin as Lugdunum. If Vieux Lyon has a distinctly Italianate air, this is because most of it was designed and constructed by wealthy Italians (most of them Florentines) during the Renaissance.

The Italians who came were good at finance, and during this period they made Lyon the banking centre of France, exploiting its geographical position as the frontier between northern and southern Europe and developing its already flourishing silk trade. Lyon was rich, powerful and cosmopolitan during the Renaissance, and its literary culture was bilingual: the poets Louise Labé, Maurice Scève and Antoine Héroet wrote in French, while the Florentines in exile, Luigi Alamanni and Gabriele Symeoni, wrote in their native tongue.

From the esplanade of the Fourvière, looking up to the left, you can see the hills of La Croix-Rousse on the east of the river Saône. Both Vieux Lyon and La Croix-Rousse are traversed by roughly three hundred *traboules* – narrow alleys and passageways, most of which were built during the Renaissance and originally meant to make it easier to move goods and people around the labyrinth. The *traboules*, which are mysterious and elegant and hard to fathom, are one of the several reasons why Lyon has the reputation in the rest of France of being a secretive city. They also had a practical application: during the Second World War, the French Resistance in the city were able to use their local knowledge to dodge the enemy.

To the right, you can see the Presqu'île, the heart of Lyon, which, as the name suggests, is not quite an island. The tip of the Presqu'île finishes at the confluence of the rivers Saône and Rhône. These rivers form a kind of 'Y' shape, which the first inhabitants thought had magical, magnetic powers. During the Renaissance, alchemists and other occultists – who thrived in Lyon – decided that the 'Y' represented a female divinity and that Lyon was a woman and a goddess. Looking beyond the rivers, you can see the city almost laid out like a map, dominated by the tower of Crédit Lyonnais, built in the mid-1970s and often called 'Le Crayon' because of its shape (although it also looks like a phallus). And then, even further beyond, on a clear day you can see the Alps, including Mont Blanc, as well as the Chartreuse, Oisans, Vercors, Jura and Bugey ranges. You really do feel as if you are standing at the very centre of France.

This was, however, all too much for me and the camera. I had stayed up late the previous night in our chic boutique hotel set incongruously in the otherwise bleak 7th arrondissement of Lyon. I drank whisky and wrote and rewrote my lines about why Lyon mattered, why it was such an enigmatic city and why its cultural politics was important to the whole of France, especially at this tense time in the country's history.

But in the morning, I stuttered and stumbled over my words. I was freezing and the cameraman was barking out expletives at each of my failures; he was freezing, too. Both of us found it impossible to fit the panorama into the frame and find the words to describe what actually went on here. We filmed a few shots which we couldn't use and then went inside to the relative warmth of the basilica to start again.

I have always found Basilique Notre-Dame de Fourvière to be quite a creepy place. The church dominates the skyline of Lyon but it is not a noble or beautiful building. Seen from the city below, it is squat and vaguely menacing, as if keeping a mistrustful eye on the citizens of Lyon and their sinning ways – more like a watchtower than a church. It was built to thank the Virgin Mary for having spared Lyon from suffering during the Franco-Prussian War of 1870, and it was consecrated in 1896. The external structure is relatively plain and unadorned, while the interior is rich and opulent, loaded with expensive gifts from the well-heeled *bourgeoisie* of Lyon to safeguard their well-being. The overall effect is sickly kitsch. Nonetheless, the church is the emblem of Lyon, and it was here that the words began to flow.

By 2015, Lyon was familiar terrain for me. I had visited countless times over the years, for work, to see friends and for love. I had also lived here for a few years in the 1980s, first at a hostel for young workers (mostly immigrants from the Middle East and North Africa) at Place Jean Macé, and later in the suburb of Villeurbanne, but for most of the time, while I was studying at the nearby Université Jean Moulin, I lived in an apartment at 81 rue de Marseille in the *quartier* of La Guillotière. This street was my introduction to Lyon, and it stood between two worlds.

At one end was Place Gabriel-Péri, a magnet for the North African population of Lyon. I loved this place, with its graffiti, street vendors selling contraband, cassette machines blaring out

Arabic pop music, and busy cafes, which might well have been in Casablanca or Algiers. It was hard to imagine a place that was so near and yet so far away from the basilica of Fourvière or the plump, stately buildings of central Lyon. And yet it was all just a five-minute walk straight into the centre of Lyon, across le Pont de la Guillotière over the Rhône.

As part of my course at the university, I had been reading *Le Pain Nu* by Mohamed Choukri, an account of the author's wretchedly poor childhood in Tangier in the 1940s. This book was published in France in 1980 in a translation by the novelist Tahar Ben Jelloun (the English translation by Paul Bowles, *For Bread Alone*, appeared in 1973). At that time, the novel was something of a *cause célèbre* in France because it had been banned by the Moroccan government for its frank treatment of sex, starvation, cruelty, drug use and poverty (this ban remained in place until 2000). Just before my arrival in Lyon, I had spent some time in Tangier on my first trip to North Africa, and I had been struck by the hardness of life there and the undercurrent of violence, both political and criminal. In the 1980s, Tangier was desperately poor and neglected. There were petty hustlers at every corner, while the town itself was dirty and half-built. Tangier is not much like that now. In recent decades, it has been flooded with money and investments from the Gulf and, with its casinos and high-end brothels, is now a playground and escape for Gulf Arabs seeking pleasures which are harder to come by in their own, more puritanical societies. Back in the 1980s, however, Tangier was still the city described by Choukri: a gritty, lawless mess, quite separate from the modern sleek streets of the richer parts of Rabat and Marrakesh. And daily life in La Guillotière did not seem so far away from Tangier. Reading Choukri in that environment was my first introduction to North African literature, and I became fascinated by the tangled politics of postcolonial France.

When I returned to Tangier as a researcher in 2002, I was

introduced to Choukri by a friend. I was taken to meet him in the Café Ritz on the rue Sorella. The Ritz was a quite rundown but homely place, where the owner, a friend and admirer of Choukri, kept a table and bottles of his favourite red wine for the great writer every night. I grew to know and like Choukri and the cafe, which had a louche but cosy atmosphere that I came to associate with Tangier nightlife.

I told Choukri I had discovered his writing while living in Lyon. He was at first amused by this and went into a long riff on France, his friendship with Jean Genet, how he loved French literature and how much he hated the French. He was flattered that his work was being studied in French universities and was keen to know what the professors said about him. I told him the truth, that I didn't think they really grasped how much of his writing came from experience and not abstract ideas. Choukri said to me that his few visits to France had made him ill. He reserved a particular hatred for Lyon; it was a city full of racists, he said. Reaching for another glass of red wine, with a low snarl, he declared that Lyon was a *'ville maudite'* ('an accursed city').

During the Second World War, there had been a real and literal truth to this description of Lyon. At the other end of rue de Marseille, nearer to my apartment in fact than Place Gabriel-Péri, was a dank and gloomy set of buildings, once a hospital of some sort but now abandoned. I learned quickly that in 1943, during the Occupation of Lyon, the hospital had become the headquarters of the Gestapo. The place was feared by the Lyonnais, who had heard rumours about the torture chambers and the atrocities that took place there. Most notoriously, the Resistance leader Jean Moulin was taken there after being betrayed and captured in the suburb of Caluire-et-Cuire. The commander of the headquarters was Klaus Barbie, who personally took charge of his torture.

Eyewitnesses attested to the cruelty of Barbie's methods. Jean

Moulin had his fingernails removed with hot knives and his hands shattered in door frames. He was beaten into unconsciousness and displayed to other inmates by Barbie as an example of what would happen to them if they did not speak. Barbie also developed new forms of torture in the Gestapo dungeons, including electric shocks and sexual abuse with dogs. In May 1944, the buildings were bombed into ruins by Allied aircraft.

In the decade after I left Lyon, the buildings were restored and turned into a museum, the Centre d'Histoire de la Résistance et de la Déportation (CHRD). But in 1984, I often passed these buildings, still a grey, dust-covered wreck, when I took up my studies at the university (appositely named in honour of Jean Moulin). Once I had come to know something of the history of this accursed site, I had a series of bad dreams about the place. I slept near a window overlooking rue de Marseille and could easily imagine the Gestapo's victims being driven along this road to indescribable pain and death.

One evening, under the influence of LSD, I was gripped by a paralysing sense of dread and panic as I was trudging across the pinkish-grey gravel of the Place Bellecour. I had been reading about the Occupation of Lyon and recalled a description of the torture of 'Jewish terrorists' in the cellars of 32 Place Bellecour at the hands of the Gestapo. Later that night, sleepless, I tried to read the opening chapters of a US paperback edition of Norman Mailer's *An American Dream*, a grim tale of pointless murder. I couldn't get more than a few pages in before the scantily clad dancer on the cover of the book stepped out onto my bedside table. A tiny semi-naked figurine. She told me not to read the book, that it would be bad for me.

I put the book down and stared at the ceiling. My mind once again moved to Klaus Barbie and his trial; he had not yet been punished for his crimes. It occurred to me that although Barbie would go on trial, there could never be any punishment that would fit his crimes. There would be no redemption either.

The LSD wore off, but in the following days Lyon seemed to me to be an uncanny, sinister, dislocated place. There is much that I love about the city – its labyrinths, the food and its fine buildings – but years on from that experience, I have never been quite able to extinguish this feeling when I am there. Certainly, it's hard to imagine a more visceral introduction to the realities of recent French history.

On a recent visit to the CHRD, I noticed a pack of schoolkids on a day out from the *banlieues* wandering around the exhibits. Their teacher patiently and carefully explained the history of the centre and what had happened. 'This is where modern France was made,' she explained. 'It was built on the suffering, the sacrifices and the bravery of the poor people who were tortured here.' The kids looked mostly indifferent, more interested in impressing their mates, messing about, flirting with each other. To them, this was all history, told in the voice of official France – the teacher, the school curriculum and ultimately the French Republic. Most of these kids were from immigrant families, the majority of them North African, and they most likely had been born in France. They were therefore future citizens of the Republic. It was a killing irony, however, that they were being forced to celebrate the courage of the *résistants*, while during the Second World War and its aftermath, their great-grandmothers and great-grandfathers had been tortured and killed by the French during the dirty colonial wars that brought down the French Empire; these were also wars that the French had fought in the name of the Republic.

This place is no ordinary museum; it is a totem of what it means to be French. But these kids didn't want to be here and hear about a France that had nothing to do with them. This was a new generation who did not have to atone for the sins of the past, and they had no interest in a past which did not belong to them.

As part of the Channel 4 film, we went to the prison of Fort

Montluc in the 3rd arrondissement of Lyon, which is also now a museum. It is a surprisingly small place, still dank and claustrophobic. There are only 122 individual cells, all impossibly cramped. You can't take more than three steps in any direction without walking into a wall or the door, and you can see nothing from the tiny high windows. Even though it is no longer in use, Fort Montluc is by a long margin the most miserable prison I have encountered and somehow retains its morally abject atmosphere.

During the Occupation of Lyon, more than 15,000 people passed through here including Jean Moulin and the historian Marc Bloch, as well as 7,500 Jews from Lyon. Under the command of Klaus Barbie, they were held here before being murdered or sent to his torture chambers at the requisitioned hospital. If they survived, they were sent on to the death camps of the East.

On 6 and 7 August 1944, forty-four Jewish children of various nationalities – Belgian, Austrian, Algerian, German and Polish, aged from five to seventeen – were brought to Fort Montluc in wagons. They had been sent to a children's home in the obscure hamlet of Izieu near the Swiss border from all over France as the Germans intensified their persecution of Jews in the south of France. The home was part of a rescue network for Jewish children in France called '*le circuit Garel*' (named after its founders Georges and Lili Garel, who were from Lyon). Photographs of children in Izieu show happy, beaming faces. Their home was presumed to be a safe haven, and the children all look as if they were on holiday.

On the day the home was raided, Sabine Zlatin, the Jewish nurse who ran the home with her husband, was in Montpelier, trying to find an even safer refuge for the children. (The Germans had already, notoriously, deported the Jewish inmates of the children's home in Marseille to the camps.) The Lyon Gestapo had been informed by a French collaborator, still unidentified but allegedly from Metz, that Jewish children were hiding there. When the wagons arrived in Fort Montluc, the children sat cross-legged on the floor as their carers were forced to stand facing the prison wall, awaiting execution at any moment. Within days, the children were sent by tram to the Gare de Perrache in Lyon, then to the internment camp of Drancy, in the north of Paris, and then to Auschwitz. The order for deportation had been signed by Klaus Barbie.

In the 1950s and 1960s, during the Algerian War of Independence, Fort Montluc housed Algerian nationalists who had been fighting against the French in Algeria or France. The *quartier* of La Guillotière was the centre of activity in Lyon for the Front de Libération Nationale (FLN), the Algerian Nationalists, and was the repeated target of raids by the French police, as well as shoot-outs between vying Algerian factions. Eleven members of the FLN were guillotined in Fort Montluc, on the express orders of President Charles de Gaulle, in the dying days of the war. There is no monument to these forgotten soldiers who fought against France, claiming that the French were employing the tactics of the Nazis, using torture as a weapon of war. There are no accounts of what happened to the Algerian prisoners here.

Although it is little visited as a museum, Fort Montluc still has great symbolic status in the Lyonnais imagination. That is why Klaus Barbie himself was imprisoned here in February 1983, when he was finally tracked down in South America and extradited to France for trial. Caging Barbie in Fort Montluc was a deliberate act, meant not to heal the wounds of the German Occupation, but to show all of France, and the rest of the world, that Lyon was facing up to its past. Among those waiting at the airport was an elderly man who had suffered at the hands of Barbie. He told the TV camera that it was important Barbie should be in Lyon because there were many still alive in the city who had given him a helping hand.

*

In January 2015, I went to speak to Richard Wertenschlag, the Chief Rabbi of Lyon at the Grande Synagogue de Lyon, on the Quai Tilsitt in the 2nd arrondissement, overlooking the Saône.

During the German Occupation, in spite of the presence of Klaus Barbie, Lyon was a refuge for Jews from all over France, and the Grande Synagogue was usually their first port of call and shelter. The German authorities did not tolerate the synagogue for long. In May 1943, the then Chief Rabbi of Lyon, Bernard Schonberg, was arrested by the Gestapo and sent to Auschwitz in his native Poland. Schonberg was an active member of the French Resistance in Lyon and was posthumously awarded the *médaille de la Résistance française*. He died in Auschwitz of 'exhaustion' at the age of thirty-five.

A few months after Schonberg's arrest, grenades were thrown into the synagogue during a service. On 13 June, the synagogue was raided by the *Milice française*, an organization of home-grown French Fascists, who arrested everyone they could find. Those detained were sent to Fort Montluc and then to Auschwitz. The *Milice* wrecked the building, using scrolls from the Torah, plaques and prayer books as target practice.

I recalled all of this as I first approached the synagogue from the Pont Bonaparte, crossing over the still, grey-green and icy waters of the Saône. Two heavily armed soldiers stood at the entrance of the building, a reminder that in the wake of the *Charlie Hebdo* murders in Paris, an accomplice of the Kouachi brothers called Amedy Coulibaly had taken Jewish prisoners hostage in a kosher supermarket in the suburb of Montrouge, just to the south of central Paris. Coulibaly was motivated by hatred for the Jews.

The Grande Synagogue is a beautiful and richly ornamented place, hidden away from the Quai Tilsitt by a discreet and anonymous entrance. Exploring the synagogue, with its intricate silver and gold carvings and exquisite coloured-glass veneers, you can't help noticing the security cameras positioned across the ceiling or hidden behind pillars. 'Every day we receive death threats,' Rabbi Wertenschlag said. 'They come in different forms – marked with swastikas or pictures of deportees to the death camps. But it's not just hate mail. In Lyon right now, you can be insulted or threatened just for walking in the street. Nazi salutes and cries of "Heil Hitler" are the most common forms of insult.'

Lyon, he said, has always been a bad place for Jews, harking back to the Second World War and earlier. But in the past decade, there had been a resurgence of neo-Nazi activity in the city. Lyon had a strange and ambiguous dual identity, the rabbi told me: it was once the capital of the French Resistance, and was now hailed as an emblem of the Resistance throughout France, but it had also been the capital of collaboration.

In the present century, Lyon has often been described as the capital of the far right in France, and certainly it has always provided a welcoming shelter for some of the most extreme groups in the country. These ideologues see France as heir to the Graeco-Roman civilization, which they claim has defined all true European history and culture. One of the most recently founded groups, and the most startling, is an organization called Les Caryatides, which is mostly based in Lyon and the Rhône-Alpes. It was set up in 2014 by a group of women in their early twenties who wanted to dedicate themselves to 'anti-feminism' and the 'salvation of the French nation'. The group was an offshoot of *Jeunesses nationalistes* and *L'Oeuvre française*, two groups banned by the Minister of the Interior Manuel Valls in the wake of the killing in Paris of the anti-Fascist militant Clément Méric in 2013. They are particularly faithful to the ideas of Pierre Sidos, the founder of *L'Oeuvre française*, a lifelong Fascist whose father, François Sidos, a *pied-noir* from Mouzaïa in Algeria, was shot for collaboration with the Germans in 1946.

After much to-ing and fro-ing on email, I managed to meet up with two representatives of Les Caryatides on a bleak January morning in Lyon in 2015. Our meeting point, chosen by the group (whose name comes from a particular style of classical architecture: columns in the shape of women supporting the higher structures of a building; women supporting men in power), was in front of the statue of Joan of Arc on the Place Puvis de Chavannes in the extremely *bourgeois* 6th arrondissement of Lyon. The statue was bordered by a scrubby and neglected little park spotted with scattered litter and dog shit.

The women gave their names as Blanche Crete and Clothilde Veyvret, such medieval and Catholic names that they sounded suspiciously like *noms de guerre*. 'I am ready to burn for France,' said Clothilde, as a combative opening remark. She was the more outspoken one, toothy and blonde, with a frighteningly strident manner that would not have been out of place in a strict, old-fashioned girls' school. 'Joan of Arc is our heroine because she got rid of the foreigners, the English, from France,' she said. 'That is what we must do now – get rid of all the immigrants and non-Europeans from France. That is the only way to save our country.'

They were dressed almost identically – leather boots, tan tights, knee-length skirts, tightly wrapped coats, scarves and prim 1960s-style *coiffures* that might have been worn by their grandmothers. They looked like a parody version of the high-*bourgeoise* BCBGs I had known in Dijon. They were also trying so hard to project an anti-sexuality that it had the opposite effect; the more you thought about what they were trying so hard to repress, the more your thoughts came back to what it was they were trying to hide or deny. Their self-conscious and deliberately styled *pudeur* was actually a sexual signal as powerful as any other. I wondered how much they were aware of this. Quite a lot, I decided after a while, given that they talked so much and with so much evident relish about sex and sexuality.

They said they were 'practising Catholics' and believed in preserving female virginity until marriage. Women who did not were no more than *'filles de joie'* (an old-fashioned term for 'prostitute'). They also believed in sexual and racial purity. One of their slogans, loudly chanted at their demonstrations and marches, was '*Les Françaises aux Français*' ('French women for French men'). 'We do not believe that the races can mix sexually,' said Clothilde. 'This does not mean that we are racist, but that we want to preserve our race.' They had another slogan, addressed specifically to the Femen movement – the feminist movement whose members I would later see in Reims baring their breasts to Marine Le Pen, their signature move. The Caryatides' slogan was '*R'habilles-toi! Tu n'es qu'une pute!*' ('Get your clothes back on! You're no more than a whore!')

They were both students of Classical Studies at the University of Lyon. 'France is a Latin country,' said Blanche, blank-faced. She had a slightly baffled middle-distance gaze, the look of a confused disciple. She seemed a bit shy, and I guessed that maybe she was happier with her Latin and Greek textbooks and a fairy-tale version of European history than with full-on Fascist activism.

She understood the ideology well enough, however. 'We are not Semites. Our civilization has no link to the Middle East or North Africa. We have a totally different civilization, a Mediterranean, European civilization from Greece and Rome, and that is what we have to defend.' In a long feature on the Les Caryatides movement in 2014, the women's magazine *Causette* had described them as 'neo-Pétainists in skirts', but I thought this was letting them off lightly.[1] Certainly, they shared the *maréchal*'s values of 'France, family, childhood' (another slogan of Les Caryatides), but the group were also Holocaust deniers (Pétain was blind to the Holocaust and only acknowledged the Nazi persecution of Jews as collateral damage from the war). As followers of Pierre Sidos, they were unrepentant about French collaboration with the Nazis, which they did not see as a cause for regret and was only a form of 'advanced nationalism'. I had heard most of this rhetoric before over decades in France, but I could not remember when I had heard it from people who were so young and so far removed from any of the historical realities – the Second World War and its aftermath – that had shaped the far right in France (and the far left too, for that matter).

Likewise, the young generation of Fascists in Lyon are proud of the collaboration that took place in their city during the Second World War. To give just one nefarious example, in 2007 a mysterious spate of posters appeared all over Lyon celebrating Klaus Barbie. This generation see no need to apologize for collaboration and throw doubt upon whether the Germans, rather than the Jews or other foreigners, were even the real enemy in the first place. They see their city in the twenty-first century as a rallying point for the next wave of anti-Jewishness, and their aim is to reclaim Lyon and France for '*les français de souche*' – the real French people who are ethnically white European and Christian.

The headquarters of the far right in Lyon is in Vieux Lyon, diametrically opposite and no more than five minutes' walk away from the Grande Synagogue on the Quai Tilsitt, though its groups tend to be based in bars and gyms. These groups have consistently attracted press attention for their street brawls, drunkenness, attacks on foreigners and vandalism of Jewish memorials. They are so notorious that the local press refers to Vieux Lyon as 'Facho-Land'.

All of this was explained to me one chilly morning in Lyon by Armand Creus, a prominent left-wing councillor in Lyon and a lifelong opponent of the far right. Armand is an open and friendly speaker, temperamentally mild-mannered, though visibly angered by fascism in France. He was born in Perpignan in 1948 to Spanish parents fleeing the Franco dictatorship in Spain and has spent much of his adult life monitoring and opposing fascism in Lyon.

As we sat on the steps of the Eglise Saint-Just in Vieux Lyon, Armand guided me through the history of the far right in Lyon, from the collaboration to the present day, and pointed out where it had bases in the area, all interlinked. 'Nobody knows where the money comes from,' he said. 'Probably a big, national group or foreign money. But there is definitely money from the outside – none of the young Fascists here could afford to pay for all this – the rent on buildings and so on. They are trying to create recruiting centres for young people here in Lyon. They are not part of a party looking for electoral gains, but are aiming to influence people's thinking about who they are, where they come from, so that this kind of nationalism enters the mainstream of political life.'

Armand Creus is unfazed by the many death threats he has received. 'It is far more important to fight these people than to be scared of them,' he remarked to me. He continued: 'It may seem that our focus is at the local level, trying to maybe clean up Vieux Lyon so that it's safe for tourists and visitors, but really what we are doing is taking on bigger forces – the far right, which is in every part of France, encouraging regionalism, local activism, and what I would call "identitarian" politics.' Here, Armand was referring to the ideology that advocates the right of white ethnic Europeans to control the 'territories' that properly belong to them by dint of ancestry. Little wonder that in 2022 the young Fascists of Lyon had thrown a party to celebrate their brotherhood with ethnic Serbs who believed the same thing and who had fought so valiantly to kick the Muslims off 'their land'.

Recently, several of the regular haunts of the far right in Lyon have been closed by the city council in an attempt to curb the violence and make the city feel safer for residents and for tourists who know nothing of its political geography. One of those shut down was a bar called La Traboule, which I visited after speaking to Armand Creus. Just off the rue Juiverie, this bar was a dingy place, where the clientele and staff were visibly not keen on outsiders. Although the name of the bar appeared only in small lettering on the door, it was easy to know where you were by the flags of Lyon fluttering from the window. Once inside, you were given a further clue by the slogan *'Rebeyne'*, which was painted alongside the flag of Lyon on the wall. This is an old word in Lyonnais slang which means 'riot'. It is a reference to the hunger riots in Lyon of 1529, when the starving people of Lyon rose up against their money-grubbing, usually foreign or Jewish, masters. Here it also refers to a far-right group who specialize in provocative demonstrations against immigrants. One afternoon, I drank a few beers there, taking in the atmosphere, noting the brusque manner of the staff and the mutterings of the few other unwelcoming customers, obviously picking up on my accent and trying to decide where I was from and why I was there. No one fell easily into conversation, and it was not long before I knew it was time to leave.

The gym L'Agogé was next door to La Traboule and hosted pretty much the same clientele, who trained there in group combat, boxing and martial arts. The ideological stance of the gym was revealed in its name – 'Agogé' comes from the Greek term *agoge*, which is the name of the military training for young Spartans in defence of their nation. One of the directors, Antoine Durand, proudly announced in 2021 that L'Agogé was 'a sort of youth club for patriots with deep roots in France and who are proud of who they are'.

When I last visited Vieux Lyon, a shopkeeper who would not give his name reflected on the city council's actions. 'The problem is that the people who went to these places are still here, they haven't gone away,' he said. 'They think that they own this territory and the closing of their bases is just another part of the war with official France – the Socialists, Communists and immigrants – which they hate. They intimidate you, and you can't answer back or your shop or restaurant will be burned down and your customers beaten up. No Arabs or Blacks come here if they know anything about Vieux Lyon.' I mentioned that I had just read a newspaper report of a well-known young

Fascist who had been spotted and cornered while shopping in La Guillotière and, by his own account, fled for his life, fearing a lynching. He escaped by pulling a knife on his attackers. 'That's probably all invented or exaggerated to make a point,' said the shopkeeper. 'The far right are trying to say that La Guillotière is dangerous for white people.' This is no doubt the case, but it is also nonetheless a fact that La Guillotière and Vieux Lyon are enemy territories within the same city.

On 8 December 2022, at about half past six in the evening, a procession of roughly three hundred people, most of them quite young, marched down the rue Juiverie, one of the thin main arteries of Vieux Lyon and, as the name suggests, once the place where Jews had been allowed to settle and work in Lyon. The dress code was mainly black. The young men wore Harrington jackets or hunting coats. Fred Perry and Ben Sherman shirts were popular, as were smart, short haircuts and occasionally a dandified clipped moustache. The young women were also dressed in black, or in slightly old-fashioned classic French *couture*. They carried flags of the city of Lyon, images of the Virgin Mary (the protector of Lyon) and flaming torches. Occasionally, you could see the flash of a banner which read '*Lugdunum Suum*' – 'Lyon is ours'.

Moving slowly and deliberately, the procession left the rue Juiverie and made its way unchallenged up the hill to Basilique Notre-Dame de Fourvière. The procession stood then, a marriage of religion and nationalism, a union desiring the 'reconquest' of Lyon, and then France, from its foreign invaders. It was like watching a scene from the mid-1930s, when democracy in France was being undermined by violent Fascist '*ligues*', who often took to the streets in bloody battles, fighting a 'war' to reclaim France. This march had been banned by the city authorities on security grounds, but there was in fact little they could do, as it was just before the opening of the annual *Fête des Lumières* – a light show in the city which runs from 8 to

11 December and attracts more than two million people to the streets of Lyon.

Families, tourists and sightseers gawped at the spectacle but no one dared to object. Some took photos or films on their phone, thinking for a minute that maybe this was some kind of quaint re-enactment from Lyonnais folklore. Most stopped short when they realized what they were watching: twenty-first-century French fascism in action.

Mourad Benchellali never goes to Vieux Lyon and rarely goes into the centre of Lyon. We were driving in his battered old car through his local neighbourhood of Vénissieux on our way to the *cité* of Les Minguettes. 'Vieux Lyon is not safe for Arabs like me,' he said, 'even if, like me, you have actually grown up in this part of France.' He went on, grim-faced and not looking me in the eye: 'Vieux Lyon has been like that for a long time: you can't go there if you're not white. The centre of Lyon is not as bad, but still you can feel people watching you. They make you feel as if you don't belong.' He did not say much more during our car journey.

Vénissieux lies only a few kilometres south of rue de Marseille, where I had once lived in Lyon, but since the summer of 1981, it has had a name for violence and lawlessness which far surpasses even La Guillotière, the mainly North African *quartier* at the far end of rue de Marseille. That summer, the *cité* of Les Minguettes, which is an integral part of Vénissieux, exploded into riots and confrontations with the police, the images of violence appearing nightly on television screens throughout France. Until then, many French people were barely aware that places such as Les Minguettes existed. However, this estate was typical of the housing which had been hastily built all over France in the 1970s, intended for an anticipated influx of immigration, mainly from North Africa and the former French colonies. What felt jarring was that the events in Les Minguettes took place only a few months after François Mitterrand, the first properly Socialist president of the post-war period, had been elected in a wave of exaltation.

The French authorities were at a loss to explain this apparently meaningless violence and, more importantly, did not know how to deal with it, or even contain it. The confrontations – car burnings and clashes with an increasingly heavily armoured police force – continued. In 1984, ever more dangerous disturbances led to the occupation of Vénissieux by more than four thousand armed police officers. There was talk in the media of a 'new French civil war'. At one stage, François Mitterrand turned up on a surprise visit to Les Minguettes, declaring that something had to be done. The problem was that no one knew what this 'something' could or should be. Since then, the conflict between the mainly immigrant population and the French authorities has only intensified.

Mourad Benchellali was born in Villeurbanne, a suburb near Vénissieux, in 1981, the year the riots started. He is the son of an imam who has a reputation for radicalism and was later suspected by the French authorities of radicalizing Muslim youths in Vénissieux. Benchellali claims that he has never shared his father's views. In the summer of 2001, aged just nineteen, he set off with a friend from the neighbourhood for 'an adventure'. Encouraged by his brother to see for himself the 'best Koranic schools in the world', Benchellali ended up in Afghanistan. He says now that he went there partly to improve his knowledge of Islam and also that he was unaware of what was being planned there (this was in the months leading up to the 9/11 massacre). Nonetheless, he ended up in an al-Qaeda training camp, where he was introduced to Osama bin Laden. He later claimed that he had been tricked into visiting the camp to meet his 'brothers' in the Islamic faith and that he had been held there against his will. Shortly after 9/11, he somehow made his way to Pakistan, where he was quickly arrested by the Pakistani military. The journey ended for Benchellali in a prison cell in Guantanamo Bay, where he was prisoner 161, convicted by the US government of 'criminal association with a terrorist enterprise'.

As Benchellali drove me through Vénissieux on our way to Les Minguettes, my attempts at small talk were met by silence or grunts. When I asked him about his experiences in Guantanamo, he told me that he had said enough in the media and that he had a new book coming in which he described his life (this would be his second book: the first was published in 2006).[2] I went on, curious more than anything else: what was daily life like in an al-Qaeda training camp? Was he ever scared? Did he have any idea what he was doing there? 'We prayed and talked about Islam,' he said. 'We did physical exercises and were disciplined. But there was no weapons training. I never saw a weapon.'

I asked how he had overturned his conviction in 2009, and at first he didn't answer. The facts were, however, that he had been interrogated in Guantanamo by French intelligence officers and that the change of jurisdiction had rendered the original charge invalid. He was extradited from Guantanamo back to a prison in France, where he felt that his sense of self was disintegrating. He did not want to mix with or be seen mixing with Islamist prisoners, who ran their part of the prison as a gang. But he was alien to the white criminals, who shunned him. He complained to his jailers about his mental health problems but received little help or support. He felt afraid and abandoned.

On leaving prison, Benchellali had nightmares about bombardments and torture. He couldn't concentrate and was incapable of holding down a job until he picked up a modest trade as a tiler. He began to give talks in schools and youth clubs in Vénissieux, aimed at dissuading young people from leaving France to go and fight with ISIS in Syria. This was, he explained, not just to help others but as a way of coming to terms with the wreckage of his immediate past. This latter subject and nothing else, it was made clear, would be the content of our interview on camera. Benchellali refused to be on trial again.

The interview took place in a run-down and draughty room at the bottom of a tower block in Vénissieux. To get there, we had to walk through a bleak and dilapidated estate. To get anywhere in Les Minguettes, you have to trudge across worn-out patches of grass about to turn into mud, or improvised unpaved paths, where you have to watch your step among the dog shit, stones and broken glass. At the foot of every tower block we passed there was a pack of youths – *choufs* – keeping watch for the local drug dealers. People drove from the smart centre of Lyon to buy drugs here. It was a tightly organized business. The *choufs* didn't like me or my camera crew, and they either melted back into the corridors of the building they were guarding, there to be unseen, or looked ready to challenge us. The sight of Benchellali calmed them down, and finally we made our way to the designated interview room, passing through a food bank, called in French *'une épicerie sociale et solidaire'*. A pocket of women in headscarves greeted us with friendly smiles and then went back to picking out something for their families to eat from shelves of out-of-date fruit and bags of couscous and pasta.

Benchellali was obviously suspicious of me – with good reason given his background – but by now I was also suspicious of him. It was less of a conversation and more of a stand-off. Benchellali wanted to tell me about the good works that he had been doing since he had left prison but his manner was hostile. His voice was flat, and as he spoke he looked beyond me into space, as if I wasn't really there.

Off camera, he was more animated. He blamed France and the French for everything that had gone wrong in the Franco-Muslim relationship. His work was an attempt to repair the damage that had been inflicted on the Muslims in France, but he didn't hold out much hope that it would be effective. At one point, Benchellali glanced up at the tough-looking 'friend' who had been watching over the interview, saying nothing, but listening carefully and projecting an unsubtle air of menace. I realized then quite suddenly that this person was not some kind of Islamist minder but actually an emotional support for Benchellali.

They exchanged a nod and Benchellali continued. He had been tortured when he was first captured in Pakistan and then tortured again, on a daily basis, for over two years in Guantanamo. He had suffered sleep deprivation, body slaps, iced water thrown in his face, and he had been made to kneel for hours and been constantly reminded that he would soon face the electric chair. He had been sexually humiliated: a female interrogator had peeled off her clothes in front of him, a provocation that had made him feel ashamed and humiliated. 'I know now that I was stupid,' he said. 'I really didn't expect any of this when I set off for Afghanistan. I knew that Afghanistan wasn't the Baleares, but I wasn't looking for that. I was looking for spirituality and then I found real trouble.' As he told me this, Benchellali was hunched and his eyes were blank.

On finally returning home, one of the things that had upset Benchellali most was that he was an object of suspicion in his own *cité*: he had exiled himself from his own people. 'Outsiders think that jihadists are heroes in the *cité*,' he said, 'but it's really not like that. People are scared. They won't come near you. To a lot of people, I'm just the "guy from Guantanamo". That's why I want to tell my story so that everyone knows that I was a fool, and that other young people shouldn't make the same mistake.'

Benchellali was now trapped, separated from his past in the *cité*, and although he was a French citizen, he was no longer at home or welcome in the country where he had been born. The conversation ended on a tense note. After the interview, as I trudged back to the main road through the mud and dusty concrete, I reflected on the journey Benchellali had taken from Les Minguettes to Afghanistan. When the *cité* was first built, and even when it exploded into riots in the 1980s, no one could have possibly predicted that its disaffected sons would have ended up in a global war.

Probably the finest chronicler of Lyonnais life is the novelist and journalist Henri Béraud. These days, Béraud is only half-remembered, but in his own era he was a star. In the 1920s, he was twice awarded the Prix Goncourt, the second time for *Le Martyre de l'obèse* (*The Sorrows of a Fat Man*), a strange and piercing tale about an unhappy housewife who cuckolds her obese husband with another fat man. Béraud himself was notably fat, a characteristic which he explained by having been born in Lyon.

During the 1930s and 1940s, as well as writing around forty novels and essays, Béraud was also the leading columnist in *Gringoire*. The political line of this weekly newspaper was not always easy to follow: although anti-Communist and supportive of the Fascist regimes in Spain and Portugal, it also offered space to such redoubtable left-wing republicans as Jean Moulin. Its line hardened throughout the 1930s, however, as the likes of Béraud saw France in imminent danger of collapse. The newspaper was also rabidly anti-English. Béraud himself published an essay as long as a book called '*Faut-il réduire l'Angleterre à l'esclavage?*' ('Should we reduce England to slavery?'). In this essay, Béraud denounced the English as a hybrid impure race at the service of capitalists and Jews, who were quite often the same thing. George Orwell regarded Béraud with contempt and described *Gringoire* as 'the most disgusting rag it was possible to imagine'.[3]

In 1945, Béraud was sentenced to death for his antisemitic writings and pro-Vichy views during the German Occupation of France. Articles such as '*Oui, il faut être antisémite . . . Le salut de la France est à ce prix*' ('Yes, we must be antisemitic . . . the health of France depends on it') give a flavour of his opinions. Béraud's sentence was commuted to hard labour by no less than

Charles de Gaulle, and he spent the rest of his life in silence and obscurity.

Béraud was a bad man but a good writer. He is a particularly entertaining and astute guide to Lyon, his native city. For Béraud, Lyon was a mysterious place, hard to fathom even if, like him, you were born and raised there. He wrote: 'This pale town of whispers where my soul searches its way; do I even know myself here? . . . Is it the labyrinth of corridors and courtyards and houses with hidden exits, all encouraging adultery and crime, where linger the vague lights of Stendhal's Italy? Lyon, my strange city, are you the austere and strict town where enlightened souls glimpse only a crossroads of traffic, never seeing what lies hidden? Is there only one true Lyon?'[4]

In translation, Béraud's prose sounds overwritten and florid. In French, however, the effect is mellifluous and poetic. Béraud wrote these lines in 1940 in a text recalling his youth in Lyon at the turn of the century. But if you wander now through Vieux Lyon, perhaps finding a hidden courtyard or getting lost in a maze of *traboules*, or gazing over the Saône from the Quai Fulchiron, watching the mists roll down over the river, Béraud's description of an elusive, dream-like city seems to be an exact description of reality.

The portrait Béraud paints of the people of Lyon is fraught with contradictions. They are, in roughly equal measure, secretive and gregarious, outwardly saturnine, puritanical and sour-faced (he often describes the typical Lyonnais as '*pissevinaigre*' – 'vinegar piss'), but they love drinking and eating to excess. They are usually politically conservative, but when roused, the working class of the city could shake the very foundations of French society.

This happened most notably in 1831, 1834 and 1848 with the '*révoltes des canuts*'. These were a series of insurrections which erupted in La Croix-Rousse as *les canuts* (silk workers) took a stand against the imposition of tariffs on their labour. These uprisings are among the most important in the early history of the Industrial Revolution and were regarded as such by Karl Marx, Pierre-Joseph Proudhon and Charles Fourier. Their revolt was, according to Friedrich Engels, 'the first working-class rising' of the early capitalist era. Their ideas were an early form of anarchism, their vision a kind of socialist utopia where men and women had complete control over their lives, free from the constraints of capital. This was the paradise imagined by Proudhon and Fourier.

The most violent of the rebellions, the so-called second revolt, began in February 1834, when the owners of the city's silk weavers' workshops decided to suppress the workers' wages, which coincided with the discussion of new laws intended to suppress republican groups. The pushback came on the day the *canuts* began using the French Republican calendar, declaring it to be not 9 April 1834 but 22 Germinal (the seventh month of the Republican year), year XLII of the Republic, which was a stand against the king, Louis-Philippe I, as well as against Paris. With the battle cry of 'live free, or die fighting', the *canuts* descended from La Croix-Rousse into the streets of Lyon. Louis-Philippe immediately sent 20,000 troops and 150 cannons to Lyon.

On arriving in Lyon, the army took over the centre of the city and all bridges over the two rivers. In response, the *canuts* set up barricades, even as they were fired on by government troops. Until now without weapons, the *canuts* looted the armoury at the barracks of Bon-Pasteur and settled into their defensive positions ready for battle. There then followed a week of hard fighting that came to be known as '*Sanglante semaine*' ('Bloody Week') until the army finally took the city on 14 April, with La Croix-Rousse the last bastion to fall. Around six hundred *canuts* had been killed and 10,000 more were sent to prison or for deportation.

The second revolt of the *canuts* was a moment of heroic deeds, comradeship and sacrifice which went deep into Lyonnais folklore. Henri Béraud was fascinated by the legends of the *canuts*, their impenetrable slang and secret codes, their occult knowledge of the hidden city of *traboules*, their independent spirit, their refusal to surrender in the face of greater force. The politics of the *canuts*, their spirit of anarchy, was less important to Béraud than how he thought they incarnated the best of the Lyonnais character. Elsewhere, the rebels have been celebrated in numerous songs, jokes and plays, always with emphasis on their wild, dangerous and Romantic nature. Probably the most famous anthem of the *canuts* is 'Le Chant des *Canuts*' ('The Song of the *Canuts*'), a German folk song which was given new lyrics by the singer and poet Aristide Bruant in 1894. The song is now part of the long French tradition of songs of resistance and rebellion. The words are plain enough to appeal to any lust for revolution: 'We will weave the winding sheet of the old world,/ for we already hear the storm brewing/ We are the *canuts*/ And we are naked and unafraid.' The most well-known version of the song is by Yves Montand, but in 2017 the veteran left-winger Jean-Luc Mélenchon added his name to the list of those who had appropriated the song when he sang the last lines at a rally in Lyon.

In recent times, the *canuts* have also been appropriated by the far right. The Fascists of Vieux Lyon in particular celebrate the *canuts* as avatars of Lyonnais wit and the urge for subversion. These are the same groups who promote the use of *le parler lyonnais*, the old dialect of Lyon (words like '*Rebeyne*', for example) and who describe themselves as *gones* or *fenottes*, two old words from the Franco-Provençal dialect used to describe the native lads and lasses of Lyon, who are also sardonic and clever natural rebels.

A less radical aspect of the legacy of the *canuts* comes in the form of food. One of the staples of Lyonnais cuisine is a dish called '*la cervelle de canut*' – *faisselle* cheese, onions, garlic, herbs to taste — which was the everyday dish of the poor *canuts* of Lyon. Literally, it means 'the brain of the *canut*', with the cheese standing in for the much more expensive sheep brain.

In the end, everything in Lyon comes down to food. Other French towns and cities make a claim for the originality, excellence and superiority of their own *'produits'*. But only Lyon claims to be the true gastronomic capital of France, and thus the world.

Henri Béraud wrote about food and (especially) drink with relish. He admitted to his readers that he was greedy, but he saw this as a virtue rather than a sin. Most of all, he delighted in *les bouchons*, the modest and traditional restaurants which date back to the nineteenth century and are the keepers of the Lyonnais cultural heritage, serving only dishes which have their origins in the region. Béraud loved not only the food in these places but also the fact that a meal would last several hours, flushed down with wine until the early hours, until the dawn even. As described by Béraud, the assembled dining company, hidden from the world by the shuttered windows of the *bouchon*, participated in an orgiastic feast with a touch of the sexual and the sacred. Béraud lovingly quotes from the poems that the greedy Lyonnais compose about their food — songs and rhymes about hams, sausages, pike, truffles, cheeses and 'the dead, green bodies, frozen and taken from the wild Atlantic' (a reference to a seafood terrine).[5]

The origins of the word *'bouchon'* are much disputed. One theory is that it comes from the tendency of restaurant owners to *'bouchonner'* ('bunch up') their customers. Another is that traditionally waiters handed out *'bouchons de paille'* ('straw hats') to their customers to absorb the sweat from their brows after too much food and wine. Yet another theory comes from the fact that *cabaretiers* (tavern owners) used to put bundles of hay in their windows to signal that horses could be cared for while their riders took food and drink (the verb *bouchonner* can also mean to rub down a horse). Most likely is the version given by the nineteenth-century Lyonnais writer and architect Nizier du Puitspelu, always a witty and erudite guide to the city's past, who in his dictionary of Lyonnais life wrote: '*bouchon*: the branches of a pine tree rolled into a ball hung in the windows of *cabarets*. This is the diminutive of "*bousche*" in Old French.'[6]

My own first encounters with the food of Lyon were not promising. In a bold moment of adventure, in my earlier days in the city, I once ordered *andouillette*. This looks delicious and smells foul. It is basically a tripe sausage: the contents of a pig's stomach rolled over and grilled. Refined food writers euphemistically describe the 'gamey' odour as the taint of the farmyard and enthuse over the *andouillette*'s earthy nature. The most exquisite part of the *andouillette* for its devotees is the pig's colon, which often contains more than a trace of what you would normally expect to find in a pig's colon. Last time I was in Lyon, in early 2023, three decades on from my first bold experiment, I heaved but tried not to show it as the man bunched next to me tucked into his roast *andouillette*. The *andouillette* smells and tastes like what it is: pig shit.

I ate this meal in Le Bouchon des Filles, a small and quite lovely restaurant in La Croix-Rousse. As the name suggests, the place is owned and run by an all-female cast, and it has to be said that everything else on the menu looked or tasted delicious. In fact, women have played a prominent role in Lyon's culinary history. The city's reputation as a world capital of gastronomy was established in the eighteenth century by the so-called *mères lyonnaises* (mothers of Lyon). The *mères* were most often cooks in wealthy households who struck out independently and took to their self-owned *bouchons* the kind of grand cooking that they had learned in domestic service, served alongside the more solid and cheaper fare that working-class Lyonnais could afford.

In the 1920s and 1930s, the *mères* became famous among the well-heeled tourists who stopped in Lyon on their way down south from Paris. The most celebrated among the *mères* during this period include La Mère Fillioux, who regularly cooked for Gertrude Stein and Alice B. Toklas; La Mère Brazier, who was the first woman chef to win a Michelin star in 1933 and the first to get three stars for two of her restaurants; and La Mère Bourgeois, who also won three Michelin stars and served Edouard Herriot, formerly prime minister of France, as well as Charles de Gaulle and François Mitterrand. Among their famed dishes were warm pâtés; chicken in succulent cream and champagne sauces; pike; eel stew; a *terrine* of larks; tripe with chervil, artichoke and bone marrow; veal with onions and bacon. Unsurprisingly, in photographs or paintings, the *mères* mostly look broad-shouldered, plump and tough, with very little of the maternal in their expressions.

The American writer Bill Buford, who came to Lyon in 2008 to learn about French cooking, recalled Mathieu Viannay, a chef with two Michelin stars, recounting how the *mères* had 'their own subculture, sharing among themselves a literature of tattered *mère* cookbooks'.[7] In his book *Dirt: Adventures in French Cooking*, Buford gives a breathless, entertaining and passionate account of his five years in Lyon trying to understand this 'subculture'. He did this by throwing himself in at the deep end, working in a boulangerie, until he got himself hired by a working restaurant, where he quickly had to square up to the rigours of Lyonnais cooking, which, for all its earthy integrity rooted in local produce, has more in common with mathematics than poetry.

The greatest of all the chefs that Lyon has produced, according to Buford and most probably the rest of France, was Paul Bocuse, who was born in 1926 in Collonges-au-Mont-d'Or, a suburb in the outlying flanks of Lyon. He learned to cook in the 1930s and 1940s from La Mère Brazier, a caustic and short-tempered woman who was not above screeching at staff or smacking her son Gaston hard in front of customers. Although Bocuse gained a global reputation and his cooking became sophisticated and intricate, he remained faithful to the basics of Lyonnais cooking – always use the best local ingredients; food should taste of what it is. Buford described Bocuse as 'a deity', and indeed he has almost mythical status in the annals of French cuisine.

Buford wanted to meet Bocuse face to face but this proved tricky, not because Bocuse acted like a superstar chef but quite the opposite: he was a man of humble habits who took his coffee at seven in the morning quietly and anonymously at Les Halles de Lyon Paul Bocuse, the central food market in Lyon which now bears his name. This is where Buford finally got to meet his hero. Bocuse was nonchalant and casual and offered Buford a tour of the market. For the duration of their short meeting, Buford was uncharacteristically without words, apart from the occasional '*Merci, Chef*'.

I got to meet Paul Bocuse one morning in July 2007 in the salon of his restaurant, Auberge du Pont de Collonges in Collonges-au-Mont-d'Or. I was there to make a film on the history of French food. Bocuse's assistant greeted me with a glass of Condrieu Blanc 2006 as I sat down with the great man to discuss his life and work. Bocuse was not at all the austere figure I had been expecting but instead rather mischievous. He loved food, women and drink, he told me, but not always in that order. He said that his aim as a chef was to take French food away from the heavy, serious feasts of the 1900s towards a lighter, fresher and more sensual cooking that was like 'a slender girl in a see-through blouse'.

Bocuse also had a beaky face and a mildly imperious manner, which grew more imperious when he later donned his chef's uniform in his kitchen, and he had the air of a kitchen general. But for now, in relaxed and comfortable clothes, he seemed almost mortal. He was friendly and kind and talked with genuine warmth about his past, his teachers and his experiences in Lyon as a young man during the Second World War (he had worked in the slaughterhouse of a Vichy-led youth camp, where he learned that brutality was an essential part of cooking, and then he was wounded while fighting with the Free French Forces).

Bocuse's most revered master was Fernand Point, who commanded a restaurant called La Pyramide in Vienne, just outside Lyon. There was a bust of Point in Bocuse's salon, and Bocuse shared some well-polished tales of his mentor and idol. He recounted how Albert Lebrun, the last president of the Third Republic, had been dining in La Pyramide in 1940 and remarked that Point seemed to have rather more *crème fraîche* than was usual in a country at war. Point responded with what he thought was unswerving patriotism: 'No one has the right to betray *gratin dauphinois*!' Point was a fat and boozy man with an intense dedication to living his art. He drank a magnum of champagne every day, as well as wine, *apéritifs* and *digestifs*. He died at the age of fifty-nine.

As part of the film, I had to cook with Bocuse in his kitchen. I am a lousy cook and the whole thing was a set-up, but Bocuse was gracious and even funny as I clumsily wielded a knife or fork in the wrong way. He allowed me to chop an onion for the camera and then threw it away when I had finished. The dish he prepared was extraordinary, probably the most stunning work of culinary alchemy that I've ever witnessed, smelled and tasted. It was *soupe aux truffes noires VGE*, a dish created by Bocuse for Valéry Giscard d'Estaing at the Elysée Palace in 1975, a distillation of truffles, *foie gras*, chicken breast, Noilly Prat, beef stock, carrots, onions, mushrooms, celery and butter. A lid of thin pastry was laid over the 'soup' so that when you pierced it with your fork, a musky aroma of truffles was your first almost erotic encounter with the dish. As I pierced the crust for the camera, I was visibly lost for words, punch-drunk on Bocuse's artistry. Bocuse modestly explained that his creation was a variation of a meal he had eaten as a young man in the home of peasants from the Ardèche.

Afterwards, Bocuse escorted us to a sumptuous dining room

and served all of us, including the five-man film crew, a seven-course lunch. There was, of course, the *soupe aux truffes noires VGE*, and dishes from Mère Fillioux (*volaille de Bresse en vessie*) and Mère Richard (*fromages frais affinés*). The centrepiece of the meal was *filets de sole Fernand Point*, which was a devastatingly unctuous composition of sole, mushrooms, white wine, *échalottes*, egg, tomato, butter and cream. It is a classic of French *bourgeois* cooking; every French man or woman is advised to eat it at least once according to a consensus of French cookery experts. We drank more Condrieu 2006 and Moulin à Vent 'Les Trois Roches'.

Paul Bocuse died in 2018 at home in his beloved restaurant, and his funeral service at the Eglise Saint-Jean in Lyon was attended by ministers of state as well as all the leading chefs of France. By the time of his death, he had not only ensured his status as the greatest French chef of his era but also bequeathed a wider legacy. One of the most commonly repeated complaints of the past few decades from those who love French food, both within France and from outside, has been that French cooking is in terminal decline, ceding popularity to fast-food restaurants and 'exotic' non-French cuisines, which have been replacing the affordable former everyday staples in France. Much of this argument is true. But great cookery still exists in France, most of it inspired by Bocuse and his followers. As much as the French language or French literature, French cuisine is a form of cultural resistance to the globalized world beyond France and the globalization that has been taking place within the borders of *l'Hexagone*, as the French commonly call France.

It struck me that during our encounter Bocuse spoke of himself in the third person. This might have been a mark of a great chef's vanity. But beyond narcissism, it was an acknowledgement that, as an avatar of Lyonnais culture and therefore 'Frenchness', Bocuse had already entered French history.

*

Arthur Young was testy and tired when he arrived in Lyon in late December 1789. This was almost the last leg of his third and final journey in France, and he was eager to get to Paris to see what was happening there as the Revolution took hold, as he put it: 'for the sake of observing the extraordinary state of things – of a King, Queen, and Dauphin of France, actual prisoners'.

Young refused to be impressed by Lyon, even though it was then the only city in France to have a population of more than 100,000 and had a reputation as a great city, standing at the crossroads between Italy, Switzerland and the south of France. Young was struck by the inward-looking nature of the Lyonnais. He remarked sharply that the tip of the confluence of the Saône and Rhône, which was a large undeveloped space, was a missed architectural opportunity. 'When a city is built at the junction of two great rivers, the imagination is apt to suppose that those rivers form a part of the magnificence of the scenery.'[8] There was nothing magnificent about the scrub and marsh which Young saw. Neither did the hard-headed agriculturist see any mystical value in the rivers.

Young was also irritable partly because he had been obliged to travel to Lyon in the company of a certain Mr Grundy, a businessman from Birmingham, with whom he was also to share the onward journey to Paris in a 'post-chaise' – a small, closed carriage – 'a mode of travelling I detest but the season persuaded me to do it,' wrote Young. On the road to Lyon, they had been stopped by the *Milice bourgeoise* – a militia organized by wealthy city-dwellers to protect their rights and property – and Mr Grundy recalled that when travelling the same road in August he had seen a corpse dangling from a tree, a peasant hung by the militia in punishment and as a warning to other criminals and insurrectionists.

During his short stay in Lyon, Young saw enough to convince him that, given the starving population of the city and the 'dreary' countryside and 'much waste', suffering lay ahead.

Accordingly, the course of the Revolution was traumatic and bloody in Lyon. Although the majority of workers, mainly in the silk industry, were inspired to acts of violence in the name of freedom by what they had heard from Paris, the merchants who really controlled the city cracked down on all attempts at insurgency. The Revolutionary Parisian press in turn deemed Lyon to be anti-Parisian and therefore counter-Revolutionary: Lyon, it was rumoured, was a city where the population was as likely to sing '*Le Réveil du Peuple*' – a song which was popular among *muscadins*, Royalists and anti-Jacobins – as '*La Marseillaise*'.

This historical moment is one of the many reasons why the sentiment persists in Paris to this day that Lyon cannot be trusted. The accepted wisdom is that Lyon is a closed city which serves only its own purposes and not those of the Republic. The Parisian view is more or less true: through its history and politics, its literature, and even its cuisine, Lyon has always been largely indifferent to the outside world, in spite of attempts by municipal city authorities to promote it as an international city taking its rightful place on the European stage.

The truth is, though, that Lyon is as hostile as it has ever been to outside influence and wary of being subservient to Paris. So Lyon still stands alone, capital of itself.

Part Three
THE SOUTH

7

Into Provence

The author and his mates, Hyères, 1985

The road to Provence begins in Lyon.

To be more precise, it starts in the *quartier* of Perrache. For many decades, this part of Lyon was dominated by the city's main train station, once the main axis for all rail traffic from Paris to Marseille. Today, Perrache is known by most French holidaymakers as the point on the map which marks the beginning of Autoroute 7 (soon to be renamed M6), 'L'Autoroute du Soleil' ('The Highway to the Sun'). This autoroute slides out of Lyon through the city's grimy edges, veering just past rue de Marseille, the street where I used to live, and then follows the Rhône for a dozen or so kilometres through a forest of petrochemical plants known locally as 'La Vallée de la Chimie' ('The

Valley of Chemistry'). As you pass the stark, scaffold-like outline of the oil refinery at Feyzin, the air hangs heavy with hydrogen sulphide and other pollutants. This road is notorious throughout France for its evil odours. I have never been driven past without gagging and then feeling nauseous for a good half hour or so afterwards, choked by the stench of bad eggs, rotten vegetables, sewers and decomposing flesh.

Despite this inauspicious starting point to the journey to Provence, the Autoroute du Soleil occupies a near-mythic place in French folklore. Since it was first properly opened in 1963, it has been the beginning of summer adventures for countless generations of French people. Its appeal is, first of all, visceral. As you travel down the autoroute you can see France spreading out and taking on its different forms before you. Lyon is traditionally known as the gateway to the south, the place where the Gothic gives way to the Romanesque. But the south really announces itself around Valence, a town about a hundred kilometres south of Lyon, where the autoroute becomes bordered by olive trees and vines rather than dense woods and verdant pastureland. The light changes – the sun seems suddenly more intense – the scent of lavender fills the air, and there is the definite feeling that you are now leaving one country for another. This is why the journey to the south can feel more like crossing a continent than a country.

The appeal of driving down to the south was most famously celebrated by the crooner and songwriter Charles Trenet in his 1958 hit recording 'Nationale 7', which was a hymn of praise to the *'route nationale'* which preceded the A7. Before the arrival of motorways, the only way that you could travel any significant distance in France was on the *routes nationales*, the long roads fanning out from Paris, which were meant to take travellers to every point of *l'Hexagone*. This road system dates back to Napoleon's *'routes impériales'*, which in turn roughly followed old Roman and pilgrimage routes.

In his book *The Unquiet Grave*, an elegiac hymn to a lost France, Cyril Connolly imagined himself 'peeling off the kilometres to the tune of "Blue Skies", sizzling down the long black liquid reaches of Nationale Sept, the plane trees going sha-sha-sha through the open window, the windscreen yellowing with crushed midges, she with the Michelin beside me, a handkerchief binding her hair'.[1] Connolly wrote this in wartime London, when a journey to Provence was a half-forgotten impossibility, and in wartime France the only journeys to be made by ordinary French people between the north and south were in clandestine fashion by refugees or resistance fighters.

When the roads opened up again in the 1950s, the *routes nationales* became a deeply loved and cherished part of what it meant to be French in the new post-war world. They offered freedom to travel throughout what had only recently been an occupied and divided nation. An increase in car ownership meant that this new freedom was now available to ever larger parts of society. Ownership of cars, along with refrigerators, washing machines and television sets, was one of the many marvels of *les Trente Glorieuses*, which had turned France into a consumer society where pleasure was now available to all (or nearly all). Now, an annual holiday in the south was no longer the preserve of a moneyed elite. Even a clerk, factory worker or teacher from Roubaix, Lille or the suburbs of Paris could afford a motor car to take his family down a *route nationale*, staying in cheap hotels which catered for these travellers, who in turn ate the local specialities and grew to know their country by its regional food as well as its great history. The journey to the south turned everyday perspectives upside down; it was, as Trenet sang, a trip which made 'Paris a suburb of Valence'.

If the journey along the Nationale 7, and then the Autoroute du Soleil, represented freedom, the destination represented earthly delight. Commonly, this took the form of *'un camping'*, a campsite usually set in parklands or woods and often near a beach. The first *campings* appeared in 1936, when workers were first able to take paid holidays. They were usually primitive and scrubby parcels of ground maintained and controlled by local municipalities to deter the newly mobile urban working classes from spilling over onto farmland or privately owned property. They were enormously popular until the interruption of war. In the 1950s, *les campings* became the first French adventures in mass tourism; they were now no longer thought of as mere campsites but rather as *les hôtelleries de plein air* (outdoor hotels). To the urbanites who flocked to *les campings*, they seemed like a little bit of heaven fallen to earth. On offer were sports, dancing, concerts, bingo, table tennis, table football (*le babyfoot*), and food and drink in a semi-bucolic setting all at far remove from the *grisaille* (greyness) of everyday life in a town or city.

Most enticing of all was the promise of romance and sex. This was not just confined to adults. The growth of *les campings* happened alongside the invention and rise of a new category of social being in France: the teenager. *Le camping* became a rite of passage for generations of French adolescents, where first love was tried out under the fairy lights of an outdoor disco (*une boum*) to a soundtrack of hit summer songs (*les tubes de l'été*). In 1972, Michel Fugain, son of a militant Communist from Grenoble who had fought in the French Resistance, had his biggest ever hit with a song called '*Une belle histoire*', the story of a boy travelling home to the north (to the '*brouillard*' – 'the mist and fog') and a girl travelling south. The two young lovers meet accidentally on the Autoroute du Soleil (presumably in a rest area or service station) and give themselves over to a night of passion in a nearby field – 'the gift of Providence'. Few French people of a certain age can listen to this song even now without a vague but intense feeling of sexual nostalgia.

Le camping remains the favourite holiday of the French nation. Little wonder then that one of the most popular French TV series of all time is the long-running comedy soap opera called *Camping Paradis*, which began in 2006 and is filmed in a variety of real *campings* across the south of France, although the television show is supposed to be set in Martigues, not far from Marseille. The series took its inspiration from an original film called *Camping*, which starred the comedian Franck Dubosc as a determined pick-up artist (and mustard salesman of the second-rate Amora mustard from Dijon, a town he says 'everybody has heard of and no one visits'), whose main job as the owner of a *camping* is apparently to seduce as many women as he can. (This first film was inevitably followed by *Camping 2* and *Camping 3*.) The television show is faithful to the artless comedy of the film. Every week an influx of new visitors provides a new storyline – a broken heart, a suspected crime, mothers who go on strike, a heartwarming family crisis – which is always resolved by the end of the programme and, as often as not, celebrated by the show's gormless and annoying dance and song 'Fiesta Boom Boom', which is a staple for line-dancing classes in the dark winter months in France.

The film and the series have now given rise to a franchise of ninety campsites across France called Les Vacances Camping Paradis, which promise the 'full Camping Paradis experience': you can wear the original sky-blue polo shirts that staff wear in the television show and even get the occasional visit from the show's main star, Laurent Ournac. The success of this franchise has been matched by a boom in specialist '*campings libertins*' aimed at '*échangistes*' ('swingers'). Across France, these places offer 'liberty and sensuality' alongside the traditional French holiday pleasures of food and sun. Probably the best known of these specialist *campings* is La Roseraie, which was the first to set up business, deep in the unlikely setting of rural Auvergne, in 2014.

The site gives access to caravans and camper vans, or you can rent a chalet. There is a toboggan run, volleyball and *pétanque*.

For all its amenities, the owner Gérard Vetter says that customers should be aware all the time of why they are there: sex with strangers. 'It's better for people to have already had experience of debauchery,' he genially explains, boasting of the recent addition of 'gang bang' beds, which are seven metres long and three metres wide. 'We pride ourselves on our conviviality,' he says, emphasizing that his establishment still has the same 'paradisiacal' atmosphere of any other campsite. The big idea is to be able to offer sexual freedom alongside all the other pleasures of a *camping*. This is, says Gérard, a halfway house between a utopian naturist colony and a free-floating sex party, which is a very different experience from the standard swingers' nightclub. 'What I like here is that you can have a sexual relationship with anyone,' says Pascale, who was on holiday here in 2017 for the first time with her husband Thierry. 'You walk around the camp, you kiss someone on the mouth, you put your hand on their arse: it's lovely! I don't know anywhere else in the world like this.'

Somewhat inevitably, the new crop of *campings libertins* has become a target for Islamist puritans. Since 2016, French counterterrorist units have foiled several planned attacks, like a sinister echo of the final part of Michel Houellebecq's 2001 novel *Platform*, whose main female character Valérie is killed in a bombing by Muslim extremists at a sex resort in Thailand. She had been planning a new business called 'friendly tourism', offering unlimited sexual opportunities in so-called Aphrodite Clubs. Not for the first time, Houellebecq's art was eerily turned into life. Attacking two popular French traditions at once – the pleasures of sex and the hedonistic holiday spirit – has now become a form of Islamist virtue-signalling. This is why Gérard Vetter points out that security and vigilance, as well as hygiene, are his watchwords.

One of the most meticulously planned and well-documented journeys along the road to Provence was made in 1982 by the

Argentinian writer Julio Cortázar and his wife Carol Dunlop. They travelled in a Volkswagen Combi, which they had nicknamed 'Fafner' after the mythological dragon in Wagner's *Siegfried*. They intended to visit each of the sixty-five *parkings* (rest areas) on the autoroute between Paris and Marseille. The journey would take them thirty-two days. They aimed to visit two *parkings* each day, travelling roughly for an hour between each one, stopping only at these rest areas. The plan was to never leave the road.

Two weeks before setting off, Julio Cortázar wrote to the director of Les sociétés d'autoroutes to ask for his permission to launch the mission and try to pre-empt any problems with toll booths along the way. He also informed him that the autoroute would be the main character in the book that he and Carol Dunlop planned to write about their journey. The director didn't reply. Notwithstanding, the pair set off. On the afternoon of Sunday 23 May 1982, they loaded Fafner up – with whisky, wine, eggs, mineral water, bread, butter, coffee, tuna, sardines, cheese (grated), mayonnaise, *choucroute*, oil, ham, spaghetti, rice and biscuits, having decided to find fresh meat and fruit where they could along the way – and set off from rue Martel in the 10th arrondissement of Paris bound for Marseille. For the duration of the trip, Julio Cortázar called himself Le Loup (The Wolf) and his wife L'Oursine (Little Bear).[2]

They left home at 2.25 p.m. and drove through the city, past République, past Austerlitz, hitting the Autoroute du Sud at precisely 2.47 p.m. At 3.10 p.m., they reached their first destination, the *parking* at Aire de Lisses, where they found a lot of English tourists (as they would on future stops), a dramatic hailstorm and then sheets of rain. They got to the next *parking* at Aire de Nainville at 6.28 p.m. By now, 'the violence of the elements' made it impossible for them to explore their surroundings. They took 'a well-deserved siesta', then awoke at 8 p.m. to clear skies and birdsong. They spotted a hare 'the size of a small dog and the colour of a chicken'. Slightly overwhelmed, and mildly depressed by the size of the task which lay ahead of them, they decided to stay the night.

By the time of this trip, Julio Cortázar was sixty-eight years old and had an international reputation as a literary polymath. He had spent his childhood in Argentina but lived mainly in France as a prolific writer of novels, short stories, poems, plays, travelogues, journals and articles. He was famous partly because he was from a generation of Latin American writers who came to global prominence beyond the Spanish-speaking world without losing a specifically Latin American sensibility. Like his peers, Gabriel García Márquez, Carlos Fuentes and Mario Vargas Llosa, Cortázar enjoyed fusing magic, superstition, folklore and avant-garde techniques borrowed from Western models such as surrealism or even non-literary forms such as jazz (Cortázar especially admired the complexity and unpredictability of Charlie Parker and John Coltrane). He also liked to mix up genres, sometimes collaborating with painters, photographers and engravers to put together text and images in poetic collision. If there was a unifying theme in Cortázar's work, it was a persistent anxiety over whether language shaped reality or whether reality shaped language. This was a tension which he never resolved.

At thirty-five years old, his wife Carol Dunlop was over three decades younger than Cortázar but every bit as playful and creative. She had been born in Massachusetts but moved to Montréal in her twenties to protest against the Vietnam War. There she became a fully fledged Canadian citizen, bilingual in French and reasonably fluent in several languages. She was variously a translator, novelist, photographer and political activist, visiting Nicaragua and Chile in support of left-wing causes. She first met Cortázar at a conference in Montréal, followed him back to Paris and married him within a few months. She was physically slight and somewhat fragile, suffering a number of undiagnosed health complaints. But she was also very witty and alive to the world, writing impressionistic, intense semi-autobiographical novels.

Julio Cortázar admired Carol's work; it was a way into the labyrinth of her mind. Both of them were fascinated by love and temporality – more precisely, the way that desire can make human beings feel as if they are stepping 'out of time', like a dream or an almost mystical experience which, when you return to the world makes you feel connected to innocent joy and wonder. This is why their co-authored book about this journey south, *Les autonautes de la cosmoroute* (*Autonauts of the Cosmoroute*), is subtitled '*un voyage intemporel Paris-Marseille*' ('a timeless voyage between Paris and Marseille'). Through an assemblage of drawings, scraps of a journal, mediations, photography and maps, the book is an attempt to capture a journey beyond the constraints of everyday reality into a more magical realm.

Le Loup and L'Oursine first began to anticipate the south on 15 June as they passed the road signs for Valence, sensing that this was a frontier, a shift of territory, language and culture. They stayed overnight at Valence, where they dined on *steak-frites* and made love, lost in each other as the lights of cars, lorries and buses flickered over them, their drivers oblivious to the unseen lovers in the shadows at the side of the road.

The next day they headed for Montélimar, with the mountains of the Ardèche on their right-hand side. They arrived two days later at the service station of Montélimar, which is not properly Provence, but it is most certainly the same terrain and, with the southern Alps now to the right, it feels distinctly 'south'. At the service station, they bought petrol, noted the restaurant, investigated the tourist office, took a shower and bought nougat, a speciality of the region, which had originally been brought all the way up the Rhône by the Romans, who called it *nux gatum*.

They had by now read all the books they had brought with them and so had to buy magazines and newspapers, which they read in the shade at a cafe *terrasse* to escape the crushing heat.

They were joined by their friends André Stil, the novelist, and his wife Odette. At 3.40 p.m. on 17 June, they finally crossed the border: they passed a 'huge and marvellous sign' which read '*Vous êtes en Provence!*' – 'You are now in Provence!' At this time of year, the grey and blue hills had just burst into the glorious colours of a Cézanne painting.

At this stage of the journey and the book, the reader, like Le Loup and L'Oursine, has become lost and absorbed in minute details, exhilarated by every new discovery. But now a new darkness begins to shadow the text and the travellers. They start to see mysterious portents everywhere. In the parking areas, they take photographs of rubbish bins, which stand 'like sentinels', or 'Teutonic knights', and the pair begin to think that the bins are watching them. They find and photograph a microphone in a rubbish bin, which they think might be listening in to them; 'they are continuing their surveillance of us,' writes Cortázar calmly. They talk of espionage.[3]

There was a reality to the paranoia haunting Le Loup and L'Oursine. Both Cortázar and Dunlop were politically active on the left and especially involved in Latin American affairs. Cortázar had taken part in anti-Peronist protests in Argentina and France and was loudly vocal in his support for Fidel Castro's Cuba, Salvador Allende's Chile and the Sandinista revolution in Nicaragua. For her part, Dunlop was known to American authorities as an anti-Vietnam dissident who had abandoned her US citizenship to take up Canadian nationality in Montréal in disgust at the war and generally at the state of America. The 1970s and early 1980s were a period when radical leftist intellectuals like Cortázar and Dunlop were constantly on the radar of the intelligence agencies of not just the United States but also their allies. This apparently mad journey from Paris to Marseille – as quixotic as the original Quijote beloved by Cortázar – would not have gone unnoticed by these agencies, even if it was incomprehensible to them.

The omens, signs and portents multiply as they head deeper south. 'Spies watch us in strange new disguises,' notes Cortázar at Aire de Pierrelatte, now into the Drôme Provençale. He illustrates his observation with a photograph of a pair of rubbish bins, which do indeed look like sinister, inhuman surveillance machines if – as you are now bound to do so if you are involved in the imaginative world of the book – you take Cortázar at his word. At a children's playground at Orange-les-Grès, the pair feel uneasy contemplating the rustic innocence of the primitive play equipment – swings like gallows, climbing frames like a torture rack. They have a sudden illumination: this is a place where witches are tortured, condemned and killed. They feel in great danger.[4]

This much turns out to be true, but it is not the intelligence agencies which are stalking them but another, more final danger that is never fully revealed in the book. Within two years of reaching the journey's end in Marseille, both Le Loup and L'Oursine were dead. Carol Dunlop went first in the autumn of 1982. The cause initially given was bone marrow failure. Cortázar died in early 1984, apparently of leukaemia. It was later claimed that both of them had died of Aids, which Cortázar had accidentally contracted from a blood transfusion. Either way, it is obvious that this journey and this book, which seem to be about life, about magically transforming their world through words, images and the poetic imagination, turn out to be about death. They wrote the book with the knowledge that they would soon die; it is this fact, deeply occluded in their account of the journey, that gives the book its startling, lingering emotional heft.

The real journey's end for Julio and Carol was the cemetery of Montparnasse. Their grave is simple, a grey-white slab decorated with a sculpture of interlocking circles representing their union. The sculpture was made specially for Cortázar a few months before his death by his friend, a fellow Argentinian in Paris called Julio Silva. Whenever I am in the cemetery of

Montparnasse, which is not unusual on a Sunday afternoon, I always make a point of passing by Cortázar and Dunlop's resting place off the Allée Lenoir. More often than not, the grave is covered in poems or scraps of prose in Spanish, French and English, photographs, home-made illustrations of their work, messages, flowers and small gifts. It is a collage of text, thought, reality and unreality, much like the work they made together.

I first travelled down the Autoroute du Soleil in May 1985 with my Lyonnais friend Michel Rabain and Les Hodge, my Scottish flatmate in rue de Marseille in Lyon. We were headed for a week or so in Marseille, Cannes, Saint-Tropez, Nice and maybe Ventimiglia or even San Remo in Italy. We set off early morning from the rue de Marseille, turning onto the autoroute just beyond the Gare de Perrache, choking our way through 'La Vallée de la Chimie', setting out for the sun and adventure.

We had hardly any money but we were travelling in an open-topped 1967 Alfa Romeo Spider. When it first went on the market, it was the most expensive car on sale that year, beating even the latest, most fashionable Lamborghini. Although we were too broke to even think about the mindless luxury of a hotel, we were able to travel in this luxury vehicle because Michel, who was a car mechanic, had bought it broken down and cheap and had just done it up. Our very rough plan was to stay with Michel's mates along the way, if we could track them down, or, like the 'Autonauts of the Cosmoroute', sleep in rest areas (though obviously I'd never heard of Julio Cortázar or Carol Dunlop at this stage). The soundtrack for our road trip was the Buzzcocks, the Undertones, the Cramps and (Michel's choice) the old masters of French rock 'n' roll, Johnny Hallyday and Eddy Mitchell. This was music which probably would have made Cyril Connolly shudder with horror. Still, we were just as full of wonder and joy as Connolly was in the 1930s, bowling down the road south to the tune of 'Blue Skies'.

Michel's musical tastes went hand in hand with his cultivation of '*un look*'. He was tall, thin and blonde and wore 1950s-style pegged trousers, vintage bowling shirts, brothel creepers or the Mexican cowboy boots which French rockers call '*Santiags*', and biker jackets or American baseball jackets (called '*un teddy*' in French). He wore his blonde hair slicked back like Paul Simonon of the Clash and '*rouflaquettes*' ('sideburns'), all topped off with shades. His 'look' was pure '*rockabilly français*'.

This musical movement has its roots in American rockabilly, a mishmash of country and early rock 'n' roll, usually pared down to a double bass, guitar and the bare bones of a drum kit, which was popular in the Deep South. Big names like Elvis Presley, Jerry Lee Lewis and Johnny Cash all played rockabilly at some point, but the new generation of young French fans also sought out hard-to-find recordings by the likes of Sonny Burgess and Charlie Feathers. These musicians from the American South were usually poor and obscure, but their music was raw and powerful and, most importantly for their French audience, soaked in authentic experience, the rougher the better.

There was a class dimension to being a self-styled French 'rockabilly' in the early 1980s. Most significantly, French rockabilly fans identified with the music of 'white trash' America because they considered themselves to be the 'white trash' of France. There was a mini-explosion of bands with names like The Teenkats and Les Rockin' Rebels. They rebelled against the stuffiness of French *bourgeois* culture by cultivating their own pseudo-American culture, from clothes to cars. America was a pure and untainted myth of a country they had never seen, but which stood in opposition to the mediocrity of everyday life in France.

Les rockabillies were also often ignorant of the fault lines in the country they idolized, so much so that the Confederate flag was worn or shown in most places they went. They were not conspicuously racist (there were enough working-class neo-Nazi skinheads in early-1980s France to soak up that tendency), but there were never any Black or Arab kids at the rockabilly gigs I went to. Coming from the atmosphere of post-punk multicultural Britain, where reggae and soul were an integral part of youth culture, it was a shock to see how far white working-class and immigrant youth tribes stood apart from each other. In Lyon, the Algerian-born Rachid Taha (later a major star in France) founded a band called Carte de Séjour, modelled on the UK two-tone movement, but they got better coverage in the UK's major music magazine NME than they ever did in France.

The favoured reading of the French rockabilly was a series of bestselling *bandes dessinées* (comic books) by Frank Margerin, which recounted the adventures of would-be rocker Lucien and his loser mates Ricky Banlieue, Gillou and Riton, who live in the predominantly white working-class *banlieue* of Malakoff, just to the south of Paris. Lucien and his pals style themselves as '*loubards*', a word popular in the 1980s to designate neighbourhood hoodlums, although in fact they are gentle, likeable, incompetent delinquents scared of *bourgeois* authority and real gangsters alike. The gang rarely or never go into central Paris, which intimidates them, they reject all official French culture, and when Lucien gets a posh student girlfriend (in the story '*Lucien s'maque!*' – 'Lucien gets a chick!') he is emasculated and humiliated by having to cut off his rocker's quiff (called a *banane* – banana – in rockers' slang) to please her.

Obviously, *les rockabillies*, all working-class sons and daughters of *beaufs*, were also sworn enemies of the BCBGs. Michel often had a go at me because of my foppish BCBG clothes, my floppy fringe and my girlfriends, who were invariably *très snob* and who made him feel uncomfortable.

Together, Michel and I made an unlikely duo, but the third person on our trip also cut a striking figure. Les, who was from Dundee, was dressed roughly in the rockabilly style, but instead of a quiff, he had a Mohican, in keeping with his love of the 'psychobilly' genre, a mutant form of rockabilly then briefly popular. In fact, it was at a 'psychobilly night' in the West Side Club in Lyon where we had fallen in with Michel and his gang.

Our first destination in the Alfa Romeo was Toulon. We intended to get there in less than a day, but this proved impossible, as Michel was the only driver. (When planning our jaunt over beers in Le Bronx bar in Lyon – the favoured headquarters of the city's rockabillies, skinheads and punks – he'd forgotten to ask whether Les or I could drive.) That first night, Michel was so exhausted that we nearly crashed several times before we settled down for a rough kip in a *parking* somewhere just beyond Montélimar. I didn't sleep much on the beautifully designed but uncomfortable seats of the Alfa Romeo, but when I woke at first light it didn't matter. It turned out that the clichés were all true: even in the grim *parking*, the air felt warmer, the light was more intense, and you could see the distant outlines of grey-white mountains which would eventually take you down to the sea. You could sense the south.

We arrived in Toulon in the early afternoon. The approach to the city was all flyovers, traffic jams and then more autoroute. But when we got to the seafront, excitement kicked in: this was our first sight of the Mediterranean (for Les and me at least), and although it was cold and churning in early May, it was still as blue as we had hoped it would be. Michel had arranged for us to meet one of his pals, who would put us up for the night, but when he still hadn't shown up after an hour or so, we decided to wander around the centre of Toulon instead. After all, we'd already survived a night in the Alfa Romeo. After a few circuits around the harbour, which seemed to be all navy shipyards, cranes and docks, we concluded that Toulon was dour and unimpressive and decided to push on to Hyères, where Michel had another friend and another promise of accommodation.

Hyères was, like Toulon, a garrison town, home to the 54th Artillery Regiment and a naval air station. But it also had a cute old town, squares with fountains shaded by *platanes* and welcoming cafes, where we drank beer. Michel's friend in Hyères, Gaby, brought with him a gang of friendly rockers, who were wearing regulation *Santiags* and leather jackets, sporting greasy quiffs and riding motorbikes. For dinner, they took us to a car park, where we ordered pizza from a truck and more beer (tins of Kronenbourg). I quickly discovered that the pizza trucks of the south of France are one of the marvels and delights of the region. The best of them are mobile wood-fired ovens which will fire up for you a bespoke pizza that is easily the equivalent of, or better than, any you will find in Naples. This makes sense, as pizza was brought to the south of France in the 1900s by a vast flux of Neapolitans fleeing the poverty of their native city and settling mainly in Marseille in the *quartiers* of La Joliette and the Vieux Port.

The pizza trucks date back to 1962, when an enterprising Marseillais called Jean Méritan, inspired by the street vendors he had seen during a trip to Spain, installed a wood-fired oven in a mobile home hitched to a small van. At first, prospective customers thought that the set-up was a municipal tar spreader, but the fad caught on and the Marseillais pizza truck had arrived. Much more than *bouillabaisse* or *bourride* (too rich, too expensive and too elaborate), pizza is the true food of the people in the south.

After the revelatory slice of pizza, we drove back to Gaby's flat – which turned out to be a broken-down squat with no furniture – with an escort of his rocker mates on bikes. There were no beds, and Gaby told us that he had mice or maybe rats. We drank more beers, listened to Gaby's music (more rockabilly, which I was getting a bit sick of by now) and smoked Moroccan dope before settling down for the night on the hard wooden floor of a bedless mezzanine. The floor felt unsafe, as if it might buckle and break under the weight of three adult male bodies, and you had to cling on to the wooden supporting structures so as to not fall off and break a limb. I remember all of these details because it was one of the most uncomfortable places I have slept, or more accurately tried to sleep, in my life. The next morning, sneezing with the grime, we emerged into the intense morning light of Provence like a trio of dusty phantoms.

Unwashed, unshaven and coughing, we drove for the next few hours, heading off towards Saint-Tropez, Juan-les-Pins, Antibes and Cannes. We stayed for twenty minutes or so in each place to take pictures and say that we'd been there. These were glamorous places which stunned and depressed us with their beauty and high prices. Arriving in Nice in the evening, we pulled up the Alfa Romeo outside a promising-looking nightclub, betting on the car to convince the doormen that we were high-value A-list players looking so filthy and beaten up because we had been playing so hard, probably with incredibly rare, exotic and expensive drugs. They were having none of it and saw us straight away for what we were: three penniless young lads on the make. Having come all this way, with hardly any money and now craving food more than drink, we made for the port and tried to blag our way into a party on a mega-yacht. Again we were turned away, this time with the swift promise of extreme violence if we did not leave immediately. From the harbour, we could see bronzed, beautiful women and ugly men on the deck of the yacht, drinking champagne, laughing, eating, and dancing to suave 1970s French disco.

That night in a backstreet in Nice, bedding down on the unforgivingly hard seats of the Alfa Romeo, starving and feeling how cold the night air can be even in Nice in May, the three of us became convinced ferocious anti-capitalist revolutionaries. We spent the sleepless night plotting to execute bloody revenge on the wicked multimillionaires who had thwarted our plan to eat their food, drink their alcohol and show their women what a good time really was. The next day, things got worse. Deciding that our luck might improve in Italy, we got to the

Italian border first thing in the morning. We were turned away at the customs. Les had forgotten his passport, and we made a collective decision to all go back home to Lyon in a spirit of solidarity. As we turned back to Nice, we passed a gaggle of stylish-looking girls our own age. We were all sporting our best dark glasses and slouched insouciantly as they cooed over the Alfa Romeo. But then, catching sight of the three of us inside trying too hard to look nonchalantly handsome, one of them uttered the damning words *'Mais ils ne sont pas beaux!'* – 'But they're not even good-looking!'

This was the final blow. The drive north to Lyon seemed much longer than it had been a few days ago when we were driving south. The soundtrack was subdued and muted – snatches from whatever local radio station was playing – and sometimes nothing at all, as we drove back in a chastened silence.

Since that first trip, I have travelled from the north to the south of France countless times, often on the Autoroute du Soleil but more often these days on the high-speed TGV, which takes you from Paris to Marseille in about three and a half hours. In the mid-twentieth century, this same journey would take eleven hours, and even the direct train from Paris to Marseille, introduced in 2001, could take me anywhere from six to eight hours. Sometimes this felt right; France is a huge country in European terms, and it is always good to have a sense of this, to grasp how the various languages and cultures in *l'Hexagone* are nominally 'French' but belong also to a wider territory which is not just a country but a whole civilization. That civilization was founded in Europe, but as the French moved through the world, conquering and occupying territories which became 'French', it has also necessarily been shaped by the non-European cultures it has been forced to absorb.

Such thoughts were in my head in the first week of May 2013, when I travelled down to Aix-en-Provence and then to the village of Lourmarin in the Lubéron, where I was to meet Catherine Camus to talk about her father. The writer and philosopher Albert Camus is, of course, now known worldwide as one of the most important figures in twentieth-century letters and a monument of French literary culture, a component part of French civilization and what it means to be French. My aim in meeting Catherine, however, was quite modest: I wanted to find out something about Camus the man, the father, the human being. I also wanted to talk to Catherine about his anguished relationship with Algeria, 'French Algeria', the country which he always thought of as his homeland.

Before travelling to Lourmarin, I had been in Algeria, looking for Camus's presence in Algiers, the city where he had been born and raised in poverty by his illiterate mother in the working-class district of Belcourt. After many detours and dead ends, I finally tracked down the tiny three-room apartment where Camus had spent his childhood with his mother, his grandmother, his brother Lucien and his uncle Etienne (who was semi-mute and who slept in the kitchen). It was at 93 rue de Lyon, more commonly known these days as rue Mohamed Belouizdad (the whole *quartier* is also sometimes confusingly referred to as 'Belouizdad'). Mohamed Belouizdad was an Algerian nationalist militant who hated the French and who grew up in this area as a direct contemporary of Camus. You wouldn't ever know that Camus had lived here and that it had shaped his whole way of thinking. There are no plaques or commemorations, you just have to find your own way to number 93 and work out where the apartment was: above what is now a phone shop whose owner shows no interest in their world-famous former neighbour.

I wanted very much to visit the apartment to be able to tell Catherine Camus that I had been there (she had never visited and would probably not be welcomed if she did), but when I asked around, in the local shops and a cafe, to see who owned the place and how I could get in, people shrugged their shoulders in indifference or ignorance. One man was hostile. 'Why do you come here? This is our country,' he barked, saying it again in Arabic for effect and for the benefit of the gathering audience. 'Why should we care if a Frenchman once lived here? We got rid of them all once. We don't want them back. Ever. Not even tourists. They do not belong here. They never will.'

I decided to move on, mildly intimidated by the positive reception the shrieking man was attracting from his public, who shouted encouragement at him. I took a few photos, made some notes and lingered long enough to be catcalled again. But I would never see inside the place where Camus had first decided to become a writer and philosopher and a lifelong champion of the poor and dispossessed. The twenty-first-century poor and dispossessed of Algiers simply did not want to remember him or know anything about him. The apartment buildings which dated back to Camus's era looked rotten, dirty and broken down, with plaster flaking off the balconies and electricity provided by a dangerous-looking tangle of wires. The street was another kind of tangle, this time of cars, scooters, dust and pollution, with people, mainly men, dodging in and out of the traffic. In the air hung the sour perfume of North Africa, long familiar to me after many years of travel in the region: the odour of petrol, black tobacco and sewage. The plane trees were dusty and tired, or just plain bare.

When I spoke to young students at the University of Algiers, where Camus had studied and taught philosophy, the reaction from them to the mention of his name was overwhelmingly hostile. 'He was no friend of the Algerians. He was a colonialist,' said a young woman called Yasmina in perfectly accented French. 'He writes about Muslims as if we were nothing. He writes about shooting Arabs and sees nothing wrong with that.' (This was a reference to Camus's first novel *L'Etranger*, in which the main protagonist Meursault does indeed shoot a Muslim for apparently no reason.) Another girl took up the argument: 'Camus does not belong here, he is not part of our tradition or culture. He is not Algerian but French.' (Camus always described himself as '*Algérien*'.) She continued: 'No French person has the right to say they belong here. They do not own us.'

We were standing in the dusty, ill-lit and mildly cavernous hallway outside an even more cavernous amphitheatre where I was about to give a lecture. Shortly, a small crowd gathered around and other students began chipping in, firstly on Albert Camus (denounced by everybody) and then on to Zionism, Palestine and the wickedness of Europe and America. This student body did not look to me to be Islamist radicals. The girls wore skirts and make-up and had their hair done up in imitation of their favourite R&B or rap heroines. The lads, too, wore the latest hip-hop fashions, or at least the versions that they could get hold of in Algiers or afford. They all looked as if they would be very much at home in France. So I interrupted the anti-Western tirades to ask them about France. Had any of them been there? Did they want to go? Did they have family there? How did they imagine life there?

A few of them said they had had positive experiences of visiting France, but they all agreed that it was not right that the French were so rich and the Algerians so poor. 'They took everything from us,' said one lad called Youssef, 'and our grandfathers worked for them like slaves. That's why they are so rich. They stole their money from the Algerians.' Those who had not been to France wanted to go there, but mainly just out of curiosity to see what it was like. After all, they had grown up with French language and culture nudging in alongside the Arabic language and Islamic culture. But mostly they wanted to emigrate to the US, Canada or Australia, 'where you could be free', said one girl wearing a white Beyoncé T-shirt.

Most of the students had family in France, some of whom had been there for generations and had taken on French and

Algerian identity. Some uncles had prospered, even built their businesses and no longer just worked in shops or factories. These people were to be envied. No one considered them as 'traitors'. They also knew that life in the *banlieues* of France was hard. 'We see it all on television and in movies,' Youssef continued. 'The Algerians, all Muslims in France, are lost. There are drug gangs and there is no morality. Young Algerians are quickly ruined by the West.' So was life better in Algeria than in France? I asked the group. The answers were full of contradictions. 'You don't die of poverty in France.' 'People have more morals in Algeria.' 'The French hate us.' 'It is bad to betray your family and tradition.' 'Algerians can never be happy in France.'

Back in Paris, I had interviewed a series of patrician and now very elderly Parisian intellectuals who, one way or another, had all been on close terms with Albert Camus. These were the writers Roger Grenier and Olivier Todd, and Jean Daniel, the founding editor of *Le Nouvel Observateur* magazine and without doubt the most distinguished journalist in late-twentieth-century France. Algeria was a central theme in our conversations. For one thing, they were all part of the generation of French intellectuals who had lived through the trauma of the Algerian War of Independence and its aftermath and been forced to make hard political decisions as the drama had unfolded in the most violent and unpredictable fashion. Albert Camus was important to them not simply as a friend and colleague, but also as a kind of moral avatar.

Roger Grenier first met Camus in 1944, when he was invited to write for *Combat*, the underground newspaper of the Resistance that Camus edited. Grenier described him as a man of deep honour. 'The first words that Camus ever said to me when I joined *Combat* was that he would never abandon me.' We were speaking in Grenier's tiny book-lined office deep in the headquarters of Editions Gallimard on the rue Sébastien-Bottin in Paris. He was editing books and commissioning new work at the age of ninety-four – a living part of twentieth-century French literary history still alive and active in the new century. 'From the moment he asked me to work with him, he treated me like a brother,' said Grenier. 'He was older than me and knew more about the world, but he never treated me as anything but his equal. Even then, Algeria was much on his mind, and he could see that relations between France and Algeria would be difficult after the world war was over, that there might even be war between them, and that the war would be vicious. He thought this would be a tragedy for both countries. He was right, of course.'

In Le Café Select in Montparnasse, Olivier Todd reminded me that although Camus considered himself a friend of the Algerian Arabs and thought that they deserved justice, he believed that an independent Algeria would be a disaster. He would constantly ask, what will happen to the *pieds-noirs*? This was their country as well. He was insistent about that. He was, of course, a *pied-noir* himself and spoke fluent *pataouète*, the language of his childhood (*pataouète* is the street dialect of Algiers common to Europeans and Muslims: a mix of French, Spanish, Catalan, Sardinian, Maltese and dialectal Arabic). It was Camus's view that 'Algeria' had never actually been a nation, that before the arrival of the French, it had been a patchwork of tribal territories variously subject to Ottoman and Arab rule. The way forward for Camus was not to separate Algeria from France (Algeria was not a colony properly speaking but technically part of France), but to build a federation which would give Muslims and Europeans equal rights but would still be under the control of the French Republic. 'This was a fragile idea,' said Todd. 'As the war went on and the violence got worse, it became completely unworkable. Even de Gaulle could see that the Algerian Muslims could never be citizens of France. That was not what they were fighting for.'

Jean Daniel, who was only a year younger than Roger Grenier, was himself a *pied-noir* like Camus, and his private office on the rue

Vaneau, overloaded with books, paintings and photos (including photos with Camus), was testimony to his lifelong love for Algeria. Daniel said that the problem for Camus was that the Algerian war was putting the French Republic dangerously to the test, exposing the limits of French universalism and the historical exhaustion of the republican ideal. Camus, however, clung on to his flimsy vision of a federal Algeria, fearing that the alternative was a newly independent Algeria brought into the orbit and under the control of the Russians or falling prey to the pan-Arab nationalism of Colonel Nasser in Cairo. Camus was wary, too, of the growing influence of what he saw as burgeoning Islamic imperialism from the Middle East. For Camus, Islam was a dead end rather than a threat, and theocracy was a form of fascism. 'Camus was right to fear all of these things, of course,' said Daniel, 'but he could not stop history. When he died he was still young, but he was exhausted. The war in Algeria had exhausted him.' Camus had been forty-six when he died.

'He said to me that the Algerian war would be a war without end,' Daniel said. 'For the *pieds-noirs* Algeria was French, it was their homeland and would always be their homeland even if they were in exile. To be forced back to France was a humiliation. Worse than that, they had been failed by the Republic, which had promised them protection, and they would never forgive this. This anger has been passed on for generations.'

We talked about Algerians in twenty-first-century France, who in 2023 made up roughly twelve per cent of the population and who are by far the largest non-European ethnic group overall.[5] 'There are Algerian families in France now,' he said, 'but not all of them have settled. Maybe the young people don't remember the struggles of their grandparents but they feel let down by the Republic, even if they do not always understand why that is so historically. They feel unwelcome and unloved, and as long as that is the case they will always be angry. I think Camus would have understood this perfectly. He always said that the Arabs needed justice and reparations as well as equality. They gained independence but not much else. So Camus saw it then as we see it now.'

From across the garden, Catherine Camus welcomed me towards the Camus family home in Lourmarin with a kind and unforced smile. She looked like a female version of her father, with the same handsome leonine features and clear, intelligent eyes. The house had been a silkworm farm (a *magnanerie*) in the nineteenth century. There are many of these old farms dotted across the Ardèche and the Lubéron, dating from the sixteenth century, when the silk trade with Lyon was at its height. The houses are square, solid and tall, usually two or three storeys high, with large deep cellars. It was Roger Grenier who had suggested Lourmarin to her father, having been impressed by the village's *château*, which stands above a winding spiral of small streets lined with fresh mint, lavender and geraniums. Camus had bought the house in 1958, flush with the money from winning the Nobel Prize in Literature the year before.

He found in Lourmarin a small literary community. The Provençal novelist Henri Bosco lived nearby. Bosco loved the Lubéron for its tough peasant ways and wrote stories which turned their hard, everyday lives into myth. Camus had a literary friendship with another Provençal poet, René Char, who lived in the neighbouring village of L'Isle-sur-la-Sorgue.

Camus knew little about poetry, and Char was not interested in the novel. But they both believed in keeping faith in words like love and beauty, not as abstractions but as living realities. They were both *résistants* whose philosophy had been forged in the equally powerful realities of the cruelty and terror of the Occupation. When Camus died, Char straight away wrote, in the numb shock of his grief, a beautiful and heartfelt poem to Camus called '*L'éternité à Lourmarin*' ('Eternity at Lourmarin'): 'There is no straight line or lightened route with a being who had left us ... everywhere is dislocated in a single blow.'

Lourmarin is now well known as one of the prettiest villages in the Lubéron, if not the whole of France. Having wandered the streets and admired the painted shutters and cobblestone alleyways, you can have a drink and something to eat at the Café Ollier, where Camus apparently used to come early each morning. It all feels authentic and inauthentic at the same time. Over a beer, I spoke to two visitors from Spain who had come here in homage to Camus. They loved the village but were less impressed by the high prices for lunch.

When Camus came here, Lourmarin had not yet been prettified and was fairly unknown to the new class of French or foreign tourists who were beginning to explore Provence in the post-war world. Camus installed his family here and thought of the house as a refuge from politics and the world, which were making him depressed and fatigued. He cherished the nights he spent here with his mother, who could neither read nor write but would tell him about family, friends and the life he had known growing up in Algiers.

As I crossed the garden to meet her, Catherine advised me not to tread on the lawn. 'Sorry. It's all been mined with dog shit,' she said. Inside the house, there were three or four dogs freely roaming.

I am not usually much impressed or interested in visiting the former homes of famous writers, especially when they have been turned into mini-museums and tricked out with phoney writers' paraphernalia (Victor Hugo's pipe, Balzac's coffee cup and so on). There seems no point, as it is all so far away from the creative process and the lived life. But this was different, a clutter of books and journals at every turn, including original copies of *Combat*, draft articles, annotated books with notes in Camus's quick, feverish handwriting. This all looked excitingly like work in progress.

That is in fact precisely what it was. Catherine had been trained as a lawyer and up until the age of thirty-four had kept her distance from the literary world. But when her mother Francine died in 1979, Catherine took it upon herself to look after Camus's vast archive and his posthumous publications. The most important and most challenging of these was a book called *Le Premier Homme* (*The First Man*), an unfinished novel about his early life which Camus had still been working on until his death in a car accident at Villeblevin on 4 January 1960. It was finally published in 1994.

Catherine told me that, as far as possible, they had kept the house exactly as it was when he died, so everything around us, the furniture, the books, was her father's. I then cheekily remarked how much she looked like him. She laughed easily. 'It's impossible to get away from *papa*,' she said. 'He gets everywhere. I can't get rid of him.'

She had also inherited her father's love of football – he had played in goal in Algiers – and Catherine told me that she had got involved with a local team and was organizing a match between a 'Team Camus' and a team from Lourmarin made up of local young people with all profits going to local '*chibanis*'. The word '*chibani*', from North African dialectal Arabic, refers to North African, and sometimes sub-Saharan, immigrants to France from the latter part of the twentieth century. Many of them live in precarious circumstances, often homeless and in poverty. They have a special welfare status to protect them under French law, as many of them do not have French nationality. Although the word now legally applies to all immigrants from these regions, it has its roots in Algerian Arabic (literally the word means 'old' or 'white-haired') and really refers to the first wave of Algerians who came to France after the War of Independence. Many of these had worked for or even fought for France and were considered to be traitors in their native country. In France, they were commonly ignored or despised, a source of shame. They were hopelessly trapped between two worlds.

Catherine encouraged me to come down and report on the

game. 'It's the first football match in homage to the winner of the Nobel Prize in Literature,' she said. 'My father would have loved that.'

As we relaxed into the morning over Camus's old desk, we drank beer, smoked cigarettes. She was funny and swore occasionally in a clear and pure diction, and I enjoyed spending time in her company, but I also caught something dark, melancholy and hidden about her. I knew that her life companion, Robert Gallimard, who was twenty years her senior and had been Camus's editor at the publishing house, was gravely ill, but we never mentioned it. We talked instead about the nostalgia that had brought Albert Camus to Lourmarin and this house. The village and the surrounding countryside reminded him of his early years in Algeria, which by 1958, when he moved here, was a lost paradise.

Catherine remembers him standing on the balcony, overlooking the garden of cypresses and the fields of olives and lavender, and saying that beyond the mountains lay the sea, and beyond the sea lay Africa. For him, this territory was not quite France, which he thought of as a dark northern European country, nor Algeria, but part of both. 'You have to understand that Algeria was not just a country for my father,' she said, 'it was also an ideal. He grew up in poverty there, but he also said that he had learned in that place an understanding of how human beings can live together despite their circumstances. He loved the light, the sea, promenading, looking for girls, playing football. It was a very physical and vital life, made more so by the beauty of the country. He thought it was a country which could teach men how to live.'

As we discussed all of this and Camus's political agonies over Algeria, I noticed that Catherine constantly used the word *'pudeur'* or *'pudique'* to describe her father's attitude and demeanour. 'He could be very stern,' she said, 'but he was also kind, and I think his severity came from a kind of *pudeur*.' Used in this way, *pudeur* means discretion or reticence, a refusal to let emotion overcome reason. I wondered if this word might also be applied to Camus's later attitude towards Algeria, when he retreated into public silence, not just because he was damaged by all the attacks that had been made upon him, but because he did not want sorrow or despair to define his thought. Catherine agreed. 'He loved balance and harmony,' she said, 'and the Algerian war had made everything disjointed in his mind. He wanted a way back and couldn't find one.'

Later, we stood on the balcony. It was as beautiful as Catherine had said it would be, but what lay beyond was a very different kind of Algeria from the one Camus had dreamed of glimpsing. The Algeria I knew was disordered, poisoned by long years of terrorism and corruption, and its beauty had long since been corroded by political and economic neglect. One way or another, most of the Algerians I met there were unhappy; they were scared of the government or scared of Islamists or feeling trapped in a country that had once been a busy, cosmopolitan pan-Mediterranean idyll but was now isolated from Europe and suspicious of the West in general. The well-heeled and well-manicured land around Lourmarin was also a long way from where most Algerians in France lived now, in *banlieues* which are often dangerously distant from the life of mainstream France.

After saying goodbye to Catherine that afternoon, I visited Camus's grave in the small cemetery which lies a short step away from his house. It is a simple affair, a stone slab, and all the more touching that there are no great monuments to the great man. He is buried next to his wife, and there are a few flowers, regularly attended to by Catherine. There are irises, roses which bloom each spring (they were in bud when I was there) and a small olive tree. Catherine told me that she was angry that so many tourists came to take pictures and even steal relics. 'He was not a celebrity,' she said, 'simply a philosopher.' When she said this, I reflected that Camus's ideas were now long obsolete in twenty-first-century France.

Camus had believed in France and Algeria together, creating a new kind of pan-Mediterranean civilization. Europeans and Muslims would be brothers, sharing what he called 'a civilization in the true sense of the word'. He said this in a speech given in Algiers during the early days of his career, but his optimism never dimmed and his belief never wavered. 'Just as the Mediterranean sun is the same for everyone,' he said, 'the fruits of human intelligence must be shared by all and not become a source of conflict and murder.'[6]

The years since his death have exposed the impossibility of this vision. The fraught relationship between France and Algeria still defines the political make-up of Provence, where so many *pieds-noirs* and Algerians had settled after the War of Independence, the Algerians seeking work on building sites and in factories and the *pieds-noirs* perhaps hoping that the North Africa-looking land in Europe might comfort them in their exile. These two populations were enemies transplanted into Provence from North Africa, bringing with them suspicion, fear and sometimes hate. Over the generations, the wounds have never really healed.

One of Camus's failings, at least according to his enemies, was that he dared to hope, believing ultimately that the human need for harmony and stability – 'common sense', as he would have put it – would overcome the impulses to murder and terrorize in the name of politics. He was a bleak optimist, and his vision of a new Mediterranean quickly disintegrated on contact with the deadly forces gathered on both sides of the Algerian conflict during the 1950s and then through the 1960s. This was a period, however, when a new type of politics was being imagined in France, a politics which sought to look beyond postcolonial conflict. Camus was dead long before this utopianism expressed itself in the near-revolution of 1968. At the very least, he would have recognized that this movement, with all its flaws and contradictions, was a return to older, revolutionary calls for absolute freedom. This too, like Camus's dreams of 'civilization in the true sense, a civilization which places truth above myth', was a universalism that never made it through to the twenty-first century.[7]

8

The Enchantment of Manosque

Secrecy and discretion in the old streets

The bus from Lourmarin to Manosque takes about three hours, although the journey is just less than an hour in a car. There are worse ways to spend three hours, however, than travelling in a local bus and idling along to Manosque, haphazardly following the river Durance, a tributary of the Rhône. Folklore has it that the Durance was once an impassable river which kept Provence separate from the rest of France. It was feared for its floods, which regularly swamped the barren surrounding land. These days, since a great dam was finally built in 1961 at the reservoir of Serre-Ponçon, the waters are mainly placid, sometimes running fast and often shallow across and around small islets of rock, shale and gravel. You'll travel through small villages and hamlets clustered alongside the road, with houses having steep-sided and severe facades which directly look onto the road. It must be strange to live here. You are in the heart of the countryside but in a site as motorized as any urban environment with the constant churn of passing traffic. There is usually just one cafe in these places (often called *Le Mistral* after the harsh, dry and cold Mediterranean wind which plagues the region), with hardly any shops and sometimes none. The names of the villages are, however, long and pretty: Notre-Dame de Fidélité, Saint-Paul-lez-Durance.

In the distance, you'll see the grey and green mountainsides and a sprinkling of *bastides*, the stocky and square farmhouses, originally built as mini-forts, which are larger and more prepossessing than the smaller traditional farmhouses called *mas* (you'll see plenty of these as well). You'll pass several *campings* buried deep in this countryside. The road to Manosque is not all bucolic charm, however. You'll also see the huge Carrefour and Lidl supermarkets which feed the population here. You'll also see artificial lakes, small local football grounds, an ironworks, a nuclear power plant, business parks, small apartment blocks and innumerable modern villas. If, like Julio Cortázar and Carol Dunlop, you enjoy making poetry of the passing panorama of everyday life, this is as good a way as any to enter into the heartland of twenty-first-century Provence.

Manosque lies between Mont d'Or and the Durance river. The Mont is hardly a mountain, rather just a hill, easily climbed in less than an hour or so. It was used as a watchtower for centuries, from the Gaulish era onwards. It was also where the local inhabitants, the Manosquins, sought sanctuary in AD 900, when the Arab soldiers invaded Provence in their wider bid to conquer southern Europe and spread the new religion of Islam. The words 'Islam' and 'Muslim' were unknown in medieval France, and the invading armies were mainly known as 'Saracens', or *Sarrazin* in Old French, meaning 'from the east'.

At the summit of Mont d'Or are the remains of a *château* built in 974 by Guillaume, le Comte d'Arles. Guillaume was called 'the Liberator' because he led the defence of the Christians against the invading Arabs. For this, he has often been claimed as the true founder of Christian Provence. The *château* here was built as his winter residence, a vantage point to watch over and, if necessary, defend his lands during the darkest months of the year. Mont d'Or has often been jokingly compared by the Manosquins to a female breast, and once you have heard this, it is impossible not to see it as you catch your first sight of the town, overlooked by what is quite definitely a breast-like hill with the remains of the *château* pointing at the sky, erect, pert and lonely as a nipple.

From the top of Mont d'Or, you have, as did Guillaume, a commanding view of the surrounding territory and in the distance the deep hinterland. Closest to hand is a canal bordered by small orchards running alongside the shining waters of the Durance. Then the eye follows the alluvial plains of the river, sweeping across the Lubéron, until one sees the peak of the mountain of Sainte-Victoire, one of the great symbols of Provence, then the *massif* of Sainte-Baume, the Haut-Var, and the Mont d'Aiguines overlooking les Gorges du Verdon. Finally, in the far distance is the first sight of the Alps. It seems as if all of the wild interior of Provence is at your feet.

You can also see the tiled rooftops of Manosque, a town built on two small hills which seems domesticated and quietly busy with its own interior life. Its nickname is 'la Pudique', which at first seems testimony to the *bourgeois* existence of the

Manosquins. The town is divided between the walled old town, dating back to the first century, and a huddle of modern suburbs linked by wide and dusty boulevards. When I first came here in the 1990s, both territories were sleepy and civilized and, above all, apparently well maintained and well ordered; 'la Pudique' seemed to be an epithet fitting its unshowy atmosphere. The use of the word to describe Manosque is, however, strictly to do with sexual modesty.

Specifically, the nickname is traced back to the moment in 1516 when King François first came to Manosque on his way back from the tiny village of Marignano, where he had defeated the armies of the Papal States and the Old Swiss Confederacy (the prize for this victory was the Italian city-state of Milan). On arrival in Manosque, the king was given the keys to the town by the *consul* Antoine Voland at the Porte de la Saunerie. François was a notorious sexual predator, much admired by his cronies for always seeking out the most delicate prey. This time it was Voland's daughter Madeleine, a virginal adolescent. François picked her out straight away and demanded that she stay by his side throughout the first day and night of his visit, making no secret of his lustful gaze. The next day, Madeleine ripped her face with her nails to wipe away her shame and make herself ugly. This was not enough. She then exposed her face to sulphur vapours, which burned it, melting her features into an unsightly and painful mask. When he saw her, François was overcome with shame and showered Madeleine with money and gifts in a futile effort at compensation. Now known as 'Madeleine *la pudique*', she had the miserable honour of providing a new title for the town of her birth.

There are many ways into the old town, but the Porte de la Saunerie is the most dramatic. The gate is named after the town abattoir, where pigs were slaughtered until the fifteenth century ('*saunerié*' in Old Provençal means 'slaughterhouse'). The Porte was finished in 1382 and is in the Romanesque style of the period: imposing, austere and with two solid towers to defend the town from attackers. When you step through the covered passageway for the first time, it feels like entering the medina of an Arab town, secretive and hidden.

The main artery of this part of the old town is the rue Grande. It is old and narrow, but the shops are all modern chain stores common to any French town of a reasonable size. Local nostalgics dislike this mediocre and dull introduction to Manosque, but it is hard to challenge the power of the corporations which own these shops. Besides, the less nostalgic locals love to shop in Nocibé, Armand Thiery Femme, Kookaï and L'Occitane, a chain of cosmetic shops which now has an international reach but was founded in Manosque in 1976 by a local soap maker called Olivier Baussan (now one of the richest men in France). L'Occitane is a great example of Provence selling its image back to itself. I have never known the rue Grande to be crowded or busy, and I always begin to saunter more slowly than my normal pace here.

Manosque is an unlikely setting for an attempt to nurture and celebrate the utopian idealism and revolutionary spirit of May 1968 ('May 68'), but that is exactly what it became for the last couple of decades of the twentieth century.

The old town of Manosque is quite small, and it is only a few minutes to the Place de l'Hôtel de Ville, which is only slightly more pompous than the surrounding squares and streets, towards the Place des Marchands. For many years in the 1990s, this was always my destination. At number 28 is the apartment where the English artist Ralph Rumney lived for the last part of his rich and 'rackety' (his own word) life.[1] I was friendly with Ralph, and we worked together on book projects and cataloguing his work (a messy and almost impossible job, which was eventually taken over by the Tate and a professional archivist). We also talked a great deal, smoked the strongest French cigarettes, unfiltered Gitanes, and drank lots of quite rough local red wine. Ralph was an open and unrepentant alcoholic, and one of my jobs each day was to go and fetch his five-litre plastic box of wine from a local store and then lug it up the three storeys of his apartment building. This was his 'daily dose', as he put it. He never touched spirits. He was in fact ruthlessly puritanical about this. I like *pastis*, and he would chide me for my early evening *apéritif*.

I first heard of Ralph because in Paris in the 1950s he had been a founding member of the legendary avant-garde group called l'Internationale situationniste alongside Guy Debord, whom I was researching. I was desperate to meet anybody who had known Debord and could unlock some of the deliberately hidden mysteries about his life. To the struggling biographer, Ralph Rumney was a godsend. He not only knew Debord intimately, or as much as anybody could know such a capricious and perverse man, but he had married Debord's first wife, Michèle Bernstein, who was another founding member of the Situationist group. Ralph could be very grave and serious, but he was funny and irreverent, liked to laugh when you least expected it, and was wildly indiscreet. This was a revelation since most of Debord's friends and admirers I had met so far had been po-faced, boring or paranoid. Ralph gave me a different form of insight into the early life of the Situationist rebels, which had more to do with free living, sex and drink than Marx or Hegel.

My first encounter with Ralph was suitably ludic. This was in January 1996, when, with a young academic friend based in Manchester, I organized a conference at the legendary Haçienda nightclub, which was known to people throughout the world as the crucible of dance music, but was also increasingly plagued by debt and drug-dealing, gun-toting gangsters. Not many of those who flocked there knew that its name was inspired by an early Situationist text from 1957 which proclaimed '*Il faut construire l'Haçienda!*' – 'The Haçienda must be built!'

For the Situationists on the Left Bank of Paris in the 1950s, the 'Haçienda' was a mythical invention, a poetic playground

The Enchantment of Manosque 199

for wild, deep and subversive pleasures in the heart of the alienated and alienating capitalist city. In the 1980s, Tony Wilson, owner of both Factory Records and manager of Joy Division and New Order and an avid reader of the Situationists when a student at Cambridge, decided to turn this myth into a reality in Manchester, the first industrial city of the nineteenth century and now a post-industrial ruin.

Wilson fancied himself as a magic-maker and a provocateur, so when we proposed a conference on his heroes, the Situationists, at the Haçienda he seized on it. The trick was to bring artists and musicians who had been influenced by situationism together with actual Situationists (there were not many left: drink, drugs and suicide had already done for most of them) and then to see what happened. It was to be a cultural experiment in the Situationist spirit; literally, in the words of the Situationists themselves, 'creating a situation from which you can't back down or back away from'.

So we invited Ralph and even sent money to Manosque for his tickets and travel expenses. Inevitably, he couldn't be bothered to show up, but he did send us a flyer for a ropey club in Manosque called the Haçienda as well as a text denouncing us as traitors and opportunists (not altogether untrue), insisting that it should be read out by a French girl from Manosque while getting undressed on stage and eating a banana. (The last part of Ralph's request was refused – my friend Emmanuelle, who was coincidentally from Manosque, laughed in scorn, saying that he was obviously an *obsedé* – 'sexual pervert'.)

But we did read out his 'denunciation', which was very funny, and that is why I set off to Manosque for the first time, to try to get our money back from this chancer (we never did get the money) and to find out more about the connection between French avant-gardes and a part of France that I had only ever passed through.

*

At first, I was charmed and enchanted by Manosque. This was mainly due to a sense of discovery. It was very different from the south of France I already knew, stretching along the coast from Marseille to Nice and then to the Italian border. This strip was technically Provence, of course, but it was also cosmopolitan, brash, modern, alternately sophisticated and sleazy, with patches of ordinary life in its *banlieues* and moderately well-heeled small towns. Manosque, in contrast, was slow, with what seemed to me to be a graceful way of life. The day was rigidly structured around mealtimes, shopping, work and siestas. In the mid-afternoon, the old town was often quite empty, and there was no nightlife after 9 p.m. It was as if the rhythm of daily life in this country market town had not quite caught up with the busy late twentieth century. Tourists found this either beguiling or boring.

The suburbs of Manosque were quite separate from the life of the old town, and people lived in a different way, more attuned to the routine of their daily commute to Aix-en-Provence or Marseille. For them, Manosque was a convenient dormitory town with no real identity or sense of belonging. Romantically, however, I wanted to believe that the old town was a place where the fundamentals of Provençal life were still intact.

One of these was food. On my first stay in the spring of 1996, I dined regularly at the restaurant of the Hôtel François 1er on the rue Guilhempierre, served by Nathalie, the young chef, who seemed genuinely concerned that I should get enough to eat and that it should be of the highest quality. The staples included *soupe au pistou*, a broth of Tarbais beans, green beans, leeks, turnips, courgettes, garlic, rind of goat's cheese or Parmesan, carrots, potatoes, basil, or any variation on the above; it is a kind of Provençal minestrone, perfect for late summer or autumn. I also relished Nathalie's *salade paysanne*, again her own invention, of *lardons*, fried potatoes in cubes, and a fried egg, all served on a bed of *roquette* with her home-made tangy vinaigrette (three parts oil, one part wine vinegar, garlic and *échalottes*).

In Le Cigaloun on the Place de l'Hôtel de Ville, for lunch I ate *agneau de Sisteron*, gently roasted in a way that softened and sweetened the already succulent lamb. This was served with green beans, and the meat was sometimes *flambé en pastis*. There was also *brouillade de truffes*: eggs, salt, pepper and a truffle left overnight and served as an unctuous cream. This food was local but never rough or rustic; even the supposedly rugged *soupe au pistou* was composed with style and mastery of the ingredients. This applied, too, to the local wines. The reds of the Lubéron can be extremely fine, balanced and delicate. I began badly by drinking the cheaper brands, which are peppery and leathery and can hit you hard, but quite soon learned to take it more steadily with the *rosés*, a wine I never drink normally but which are more composed, more forgiving and easier in the summer heat (which could start in late March or early April). When I could afford it in those days, I favoured Château La Tour de l'Evêque, which is almost transparent and lovely at midday when served with ice.

For a while, I regularly rented a studio on the avenue Jean Giono in an *hôtel particulier* called the Grand Hôtel de Versailles, which dated back to the eighteenth century and had once been a stables and a staging post on the road from Paris to Marseille. The place was now run by Marie-Christine Bourdeaux, an energetic dark-haired woman in her fifties who had inherited the *hôtel* and who was trying to make a business out of the place, half as a hotel and half as rented apartments, and had a particular interest in attracting artists. The building was beautiful inside and out and cared for with an attention to detail that included flowers in the lobby, beautiful photographs and paintings of nineteenth-century Manosque or the wilds of Haute-Provence on the wall, elegant pottery from the region, right down to the porcelain coffee cups for your *café crème* in the morning. If you asked, she would also make up a picnic dinner of the best local cheeses, charcuterie and wine, and as far as I knew she never made a profit.

Sometimes, her husband Fred (whose real ambition was to be a painter) would pick guests up at Marseille-Marignane airport for no extra cost, just to be hospitable. That was her and Fred's trouble; they both had refined, good taste and excellent manners but were clueless about business. Every time I came back over the next few years, I could see that Marie-Christine was sinking deeper and deeper into debt. One evening, she invited me over to their house (a lovely *bastide* a mile or so beyond the old town), and over *rosé* and grilled merguez sausages, she told me that she was selling up and asked if I would be interested in taking over the place. I choked over my glass of wine: was she joking? She said she might be, but I sensed that it was just a way of covering her embarrassment at bringing up the subject. I was not surprised that she wanted to give up the business. Every time I came back, the building was emptier than it had been a few months before. And this was a generous offer she was making. She wasn't looking to make a profit, she said, she just wanted to move on.

Marie-Christine thought I would be interested because, as an academic and a writer, I was almost an artist myself, and I clearly loved the place, but these were the worst of all qualifications for taking on such a project. And, aside from the fact that I had no money and no interest in or knowledge of how to run a business in France, I could see no way that the *hôtel* could be a viable financial enterprise in a town with so little passing trade. In the 1950s, the Grand Hôtel de Versailles had been the heart of the cultural life of Manosque, but it was already dying by the time I knew it, and Marie-Christine finally abandoned the *hôtel* in 2007. When I went back to Manosque in October 2023, after almost a twenty-year absence, one of the large eighteenth-century doors to the entrance had been removed and bleakly boarded up. Next to the other door was a modest plaque signalling the consultation rooms of a physiotherapist. There was no sense or memory at all of the bohemian and creative life

Marie-Christine had so quixotically tried to cultivate there (I had not been her only pet 'artist').

For all its seemingly staid and solid character, there is also a deep vein of pleasing weirdness in Manosque. This is most visible in the works of the writer Jean Giono, who lived and worked here and is known for his unpredictable, beautiful and often violent stories of life in the wilderness of Haute-Provence. He was not, however, a folkloric writer; he was much stranger and more intriguing than that. Giono scorned the revival of the Provençal dialect in his lifetime and the fake renaissance of Provençal culture that went with it. Instead, his world was full of portents, cruelty, dark apparitions, signs and omens that don't make sense, and then do make sense in the most astonishing and jarring fashion.

Reading Giono is like reading the Greek myths stripped back to the raw reality of the natural world of Haute-Provence. Giono's great theme is the tragedy of existence in such a setting. He was a reader of Friedrich Nietzsche and particularly admired the German philosopher for his notion of *amor fati*, the love and embracing of one's fate in all its totality. Nietzsche, who briefly lived near Nice, had developed this notion on his long walks around the mountain village of Eze. Like Giono, Nietzsche thought of Provence and the Provençal peasant as incarnating a savage pagan and poetic wisdom.

Giono had a long career as a writer. His first novel, *Colline* (translated as *Hill of Destiny*), was published in 1929, and its immediate success meant that he could leave his job in a local bank to devote himself to literature. He went through several periods of philosophical and stylistic change throughout his career and, along the way, acquired a reputation as a Nazi sympathizer during the Occupation for his political quietism and pacifism (he was even arrested by the Allies in 1944 as a suspected collaborator). There is, however, a unity in Giono's work: all of his stories are haunted by the 'enchanted land' of Haute-Provence, which is alternately savage and magnificent but always the chief protagonist in his writing and always more powerful than the men and women who live there. His human characters are peasants who can only guess about life and nature, and fear and superstition are the controlling forces in their destinies. Their only religion, if it can be called that, is a kind of bleak pantheism.

Edmund White, an admirer of Giono and an occasional visitor to Manosque, saw in Giono's depiction of Haute-Provence that human beings are indivisible from what he describes as 'the beauty and terror of nature in its raw state'.[2] Giono wrote that there were two fundamental truths in his work: 'The first of these truths is that there exist people who are simple and nude; the other is that this earth [is] fleeced with woods ... this living earth exists *without literature*.'[3] Giono elaborated on this theme in his late work *Le Haut Pays* (The High Country), where, echoing Walt Whitman (Giono greatly admired Whitman and called him 'the American Homer'), he saw the landscape as all alive.

Ralph Rumney was no fan of Giono. He had tried to read a few books when he first arrived in Manosque in the 1980s but dismissed them as 'rural nonsense' and 'the ridiculous fantasies of a Nazi collaborator who loved Nietzsche too much'. This was going a bit far, I thought. Giono was (like Ralph) a dedicated pacifist and an anti-nationalist who never even really believed that such a thing as the French nation really existed. Reality for him was the life lived outside of such an abstraction – 'life without *literature*' – and so he was indifferent to the German Occupation of France, famously and notoriously wondering in 1940 what difference it would make.

Ralph was impatient with this argument, as he was with all arguments that contradicted his way of thinking and the diktats he would lay down about life and art. Nonetheless, Ralph loved Manosque and it loved him back. Until he was confined to bed in 1999, laid low with an undiagnosed paralysis in the legs, he was well known in the cafes and bars of Manosque as a great artist and a drinker. Nobody had ever seen much of the art but they had seen plenty of his drinking. He was generous with money and stories, all enunciated in a slow and superb formal French, which he had never studied but acquired from his literary acquaintances in Paris.

His life before Manosque had the air of fiction. He had been brought up in Halifax, where he was a lazy and rebellious student of art at the local college. Tall, lanky and charismatic, he suddenly left for Paris in 1953, at the age of eighteen, and fell in with a crowd of hard-drinking, like-minded would-be avant-gardists, who clustered around a bar called Chez Moineau on the rue du Four. Among their number was Guy Debord, the future founder and theoretician of l'Internationale situationniste, who would play a key role in Rumney's life. He also met and knew André Breton, Henri Malraux, John Cage, Yves Klein, Alexander Trocchi, Jean Cocteau, the Guggenheims, Gregory Corso, William Burroughs and Allen Ginsberg, and had even been a regular babysitter to the daughter of the librarian, writer and mystic Georges Bataille at his flat on the rue du Dragon.

Soon Rumney was enjoying what appeared to be a gilded life, living in a swish apartment on Ile Saint-Louis and married into one of the richest families in America, with Peggy Guggenheim, the world's most important art collector, as his mother-in-law. His relationship with his wife Pegeen was, however, troubled and stormy, not just because of her depressive tendencies but because from the start Peggy was against her daughter's marriage to this feckless and impertinent Englishman. And then, on 1 March 1967, it all changed. That evening, the couple had argued. Rumney had been away in Venice, where in a dispute over his papers he had found himself handcuffed and deported. He had returned to Paris to a distraught Pegeen, who thought that Venice, where her mother lived, was now closed to her. Angry at Rumney for his carelessness, and fearing that this marked a final break with her mother, she started weeping and remonstrating. She finally wished him goodnight and went to sleep in the maid's room. The next day, Rumney found her dead from an overdose of sleeping pills.

This was only the beginning of the nightmare for Rumney, who found himself accused by the Guggenheims of aiding and abetting her suicide. The press was alerted straight away, and Rumney, to avoid journalists clustering at the door of the flat, was forced to flee across the rooftops, pausing only to give his side of the story to a trusted reporter friend from the Italian newspaper *Il Giorno*. In the following days and weeks, Rumney was forced to live undercover in Paris, where he was constantly trailed by the Guggenheims' private detectives. The family's prestige, money and lawyers made it impossible for him to overcome the slurs. Sensing that the police and possibly a jail sentence were coming ever closer, he admitted himself to La Borde clinic, which was effectively a psychiatric hospital. After several months there, he made for London, where he was out of reach of the Guggenheims' lawyers but penniless and desperate. He washed up in Paris again in the early 1970s, his alleged crimes now apparently half-forgotten or at least abandoned by the police and private investigators. He lived off his wits, made art when he could, but devoted himself mainly to drinking, usually in Le Rosebud on the rue Delambre, a favourite of Samuel Beckett, whom Rumney inevitably claimed to know well.

In the 1980s, Rumney tried to reinvent himself. He was not yet entirely broken down by his life experiences and was eager to begin 'a second life' in Manosque, but his reputation followed him. The French police began once more to note his activities and contacts, partly because of his Italian links but also because the Situationists were rumoured to be sponsors of terrorism. It did not help that the likes of the Angry Brigade, the Red Brigades and the Baader–Meinhof gang all quoted Guy Debord's 1967 book *La Société du Spectacle* (*The Society of the Spectacle*) as a manual for revolution. In the 1980s, Debord and the Situationists were also being considered by some historians as the strongest cultural and political influences on the near-revolution of May 68 in France. Ralph joked about all of this. 'Of course we were revolutionaries,' he said, 'and, of course, we were involved in May 68. It was our ideas that turned it into a festival rather than a war. We would rather fuck and drink than fight the police, as anyone in their right mind would prefer.' Rumney told me that he had been arrested by armed police and spent a few nights in jail in Marseille. He was suspected of links to terrorism, but no charges were made. 'I refused to take it seriously,' he said, 'and that, of course, only made them angrier.'

Inevitably for his French neighbours in Manosque, Ralph was the very epitome of an 'English devil', someone who has moved to the south of France because he has something to hide, needs to change his name, or at least cultivate a discreet anonymity, and soon goes to seed in drink and regret, like a character in a novel by Graham Greene or Lawrence Durrell. Ralph was aware of this cliché and mostly laughed at it, but he also enjoyed maintaining an air of deliberate mystery. 'M. Rumney is a splendid man,' I was told by someone who had regularly passed drunken evenings with Ralph in the cafes of the old town, 'but we really don't know anything about him. We think he must be very rich, but how? Is he a murderer? He says he's an artist, but I have never seen any of his paintings. Where are they? Do they exist?'

In fact, when it was not being exhibited around Europe, in storage or for sale at Galerie Lara Vincy in Paris, most of Ralph's work was kept in his apartment in Manosque. 'I am not some sort of a local artist,' he would insist huffily when his drinking companions asked to see his work. 'My work is either for the world or private. It is not to be taken lightly.'

Although Ralph retained the attitude of a creature who had spent most of his life in European capitals, he did have one thing in common with Jean Giono, which was a hatred of the late twentieth century and especially its consumer culture. He had decided to settle in Giono's Manosque precisely because, at least in the old town, if you ignored the clutter of modern shops, it was possible to never have to look at anything too vulgar.

Ralph had chosen his apartment with this in mind. It was a large, airy space with big, wide rooms and high ceilings and, most importantly, as he pointed out to me when I first went there, you could see no trace of the twentieth century from its large and sunlit windows (always lined with a balcony of geraniums and herbs). You were almost at the same height as the Porte de Soubeyran, the thirteenth-century gate to the town, which was adorned by a lovely *campanile*, added in 1830, in the shape of a pear and a bulb as a memory of the ramparts of the old walls. Beyond that were the rooftops, then the hill of Mont d'Or (which Ralph had climbed) and then the wilds of Haute-Provence (where Ralph had never ventured, not even once). The effect was sublime and elevating; you really did feel transported into an older reality. This was where Ralph had decided to spend his last years with alcohol, tobacco, art and friends.

Jean Giono loved Manosque for this reason. He was nostalgic for the town when it was still poor and unsullied by the twentieth century – with its 'badly paved streets' and its 'convents, hidden interior gardens, courtyards, wells and magnificent fountains'.[4] At least until the Second World War, it had actually been a self-contained world, where people spoke the local *patois* instead of French, and Marseille, Paris and Europe were distant abstractions.

In Rumney's imagination, the old town resembled his ideal of a city, which was the city-state of the Renaissance. The Situationists dreamed that this could be a model for future cities: as autonomous, self-ruling places where art, politics and philosophy were more important than capital and labour, and which opposed all of the commodity culture of the twentieth century, the stultifying and all-powerful system which they called 'the spectacle'. In truth, the Situationists were nostalgics and romantics; they knew that their ideal city could never be realized but that didn't stop them from dreaming about 'the Haçienda'. And if they could, they built their own versions of reality around this poetic fantasy. This is what Ralph had done in Manosque. In his exile, Ralph had more than a touch of the raffish con man. But he was deadly serious about his art and his philosophy of life, which was the Situationist *credo* – the refusal to give in to the society of the spectacle, where image and illusion had replaced real life (writing this in 2023, it sounds more prophetic than ever). He fused his life and art into one indissoluble fact, which had always been another Situationist ambition. I found this quixotic, moving and slightly heroic.

By 2000, Ralph was dying. He knew this and so did all of his friends. He was in the later stages of prostate cancer and he was frustrated at this. 'I thought I would die of drink,' he said. 'That was my ambition. Now I have been cheated by this mediocre, crappy disease.' In July and August of that year, quite spontaneously, his friends gathered in Manosque in a kind of unspoken homage. I went, too, renting the studio from Marie-Christine.

Ralph gave the gathering the grand title of a '*colloque*', but really it was more like an extended dinner party spread over several weeks. There were no papers, lectures or plenary sessions, simply a free-floating, ever-changing group of people meeting for walks, drinks, meals and discussions. The atmosphere was enhanced by a mild sexual charge; people were flirting with each other intellectually and also with the faint promise of another type of promiscuity. The *colloque* was convivial but also serious: everyone was there to participate a little in the end of Ralph's life and also to engage with the ideas that had defined that life.

Throughout August, his friends helped Ralph organize a series of events in the town – an attempt to 're-enchant' Manosque. Much to my surprise, the events were financially supported by the *mairie* of Manosque (but it helped that he was a drinking pal of Ralph's and considered the town honoured by the presence of this 'great British artist who was almost a Frenchman'). One of Ralph's first activities was to 'restore' the statue called *La Femme Assise* (Sitting Woman), which stood in the small square outside his apartment. Ralph did this by covering the statue, a delicate, figurative piece, with cling film. Small children delighted in touching the statue as they passed and giggled when it made a noise. The local press didn't know what to make of it but ran pieces on Ralph and his association with revolution and May 68, while the artist himself gave long, alcohol-sodden interviews in local cafes. Above all, Ralph exalted in the fact that *La Femme Assise* had been sculpted in 1942 by Karl-Jean Longuet, the great-grandson of Karl Marx. Ralph, ever the mythomaniac, now saw himself directly involved in the Marx family tradition.

On the Place Marcel Pagnol, in a shop called Le Royaume Animal (which used to be a pet shop and retained the smell), a small temporary gallery was installed to show works by the early Situationists Piero Simondo, Giuseppe Pinot Gallizio, Asger Jorn, Gil Wolman and Ralph Rumney. It was intriguing to sit with a drink at the cafe opposite and watch as curious, casual tourist visitors looked into the 'gallery', possibly expecting some Giono-inspired folkloric art, and emerging, sometimes smiling or baffled, or both, having been exposed to the primal punk energy of the Situationists in their young iconoclastic prime.

The visitors to Manosque came from all over Europe. They included a cohort from Hamburg which consisted of former members of Gruppe SPUR – a German Situationist offshoot – and a younger female cohort from Berlin. There were those interested in the revolutionary spirit of the Situationists, and there was an anarchist delegation from Arles, where Guy Debord had once lived and where he had known and inspired the group. They were very funny and very serious, describing their vision of the world as total freedom, which meant entirely detaching yourself from society in order to reinvent it.

Closest to the antic spirit of the Situationists were a group who called themselves the Banalystes. They had been founded in 1982 at a 'congress' of like-minded souls at a railway stop called Fades in Auvergne. This was, they said, 'the most boring and characterless place in France', which is why they met there for the next ten years to discuss and plot against the 'colonization of life by the banal'. They blamed 'banality', a side product of Debord's 'society of the spectacle', for most forms of contemporary alienation, leading to boredom, depression, anger, violence and maybe even suicide. Their tactic was to visit places all over France, find the 'banal' and write witty, pseudo-official 'reports' on the level of 'banality' in any given region, using data on public services and consumer activity to produce *'un indice de banalisation'* ('an index of banalization'). Manosque stood at 126, which was bad, they said, and a disgrace to the ghost of Jean Giono, whose Manosque was made up of aura and atmosphere.

Some evenings, Silvia, who had been one of Ralph's lovers in Venice and who still lived there, cooked local roast lamb, which we all shared with glasses of wine around Ralph's bed, where he lay unable to move but still holding forth. A film crew came from one of the Italian TV channels to interview him and the rest of us, his 'disciples'. For the interview, Ralph wore a Hawaiian shirt and a fedora, spoke beautifully enunciated Italian and, despite his sick, broken-down condition, sat upright at a table, smoking, looking every inch the arch-dandy and gentleman Situationist.

The *colloque* in Manosque was inspired fun but it was also an exercise in nostalgia. The Banalystes, most of whom were only slightly older than me, all knew this. They were all university teachers, civil servants, journalists and even town planners, who had been just too young for the promises of May 68 but wanted to preserve the utopianism of that era in the coming century.

But they understood that their mission was not only quixotic but doomed. By the end of the twentieth century, the 'spectacle' was everywhere and in control. This was why in the end, the *colloque* – an attempt to 're-enchant' Manosque, to rebuild the Situationist Haçienda there – was not a festival but a wake.

The legacy of May 68 is now an integral part of the French cultural imagination, but only as a relic of a bygone period whose last surviving participants are now irrelevant curios. It is the subject of academic treatises, conferences and exhibitions, confined to a museum, or as an *ex-soixante-huitards* lament, a mausoleum. For historians, it is usually discussed as the last of a long line of insurrectionary moments, from 1789 to 1830, 1848 and 1870.

Most significantly, although the insurrection of May 68 was a threat to de Gaulle's government, it was not a threat to the ideals of the French Republic. In many ways, it was an extension of them. The various factions involved – Marxists, Communists, anarchists and artistic avant-gardes like the Situationists – all had freedom as their priority and were faithful to the ideals of the European Enlightenment. Their priority was sexual, economic and individual liberty, a renewal of the promises of the Revolution of 1789. One of their guiding slogans, also dear to an earlier generation of freedom-loving Surrealists, was the famous exhortation made by Marquis de Sade, who declared in 1790, in a sermon inserted among the scenes of buggery and coprophagy in *La philosophie dans le boudoir*, '*Français, encore un effort si vous voulez être républicains!*' – 'Men and women of France, one more effort to become republicans!'

One of the difficulties of reading Marquis de Sade now is that he is one of those few writers who have given the world an adjective, and this has become a kind of shorthand: without reading Sade, everybody presumes to know what he is all about. It is only when you pay close attention to his work that you begin to understand that his writing is not erotica, not even really pornography, but something else much more monstrous, grotesque and nightmarish. His masterpiece was *Les Cent Vingt Journées de Sodome* (*The 120 Days of Sodom*), a fictional compendium of murder, torture and sexual crimes which tests the limits of the human imagination. This is not an easy book to read; its viciousness is occasionally breathtaking. But what really threatens to break the reader's nerve is the overwhelming atmosphere of claustrophobia. Sade is in this sense Kafkaesque – the Kafka not just of *The Trial* or *The Castle* but also of *In the Penal Colony*, a world ruled by cruelty and evil, where all hope of redemption or release is impossible.

Sade wrote this book in 1785 while he was a prisoner in the Bastille. On his release, he embraced the French Revolution with a passionate zeal: what could be more liberating for a prisoner held in a dungeon, imprisoned by tyrants, than to emerge into a new world of absolute limitless freedom? If the novel was Sade's allegory for the nightmare of confinement, then his call to 'make one more effort' was a call to make the revolution even more revolutionary, throwing off all sexual and religious morality, abolishing religion and division in a world where men and women are masters of their lives and destiny, a dream of the universal and absolute right to freedom. To talk in these terms in twenty-first-century France is, however, an absurd anachronism, as remote as the rituals and beliefs of antiquity. Universalism is now mostly alien to much of the Left in France, which has, confused by the politics of race and religion, suffered a loss of faith in the project of the Enlightenment as a universal ideal.

But briefly, in Manosque in 2000, in the company of Ralph Rumney and his friends, who were faithful to the spirit of May 68 and embodied the idealism of that moment, I glimpsed what it might look like to have been a French revolutionary in the mid-twentieth century, a true 'republican' in the language of Marquis de Sade – who, after all, had his family home in a *château* perched on a steep hill in the village of Lacoste, an hour or so west of Manosque. This is where the locals greeted the reprobate with reverence as 'Moussu lou [Monsieur le] Marquis de Sade', protecting and defending him from the slurs of his enemies in Paris. Ralph, a keen reader of Sade from his adolescence onwards, often mentioned this fact with some relish, making the point – and for once agreeing with Jean Giono – that life in Haute-Provence had never been as carefree, innocent or *pudique* as outsiders liked to think.

I arrived back in Manosque, after nearly two decades away, on a blustery and rainy morning in late October 2023. There were some problems reported with the trains at Gare Saint-Charles in Marseille, so I hired a driver to brave the predicted storms and drive me the seventy kilometres up the A51 to Manosque. On the way, the storm became a tempest, and for stretches of the journey we could hardly see thirty or forty metres ahead. My Corsican driver, Lucca, said that this reminded him of the autumn weather on his native island. He wondered whether we should turn back, but since we were halfway to Manosque when the storm reached its terrifying height, I suggested that we should push on.

The clouds cleared and the rain became a steady drizzle rather than a hard, driving cascade as we neared Manosque. I caught my first sight of Mont d'Or as we reached our turn-off on the motorway and was excited. That feeling ebbed quickly as we got lost in the new suburbs of the town. Lucca asked me for advice but I was lost. Hardly any of this had been here twenty years ago, when even then Manosque had a sizeable number of outlying suburbs and a reputation as a dormitory town. These new developments were different; they were not just standard facilities for commuters who wanted to live in a quiet backwater but were a kind of sub-city in themselves: a forest of malls, cinemas, fast-food restaurants, car lots, business parks and squat apartment buildings formed in grim phalanxes around a busy arterial road. It did not look much like Provence but a charmless and characterless suburb in North America. My immediate thought was that the Banalystes would have been horrified and also vindicated.

I hoped that old Manosque was still there, and it was. Lucca dropped me off at the Place du Terreau, and I made my way to the only hotel available, which was unsurprisingly called Hôtel du Terreau, an establishment with few or no amenities. I loved it straight away. To get to my room I had to climb a twisted and tricky stone staircase, which along the way revealed hidden delights: a dark, windowless room, cosy with leather chairs, a table and a pile of books; and then a strange interior herb garden you could only see by peeping through a small window in the corridor. My own room was a double-L shape with two large shuttered windows, which when opened gave you a view of the hills beyond Manosque. Black clouds were moving over the hills in a dramatic, swooping formation. In the morning, as I drank my coffee and munched down a tartine slathered with honey, these hills were glowing green in the bright morning sun, and you could make out the not-so-distant Alps.

Madame Laurence, who ran the establishment, had only been in Manosque for eight years but she had a dim awareness of the legend of Ralph Rumney. 'He was a painter, I think. A Communist, no?' Monsieur Laurence, a dour, thin man seated at an old-fashioned computer, chipped in. 'I have been in Manosque longer than Madame,' he said. 'I know of this Englishman. He was a drunk [M. Laurence here used the quaint archaism '*poivrot*']. He never paid his bills. That was his communism!'

I found Ralph's old studio and apartment quite easily, after slithering down greasy side streets until I suddenly found myself on familiar ground in the Place des Marchands. I was delighted to see that directly below the apartment was an artist's studio called Atelier Lupi and that the artist himself, Benoît Lupi, was hard at work in the brightly lit paint- and ink-spattered space. I introduced myself, and Benoît was straight away friendly, welcoming me out of the mid-morning drizzle (the rain had started again). We chatted and he showed me his latest works, which were impressive – mid-size canvases of oil and ink, blurry seascapes and cityscapes in muted colours, no hint of the bucolic or the folkloric here. He was, he said, an artist interested in colour and form rather than figurative landscapes. This was what the world looked like to him.

Benoît was forty-four years old and a native of Gordes in the Vaucluse, not far from Avignon. Gordes is a pretty hilltop village, called in French a *village perché*, and is in fact one of the prettiest in all Provence, and has often been filmed, painted or photographed. The village is famous for the way it seems to tumble down a steep hill, which catches the sun in the late afternoon, giving the old stones a golden hue. The village itself is a maze of covered arcades and passageways, quiet squares and unexpected shadows. The photographer Willy Ronis lived here for a while and captured this quality of light and shade in his most famous photograph, *Le nu provençal*, of a naked woman washing at a sink next to an open window. Among the artists who came to Gordes was Marc Chagall, who fled to the village in 1940, fearing for his life as a Jew and what the Nazis called 'a degenerate artist' – that is to say, a modernist and a potential subversive. Still, he was not safe in Gordes, where the Resistance was busily active, making the village a target for the Gestapo. Chagall loved Gordes but knew he had to leave, and he was eventually smuggled out of France to America via Marseille and Lisbon in 1941. Abandoning the beauty of Gordes was, for Chagall, the most tragic form of farewell to France.

Today, the place is a magnet for the well heeled and the fashionable, mostly Parisians and Marseillais who have second homes there. Benoît was not angry that his home village had been 'colonized'. He reasoned that the outsiders brought money to what might otherwise have been a poor, forgotten village in the south – when Chagall was there, it had been literally crumbling to pieces. But Benoît could not afford to live and work there, so he moved to Manosque, where he could live quite comfortably with his family, making occasional trips to Paris to see his dealer or a client, before returning to the Place des Marchands to make canvases.

While I was drinking coffee in Benoît's cosy studio as the rain spattered against the windows, Manosque still felt like a special place. I was nostalgic and pleased that Benoît was working there, just below Ralph's former studio, seemingly carrying on the artistic tradition. Benoît knew about the Situationists, admired them, and knew a little about Rumney, although he had not before heard the whole ragged story of his life. 'It is not possible to live like that now, however,' he said, arms folded and looking serious. 'France is not the same. The art world is not the same. You can't be heroic any more. The world won't let you.' He explained that although he was inspired by the dreams of the old avant-gardists, he did not believe in their revolution, or rather, he understood that their revolution had failed. 'I had teachers who were part of May 68 and thought that they could create a new France which would be more equal and freer than in any other part of history, and I wanted to believe them, but even as a child and then as a student, I could see that the France I was growing up in was not going to be like that. More and more people have become divided and angry. Even in Manosque, which looks old-fashioned and peaceful where we are sitting, is not always like that.'

As I continued to explore Manosque I began to see what he meant. The old town, for example, was beautiful, but parts were also in a state of severe neglect. You only had to wander off the main streets to find yourself in narrow, dirty streets which stank of piss and shit, and where even in daylight it was quite common for a fearless rat to cross your path. Checking out the property prices, I fantasized about leaving my modest Paris flat and living in lordly splendour in one of the Renaissance houses, but when I got up close, I could see that many of them were half-wrecked and beyond even the most expensive repair. Over the past few decades, the *mairie* had not invested seriously in the old town, and the middle classes of Manosque had moved away to new-build villas with swimming pools and garages, settling in clusters around the hills. The inhabitants of the old town were too poor to move out and so endured the bad sanitation, bad smells and broken pavements.

Many of them were Arabs. I had first become aware of this population in the 1990s during my walks through and across the town. That feeling of being in a medina was compounded by the fact that so many Arabs seemed to live here and were even possibly – it was hard to tell – the majority of the old town's inhabitants. At lunchtime, you could catch the smell of woodsmoke and North African cooking in the backstreets. Women in traditional clothes walked the narrow lanes alone or in pairs, discreet and furtive as if they shouldn't have been there. Older men in elderly suits, often sporting the wide flat caps favoured by North Africans of an earlier generation, loafed at cafes, gossiping, smoking, drinking coffee. The sound in the air was Maghrebi Arabic, not Provençal. There were few young people to be seen, but there were straggly groups of snotty-nosed small children presumably being looked after by grandparents. This was not like the Arab quarters of Marseille or any other reasonably sized town in France, which were busy, bustling, showy and noisy. Instead, the atmosphere was muted and hushed, as if the Arabs who lived here did not want to be seen or have their presence signalled in any way.

Later I learned that the Arab population was mainly made up of *harkis* and their descendants. The term comes from the word '*haraka*', meaning 'movement', which in Arabic military parlance was a strategy commonly used to conceal small groups of guerrillas from external enemies. The word was picked up on by the French military during its conquest of Algeria in the 1830s. During the Algerian War of Independence, the term *harki* was applied to the groups of auxiliary police formed by the French army to provide police and military cover at a local level, defending towns, villages and tribes against the Algerian nationalist insurgents, the FLN ('Front national de libération', or 'National Liberation Front'). By 1962, some 26,000 men were playing a number of roles from local policemen to conscript troops in the field. The *harkis* were mainly peasants themselves, and most had no real interest in national liberation, still less the politics of national liberation.

In the summer of 1962, in the wake of Algerian independence, the *harkis* became the focus of revenge and anger for the victorious Nationalists. There were terrible stories of crucifixions, gouged eyes, castrations and other atrocities. In the end, France grudgingly allowed 15,000 *harkis* and their families into France. There, they were treated as pariahs, a source of shame to the native French, as well as to Algerian immigrants with direct living connections to the Algerian war and their own sense of alienation towards France. They were herded together and left to rot in wretched camps outside French cities and towns. The legacy of this time lingers on: these days in the *banlieues*, to be called a *harki* is the deadliest insult; you are a traitor to the Arab cause, still dancing to the tune of the colonial master, still blindly obeying orders and betraying your compatriots. The footballer Kylian Mbappé was only the latest prominent *banlieusard* to be insulted in this way when the Parisian-Senegalese rapper Booba publicly accused him of being a *harki* for voting in a French election.

Manosque is well known as a '*ville-harki*', a '*harki* town'. It is where hundreds of displaced and disorientated *harkis* were billeted, having made the crossing from Algiers to Marseille. They were settled in camps in four forests and in two run-down housing estates called Saint-Martin and Les Quatres Saisons, where the conditions were filthy and cramped. Living close to nature and subject to its cruelties, the *harkis* of Manosque were as separate from the life of modern France as any of the tragic Provençals whom Giono took as his subjects. A *harki* archive quoted 'Moussa', who arrived in France at the age of five, as saying, 'You could live your whole childhood not knowing that France really existed, and when you realized it did, it made you feel less than human, a citizen without citizenship, an illegitimate child of the Republic.'[5]

As part of the drive to reabsorb the *harkis* back into society in the 1970s, the *harkis* of Manosque were mostly rehoused in the old town. There, they reconstructed their old lives in the medina-like maze of streets, having now acquired the habits of stealth, secrecy and avoiding contact with outsiders. Their descendants are still there and identify as *harkis*, both as a show of defiance and to shame the Republic that abandoned them to massacres in their homeland and betrayed them in France. There are now political organizations to defend these families, to ensure they have rights and justice. In June 2023, there was an official visit to Manosque from the National Commission in Paris, which looks after the affairs of *harki* families. The Commission met with the families of Manosque, discussed historic reparations and visited the former *cité* Saint-Martin, now called Les Grands-Prés. Such gestures are good and necessary, but the feelings of humiliation and outsiderdom that come with being a *harki* are still passed down through the generations.

One afternoon in the park of the Place du Terreau, I came across three women sharing a picnic lunch, smoking and complaining loudly in French and Arabic about a rogue sister-in-law (I was not earwigging; they spoke so loudly that it was hard not to hear what they were saying). They were sitting on a bench next to a modest stone monument to the 'Harkis Morts pour le France 1954–1962', which had been placed there in 2020. As I started to take photos of the monument they laughed and asked me why. I told them I was interested in the history of Manosque and its *harkis*, and, after ten minutes or so of chit-chat, I finally dared to ask if they were *harkis* themselves. They were three different generations of the same *harki* family: grandmother, mother and daughter. The oldest woman wore a headscarf and traditional clothes; the two younger women wore loose black hair, tracksuits, gaudy jewellery and trainers. All three were quite plump and enjoying their lunchtime feast with vigour. They asked me to join in and I did.

The oldest woman had come to Manosque as a small child in the 1960s, originally from a village in the Aurès Mountains. The younger women had been born in Manosque. All three of them said that they attached no shame to their identity, but that they didn't have any connection to the wider Arab community which had been moving into Manosque from Marseille and other centres over the past few decades. 'For us, they are outsiders,' said Farida, the granddaughter. 'They have a different life to us. We are all Muslims, but we are still separate. They have come from big cities and live in a different way.'

'We have a different history,' said her grandmother, Madame Touria. 'We do not speak to each other. We are not connected.'

But they were, and this was their tragedy. The *harkis* were sent all over France, but most of them were concentrated in Provence, as were many of the first Algerian emigrants who left Algeria after the War of Independence. The *harkis* were hidden in forests and the outskirts of obscure towns while the much larger Algerian population settled in city spaces mainly along the coast. The two communities avoided each other, but they were linked by war, race and religion and were part of each other's cultural identity whether they liked it or not. The grandmother had never been back to Algeria, although she followed news of her large cast of relatives there. The younger women had never been there. They said that they felt 'Algerian' – it was their language, their religion, their superstitions, even their food – but had no wish to be part of a wider Algerian community. Nor did they wish to assimilate; they all responded with horror when I asked if they thought of themselves as 'French'.

That evening, I ate in a small restaurant called Le Mirador, which was opposite the Porte de la Saunerie. Even at dinner time, the restaurant was mostly empty, although the food was excellent (I ate *sauté de veau aux épices* with *gratin dauphinois* – veal, spices, cheese, cream, potatoes, garlic). The chef Thierry, another Corsican, came over to chat.

Thierry had been working in Le Mirador for nearly twenty years and during that time had seen Manosque change. 'This used to be a really busy place every night,' he said, 'but then people stopped coming. It's because the town has changed so quickly. This place is a perfect spot to come in the evening, right in the centre of town. But nobody comes into town anymore. For all the young people, their lives are out there in the *banlieues*, or in the shopping malls. They're not interested in leaving their ghettoes. So we're struggling here, like everybody else in the old town.' I wondered about this exodus, especially as the centre-right *mairie* of Manosque had lately been pushing the notion of Manosque as a *'ville-idéale'*, 'the perfect town', old enough to be historic and young enough to be looking to the future, small enough to be away from big-city pressures and large enough to be interesting.

'The problem is that none of that is true,' said Thierry, before going on to make a list of complaints that I had heard already from the Manosquins. In the past two decades, the town had been expanded to accommodate a new population largely made up of refugees from Marseille and other coastal towns. This population was different, by race and religion, from the indigenous population of Manosque, those who were too old or poor to leave (Thierry called them *'pacoulins'*, a Marseille slang term for country yokels). Like many medium-sized towns across France, there was a severe lack of medical services or educational provision and incoherent public transport. Unemployment was a problem. In this way, Manosque was fairly typical of '*le désert français*'; despite its beauty and location, it was quite definitely now part of 'peripheral France'.

Worse still, according to Thierry, many of the new citizens of Manosque were 'problem families' who had been decanted into Manosque, bringing all of their problems with them. During the pandemic, the drug culture took off, with young kids cycling around the town delivering packages. The noble summit of Mont d'Or was now well known as a daytime refuge for crackheads and was strewn with drug litter. The new *banlieues* were disorganized, as I had discovered with my Corsican driver Lucca, and traffic was a nightmare. Manosque was a town that seemed to have also taken a wrong turning in its history. As Thierry said, its culture was dying in front of your eyes.

I had heard this before and could see it for myself. Manosque had been encircled and then strangled by its suburbs. The place now had a forlorn and dusty feel, as if real life was taking place elsewhere. I still felt a residual affection for the place but the enchantment had worn off. Whatever traces of Ralph and Giono's old dreams that still lingered in the old town were actually just phantoms, quickly glimpsed and suddenly gone.

British visitors to pre-Revolution France were mostly unimpressed by Provence. The philosopher and physician John Locke came to France in 1675 at the age of forty-three and spent three years, mainly in the south, trying to recover his health (he was consumptive), although there are mysteries around his prolonged stay in France: was he, like Christopher Marlowe, another English spy? He wrote a journal packed with splenetic texts written in a crabbed style, partly in bad French and cryptic English, possibly so that they could not be easily deciphered. Like most Englishmen in France, he complained about the food.

(One bill of fare was no more than 'a cabbage and a frog that was caught in it', he noted bad-temperedly.) On leaving Provence, Locke wrote:

> Here we passed the Rhosne again and left Provence, a country, however commended, wherein I had seen more barren ground than fruiful, & yet had passed the best part of it. The people too, if one my judge by their clothes & diet had, like the country, 5 acres of poverty for one of riches, for I remember at Aix in a gardiner's house where we found them eating, their Sunday dinner was noe thing but slices of congeal'd blood in oile which an English gent, was with me would needs tast, though to the turning his stomach.[6]

Arthur Young passed through this part of the world in August 1789. He suffered from the heat and the wind of Provence: 'The *vent de bize* has blown strongly for several days,' he noted in mid-August of 1789, travelling from Orange to Avignon, 'with a clear sky, tempering the heats, which are sometimes sultry and oppressive; it may be, for what I know, wholesome to the French constitution, but it is diabolical to mine'. He complained about the extremes: at five in the morning it was so cold that 'no traveller ventures out'. Later in the day, the hot, windy climate reduced a man to 'cutaneous perspiration . . . this piercing through the body seems, by its sensation, to desiccate the interior humidity'. For Arthur Young, despite some scant examples of 'excellent irrigation', Provence was bare and barren, scarred by 'bad husbandry' and 'scandalous conditions'. The interior of Provence was one of the hardest parts of his journey through France.[7]

It was only in the nineteenth century that the British began to see Provence as an enchanted land, but its invention as a kind of earthly paradise for the Victorian tourist was in fact a slow process, following the politics and developing technologies of the era. After the end of the Napoleonic Wars, when France was again open and safe for British visitors, it became fashionable to boast of visits to Paris, which to the foreigner was as fascinatingly brutish as it was elegant: 'a city replete with vice and dissipation,' wrote the French-born British artist Francis Hervé in *How to Enjoy Paris in 1842*, a satirical and sometimes sarcastic guide to Paris for the English visitor to Paris. 'I hate them,' said a certain Mr Lewis to Hervé, speaking of the French while en route to Paris. But this did not stop Mr Lewis from extolling the French art of living, especially the food (and quite likely, he hints, the sex).[8] Moving further south for the British traveller offered even more exotic, sensual delights. It was also considered prestigious and adventurous to change climate and terrain. However, these travels were not without discomfort and danger.

British visitors to the region echoed Arthur Young in complaining loudly about the terrible heat (or cold) and the cruel wind (*le mistral*) as well as poor hygiene, bad water, the frighteningly foreign food (garlic and herbs especially) and ugly, gnarly-faced peasants who spoke a barely comprehensible, possible barely human, dialect. The growing number of travellers who journeyed to the south of France despite these travails also offered an opportunity for an enterprising publisher called John Murray to make money. *A Handbook for Travellers to France*, first published in London in 1843, became the essential guide for travellers. This was the prototype for what would become the modern travel guidebook, and Murray himself contributed several sections to the book. These first descriptions of Provence are surprisingly off-putting for an audience presumably in search of pleasure and the thrill of the foreign. The book compares the scorched landscape to the 'dry, wasted bones of a skeleton'. It goes on, patriotically: 'the inhabitant of the North would not readily purchase the clear cloudless sky of Provence with the misty verdure of England'. The locals are primitive and sometimes vicious, a result of the climate: they are 'rude in manner' and 'harsh in speech' and given to 'the committal of acts of violence unknown in the North'. The 'venomous bite' of the mosquito is another hazard for the traveller.

Murray's book also pandered to a generalized suspicion and dislike of the French among British travellers. The *Handbook* made much of the violence associated with religious and political extremism in Provence. A description of the papal court in Avignon lingers on a torture chamber used by the Inquisition, where prisoners were trapped in a funnel-shaped dungeon which had a furnace for 'heating torturing irons'. Nearby was 'the instrument called La Veille, a pointed stake, upon which the condemned was seated, suspended by cords from above, so as only to prevent his falling, but allowing his weight to bear upon the point'. This description, and the reality of the dungeon itself, impressed Charles Dickens so much that he lifted it and used it practically verbatim in his *Pictures from Italy*.

The French Revolution was within living memory for some of the first British travellers, and they would have been aware of the gory scenes that played out in the places they were visiting. The people of Provence, it seemed, went quite mad during the Revolutionary period, committing endless massacres and 'atrocious crimes'. At Orange, it was reported that 378 people had been executed by guillotine in the space of three months. Revolutionaries sacked the village of 'Badouin' (in French this is the village of Bédoin in the Vaucluse), killing all its inhabitants as a public spectacle. Even as late as 1815, on hearing of Napoleon's defeat at the Battle of Waterloo, the natives of Provence were bloodthirsty and vengeful. In Avignon, Royalists, who hated Napoleon, murdered Maréchal Brune, one of Napoleon's senior Marshals of Empire, who had the bad luck to be found carrying the passport of Lord Exmouth. He was beaten to death by a mob and his body thrown into the Rhône.

The road to the south became less dangerous for British

travellers, or those with British documents, with the development of the railways. France was at first behind Britain, Belgium, Germany and Switzerland in developing any kind of network, having squandered so much money and so many men on wars during the Napoleonic era. Nonetheless, French ambitions to connect the entire territory began to be fulfilled in 1855, when the first full connection to the south was laid by two companies, *Compagnie du chemin de fer de Lyon à la Méditerranée* and *Compagnie du chemin de fer Paris à Lyon*. Napoleon III described the line as 'an imperial artery'. A few years earlier, the Gare de Lyon in Paris, the true gateway to the south of France, had opened. Now the perilous four-day journey took only a day, a night and the next morning, unless you stopped off along the way to rest. This railway line would soon become the busiest in France.

As France advanced economically, the updated edition of Murray's *Handbook* began talking about the French Riviera as the 'garden of Provence', a sanctuary for invalids and a playground for everyone else. The British rushed to spend their money on the Côte d'Azur, but they were not popular. 'There is an innumerable quantity of Englishmen and Russians of low quality here,' wrote Prosper Mérimée, writer, archaeologist and (among other duties) a sybaritic Inspector General of Historic Monuments for the French Government.[9] He went on: 'The avalanche of foreigners brought by the railways is ruining the beautiful promenades of this country [Provence].' The Russian writer and proto-socialist Alexander Herzen was equally blunt, observing in 1841 that 'consumptive Englishmen and Englishwomen with broken spines make up most of the population of Nice'.[10] This was, of course, wildly inaccurate, but it did capture the genuine European contempt for the English, who were polluting the 'garden of France' with their money, illnesses and general ugliness.

Still the British came. At one point in the late nineteenth century, it was estimated that there were at any one time approximately 20,000 British residents occupying the strip between Hyères and Menton. They acted in an imperial manner, as though Provence was a British colony, and brought with them their own doctors, religion, cooking and myths about the place. Eventually, the British visitors, '*les English*', would become part of Provençal folklore and, in this way, would finally settle into being a composite part of French history. That is how an Englishman like Ralph Rumney, who, like so many of his compatriots, dreamed of Provence as his perfect place of exile, would also ultimately be absorbed into this patrimony.

Ralph died in 2002 in a hospital in Marseille. A friend contacted me to say that Ralph wanted to say goodbye, but when I spoke to him on the telephone he had already lost the power of speech and could only make tortured noises, evidently in great pain. In an obituary for the *Independent* newspaper, I described how much Ralph had loved southern Europe and especially Provence as an act of defiance against his northern upbringing. I also recalled the *colloque* of 2000 as his final artistic action, his last act of lucid dreaming. He would have said that he could only have done this in Manosque, his imagined urban utopia in Haute-Provence.

Provence is, of course, now a dream territory for the French as well as the British. There is an often overlooked but fine demonstration of this in the Gare de Lyon. This is *La grande fresque de la gare de Lyon*, a mural which runs the length of the corridor of a hundred metres or so, between Hall 1 and Hall 2 in the train station. It was commissioned in 1900 by the two companies that founded and operated the lines south. The first version was painted by Jean-Baptiste Olive (it was touched up in 1980 by the artist Jean-Paul Letellier), a native of Marseille mostly noted for his fascination with the Vieux Port of Marseille and the surrounding countryside. The mural is in shimmering soft shades of pastel and oil, lit up by daylight from *verrières* (ingeniously situated glass panels in the roof) in the otherwise gloomy and dimly lit hall. It depicts the full sweep of cities accessible on the line from Paris to Menton, just before the border with Italy (and then leaps inexplicably to Venice). The *fresque* will show you, among other marvels, Basilique Sainte-Marie-Madeleine at Vézelay, Cathédrale Saint-Bénigne in Dijon, the Hospices de Beaune, Basilique Notre-Dame de Fourvière in Lyon, as well as the better-known and obvious glories of Avignon, Marseille and Nice. It is a celebration of the totality of France at the cusp of the nineteenth and twentieth centuries. Like the Eiffel Tower, the railways were a coming together of art, technology, engineering and a vision of modernity, showing the world what the French were capable of and why France was now so special and so powerful. The *fresque* was a vision of the 'Great Nation' for the new century.

Over a hundred years on, the best way to appreciate the journey south is now from the buffet car of the TGV train, which so smoothly cuts through and glides across the real landscape depicted by the *fresque*. There are windows on either side of the wagon, which are enlarged to allow a panoramic view of the passing countryside, and if the train is not too packed it is pleasant to perch yourself on one of the stools facing outwards onto a little table below the window, drink a beer and watch France unfold before you at three hundred kilometres per hour. It is like watching a speeded-up travel film designed to show off the country's variegated scenery all at once. The journey is a blur of grey-tiled houses, then red-tiled houses, small farms, bridges, industrial plants, car parks, industrial scrapheaps, business parks, marshes, aqueducts, vineyards, distant mountains, green fields, dairy cattle, fields of olives, graffitied hoardings, the backsides of urban apartment blocks with their balconies of dried-out plants, flowers and old garden furniture, and then Marseille.

Getting off at the Gare Saint-Charles in Marseille is a visceral experience. For the past three hours or so from Paris, you have seen France but neither smelled it, tasted its air nor heard its languages and dialects. If it is good weather when you arrive at the station, it will be heavy with heat, and you will feel that you have travelled properly to a southern zone. The dusty and faded palm trees tell you the same thing. You'll hear the tangy accents of Marseille and the south, and North African Arabic in all its variants and musicality. Of course, you can hear these African languages in Paris, but here they seem to belong; they seem to be at home. The warm air is scented with petrol fumes and the faint rumour of the sea. When you emerge from the station onto the beautiful stage-like *terrasse* on a spring or summer day, and sometimes in other seasons, the sun can blind you. This is an African sun. You are nonetheless still in Europe.

But only just.

9

The 'Wicked City' of Marseille

Entering Marseille from the sea

If food is travel, to my mind the best way to taste the spirit, the electricity, of Marseille when you first arrive in the city is with a can of Kronenbourg and a simple Margherita from the Pizzeria Gare de l'Est near the Marché des Capucins. Like all the best working-class food the world over, it is hot and greasy, melts in your hands, and is unbelievably tasty. This hole-in-the-wall place is in the *quartier* of Noailles, one of the liveliest neighbourhoods in Marseille, bustling with fruit sellers, kebab shops and teahouses and largely populated with immigrants. They are mainly Tunisian, Algerian and Moroccan, although latterly there has also been a strong West African presence. I have always loved this part of Marseille.

It should be noted, too, that the pizzas in Marseille, and across the south, are not always Italian in origin. In the back country of Provence, the locals favour *moitié-moitié* (half and half), which is half anchovies and half French Emmental cheese. On the seafront at Marseille, I've eaten *pizza aux figatelli et à la brousse* (pizza with Corsican boar sausage and curds) and Armenian pizzas with shredded meat. A fairly recent innovation is the pizza-kebab, which is a pizza layered with roasted kebab meat and can also include the spicy North African sausage called merguez. Some of the best and most popular pizza trucks are in the badlands of Marseille: in the *quartiers nord* and other lawless places. Here, it's not unusual to find several varieties of dope or cocaine on offer with your slice. All of this food, and how to eat it, is very much how modern Marseille comes alive, but really people have lived like this here – on the street, faces turned to the sea and the worlds beyond – for a very long time.

Marseille is an old city, even older than Paris. The city was born from the sea twenty-six centuries ago when it was founded by Ionian Greeks from Phocaea in Asia Minor. (Phocaea is today the town of Foça in the Izmir region of Turkey. The name Phocaea comes from the Greek word '*fókia*', referring to the seals that lived on the islands around the settlement. This sound has echoed down the ages and persists in modern French as the word '*phoque*', meaning seal, with similar variants in Catalan, Spanish, Italian and Romanian.)

Appropriately, these Phocaeans – these men like seals – were master navigators and the first in the Hellenic world to sail to all ends of the Mediterranean in search of colonies and trade, founding settlements in Corsica, Italy and Catalonia. The greatest of these was Marseille, which the Greeks called Massalia and the Romans Massilia. When the Phocaeans arrived here, there were already southern Gauls and Ligurians with their own relatively sophisticated culture. But it was the seafaring Greeks from the other side of the Mediterranean who turned the natural harbour of Marseille into a *polis* – an organized and independent city with its own political life, economy and religion – which looked outwards to the Mediterranean and, with Carthage, dominated the sea trade of the era. Massalia was built where the area called Le Panier is now and would have tumbled down from the hills to the sea much like this old part of Marseille, with its hidden alleyways, narrow streets and steep staircases, does today.

The oldest approach to Marseille is still from the sea. This is how the Phocaeans came here and, after them, countless mariners, merchants, soldiers, immigrants and others, travelling from the furthest edges of the known world. Nowadays, you'll see fishing boats; the regular roll-on roll-off ferries to and from Corsica, Sardinia, Morocco, Algeria and Tunisia; and the huge and ugly cruise ships that are a contemporary blight on ports across the Mediterranean. But there is still freight being unloaded at the massive docks of Marseille Fos port, which runs west for fifty kilometres from La Joliette and L'Estaque, making Marseille the second-busiest port in France and the eleventh busiest in Europe. Marseille is France's nearest port to the Suez Canal, and sixty per cent of France's oil comes through here. As does much of France's illegal supply of cannabis, heroin and cocaine, as well as the massive trade in black-market cigarettes, which you can find on sale for half the price of a regular packet from the street vendors in the *quartier* of Noailles.

The first glimpse of Marseille, from a few kilometres out at sea, is dramatic and seductive. The city reveals itself slowly as you approach: first, a long grey-white line that stretches across the bay from L'Estaque to the Plages du Prado, then, as you move closer to the Vieux Port, which is really just a long and narrow oblong-shaped channel carved into the right-hand side of the bay, you begin to make out the *calanques, anses* and *vallons* – local words for narrow valleys or coves, crinkles and creases – which are carved into the craggy coastline (these stretch for roughly fifteen kilometres, to the town of Cassis, and are all, despite their wildness and inaccessibility, amazingly still part of the 9th arrondissement of Marseille). Suddenly, the long vague white line takes on a definite shape – like a cracked porcelain bowl, or as Richard Cobb put it, 'a huge amphitheatre open ... seawards'.[1]

To the left, the skyscrapers of the *quartiers nord* are set into relief against the high, grey-green limestone hills of Provence, while your view of the Vieux Port is now dominated by Basilique Notre-Dame de la Garde, crowned by a golden statue of the Virgin Mary. The church stands over 150 metres tall on a limestone hill overlooking the city from its southern side. Built in the mid-nineteenth century, the basilica is a mishmash of neo-Byzantine and Romanesque architecture styles. When you first arrive in Marseille, whether by sea, road or train, you can't miss the basilica, which dominates the skyline. Accordingly, the church has become an emblem of the city; it is to Marseille what the Eiffel Tower is to Paris.

The church exactly mirrors the Notre Dame d'Afrique in Algiers, which was built roughly at the same time and also stands on a hill, overlooking the bay of Algiers, beckoning the sea traveller to port. I have climbed up both hills, and each time I have done so, the mirroring effect felt very real. This was almost certainly what the architects had intended and was quite definitely the ambition of Louis-Antoine-Augustin Pavy, the Bishop of Algiers who commissioned Notre Dame d'Afrique. (Pavy also said that he wanted the church modelled on the Basilique Notre-Dame de Fourvière in Lyon. And appropriately enough, Notre Dame d'Afrique does indeed stand over the city like a watchtower, like the Fourvière does in Lyon.)

In 1966, the *pieds-noirs* who had recently arrived in Marseille, in bitter forced exile from 'French Algeria', petitioned the city authorities to name a square in the 10th arrondissement in honour of the Algerian basilica. The Square Notre Dame d'Afrique is regularly graffitied with anti-*pied-noir* and anti-French insults in French and Arabic, respectively, as is the nearby rue du Cardinal Lavigerie, another public space demanded by the *pieds-noirs* and named after the archbishop of Algiers who, on the orders of the Pope, commanded the Catholics of North Africa in the 1860s and sought to make Algeria a Christian country. (In 1991, the statue of Jesus outside Notre Dame d'Afrique in Algiers was torn down and smashed by Islamists consumed with this same iconoclastic fury.)

The last time I entered Marseille by sea, I noticed two Algerian ferries crossing each other in the port, one on the way to France and one on the way to what used to be France. Noting the same sight as I did, a young French-Algerian girl sitting next to me quietly said '*Vive l'Algérie!*' to herself and her family. When I asked why, she said, 'It's just a little joke.' She explained, 'My family are in both Algiers and Marseille. In Algiers, I can stay with *al-Jaddi* and *al-Jaddati* (grandfather and grandmother). I am at home in both places, and neither of them is really all French.' This did not mean that she was anti-French or hated France, but that Marseille, as a city of the sea, of perpetual comings and goings – in French, '*une ville d'escale*' – belonged as much to its travellers, immigrants and emigrants as it did to the French state.

The ferries and the freighters all make for the docks. But the tourist boats, fishing boats and pleasure cruisers enter the Vieux Port, which feels like you're entering a stage set, or Richard Cobb's 'amphitheatre'. The entrance to the harbour is guarded on both sides by two forts, Fort Saint-Nicholas and Fort Saint-Jean, which are empty and unarmed these days but still imposing. The harbour is overlooked on the southern approach by the Pharo Palace, commissioned in 1852 by Napoleon III, a frequent visitor to Marseille who wanted to mould the city to reflect his glory, much as he had already started to do in Paris by rebuilding the city according to the plans of Baron Haussmann. The palace was intended as a residence for Empress Eugénie but was dismissed by architectural critics of the day as vulgar and mediocre, much like Napoleon III himself. In 1872, just before the death of the Emperor, it was surrendered to the city of Marseille, which first turned it into a cholera hospital and then the School of Colonial Medicine. It is now a park with views of the sea, the city, and the mountains which rise above Marseille from behind as if to shield it.

On the bank opposite the Pharo Palace is the main building of the Musée des Civilisations d'Europe et Méditerranée (Mucem), a huge charcoal-coloured cube made of fibre-reinforced concrete. The architect was Rudy Ricciotti, a *pied-noir* born in Kouba, a *banlieue* of Algiers. His conceit is that the lattice looks like a mantilla, concealing the treasures within from all points across the Mediterranean. Up close, it looks elegant and fragile, exactly like the lace of a mantilla, creating a dappling effect, with the light inside the cube transforming the formal museum space into a shady, sleepy southern square.

In old photographs of Marseille and a few paintings (notably by Albert Marquet), you will see that the jetty of the Mucem was once the base of a huge transporter bridge, with a tower almost a hundred metres high, that was built in 1905 and spanned the mouth of the harbour. The design was based on a bridge which once spanned the Mersey between Runcorn and Widnes. The bridge in Marseille was a superb piece of modernist engineering, defining the entrance to the city as an exciting living machine. The Nazis blew it up when they left in 1944, but the bridge is still part of the long historical memory of Marseille, admired and loved by its working class as their own Eiffel Tower, a perfect blend of art and technology (they considered the Basilique Notre-Dame de la Garde too *bourgeoise* and Catholic). The Mucem is in many ways an impressive building, but there is a certain twenty-first-century melancholy in the fact that it is a postmodernist museum where living industrial art once stood, worked and defined Marseille.

The Mucem ends at the northern tip of Fort Saint-Jean, which is where in John Frankenheimer's 1975 film *French Connection II*, the hard-boiled New York detective 'Popeye' Doyle, a stranger and misfit in Marseille, finally gets to shoot at 'Frog One', the crafty and elusive drug lord who has led him a dance throughout the film. This moment is one of the most exciting climaxes in cinema history. Doyle has chased him on foot from La Canebière, dogged and sweating, down the length of the Quai de l'Hôtel-de-Ville, climbing over barriers, losing sight of his quarry. Finally, in the last few seconds of the film, when 'Frog One' emerges from his hiding place on the boat as it is about to leave the Vieux Port, thinking that he is safe, Doyle aims, fires and the screen goes blank.

Frankenheimer's portrayal of Marseille was of a dirty, dangerous and brutally violent city with slums and African-looking street life. It was realistic – this was what Marseille really looked like in the 1970s – but also romantic. Even French audiences were rapt, bedazzled by this portrait of a city which was in France but which they did not know.

Seeing the film in 1978, before I'd ever been to France, made me want to go to Marseille. When I finally got there, a decade later, I was not disappointed. I arrived late at night, on my own, with hardly any money, and took a no-star hotel in Belsunce, the first one I saw as I made my way into the city from the Gare Saint-Charles. My room was small and musty and smelled of damp. I was the only European in the hotel and can now see that my fellow residents were *chibanis*, poor, quiet and discrete men who lived here permanently in exile between two worlds, Africa and Europe. I stayed there for a week, getting to know the owner, an Algerian Marseillais called Hamid, and the life of the *quartier*, which seemed to me to be just as intricate, unknowable and exciting as the bigger life of the city I was exploring on my daytime tourist expeditions.

Belsunce, then as now, was dilapidated and rotting away, its wretched hotels serving as a home for this static population of *chibanis*. I was then earnestly trying to learn some Arabic and I remember being confused by the Arabic term for the Mediterranean Sea in my textbook. This was '*al-Bahr al-Abyad al-Mutawassit*', an old usage dating back centuries, to be found on Arabic and Ottoman maps, and which translates as 'the white in-between sea'. When I pretentiously tried it out with Hamid in a conversation about travel and how to book a ferry to Algiers, he smiled in sympathetic recognition and assumed that I knew more Arabic than I did. Noticing straight away that I couldn't understand his reply and that my Arabic was childishly limited, he gently moved back to French. He also assumed that, since I knew this term, I also knew more about the Arab world than I did. But I was still learning. This was a start, however, a view of the world from the south and not the north.

During those first few days in Marseille, in the spring of 1988, I was intoxicated by the city. I walked for hours, climbing hills and poking around backstreets. None of it seemed beautiful, but I was endlessly intrigued, trying to work out exactly what made this place feel so unique.

I was then living with Sylvie in comfortable, safe, *bourgeois* Dijon but I had come on my own to Marseille for an adventure. (Like many French people, Sylvie had never been to the city and never wanted to go there. She had already decided that she would hate it – too '*prolo*', too '*vulgaire*'.) In every way, Marseille was the opposite of Dijon. I deliberately sought out its non-French spaces. Many of these were Arab or African, but also Turkish, Armenian, Italian, Sardinian, Corsican, Spanish or Greek, making the city feel for me, with my sincere passion for this mix, more Levantine than French.

These spaces were reflected not in the architecture of central Marseille – which, aside from the grand seventeenth-century *mairie* commissioned by Louis XIV, whose motif adorns the front of the building, is mostly the classical nineteenth-century

French style – but at the level of the street: in the languages and behaviour of the people, their food and their music. You could find these cultures in cafes, bars, *bistrots*, takeaway joints, barber shops, grocery stores and street markets. The people who used and lived in these places had all, at some time, come from somewhere else beyond French borders, but they were also somehow at home here. What I discovered on that first trip was that while Marseille is the second city of France, it is also, perhaps more importantly, the first city of 'the white in-between sea'.

The city's connection to the sea is easiest to feel, and smell, on the Quai des Belges, the end point of the Vieux Port, where a fish market is held most mornings. The market, called *La Criée*, is noisy and colourful and not at all folkloric – about a dozen or so fishermen are selling their overnight catches for the highest price, mostly to restauranteurs. Alongside the market is the so-called L'Ombrière – 'the shade catcher' – a large mirror made up of polished steel plates facing the ground, constructed in the shape of a canopy, which provides much-needed shade on the Quai. The installation was designed by the architect Norman Foster and set up in 2013. It is literally quite dazzling (the light bounces off the steel at all angles) and can make you feel dizzy if you look up too soon to see the street life that you are part of being reflected back at you from above. It is a simple but stunning idea, a perfect way to capture the endlessly changing movement of the Quai below.

The street life of the Quai is restless at all times of the day or night. This is partly because it is a kind of crossroads between La Canebière, the long road that leads down to the sea from the centre of Marseille, and the rue de la République, with its heavy traffic comprising cars, taxis and buses (which all stop here) heading for the Pharo Palace, the Corniche or the autoroutes to Prado and out of town. The Quai des Belges is also an international crossroads: Marseille is at the centre of three autoroutes which can take you to Spain, Italy or northern Europe.

This is where Julio Cortázar and Carol Dunlop ended their mythic quest at 10.40 a.m. on 23 June 1982, welcomed in their triumph (and 'anguish' at ending their journey) by 'a guard of honour' of the local seagulls – *les gabians* of Marseille folklore, the birds who watch over the city. They stayed only an hour or two, drinking a *pastis marseillais* at a cafe (most probably La Samaritaine, the 1900s-style brasserie at 2 Quai du Port) before setting off again for Cadenet (near Lourmarin in the Var) and then to the tiny village of Serre to stay with the Surrealist poet and painter Jean Thiercelin and his wife Raquel in their house, which looked like a medieval fortress. Thiercelin's greatest ambition as an artist, he often said, was to find the Holy Grail. Cortázar wrote that he and Dunlop had found this on the Quai des Belges.[2] After deliberately disconnecting themselves from the regular rhythms of everyday life and delving deep into their own subjective experience, the maelstrom of the Quai des Belges in mid-morning must have come as an electrifying shock.

Here, all is relentless motion as people move between the fish market stands, the bus stops and the street vendors selling *crêpes*, ice creams, soft drinks, gaudy children's toys that make loud noises, chestnuts (in the autumn), fried fish and shrimp. Even at mid-morning there is a smell of marijuana, coffee and pastis, which when mixed with the fish smells and the oily engine smoke of the tourist boats is alchemized into a heady, unforgettable perfume. The soundtrack is rap or Arab pop music blasting from portable Bluetooth speakers (sometimes used to accompany busking hip-hop dancers or, later in the day, a spontaneous rap battle), all punctuated by the unceasing blare and buzz of traffic. The crowd is an ever-shifting kaleidoscope of classes, races and religions: commuters, shoppers, beggars, drug dealers, lads and girls lounging about and flirting, skateboarders, old men sitting on benches staring at the sea. It is all fast and contemporary, but there also seems something ancient about the way in which so many different people gather here to be separate and together in an open space by the sea. This is how Mediterranean people, on all sides of 'the white in-between sea', have lived for centuries if not millennia.

The ancient world nudges at the edges of modern Marseille. The Phocaeans are a fundamental part of the city's identity. The football fans of Olympique de Marseille (OM) are known as '*les Phocéens*' throughout France. In tourist propaganda, in the media, and even in official documents, the city is referred to as '*la cité phocéene*'. Louis Brauquier evoked an idyll of Massalia in his poem '*La Fondation de Marseille*' ('The founding of Marseille') as 'an immense plain, guarded by sheer mountains . . . there were gardens and vines, women and warriors'.[3]

But it is hard, in concrete terms, to find much real evidence of ancient Massalia. Prosper Mérimée, ever pernickety and pained, noted as much in his journal, complaining that 'it is surprising that, in a town as antique as Marseille, one finds hardly any vestiges of Greek or Roman rule'.[4] In 1967, some broken Greek stones were discovered during building work for a new shopping mall near the Vieux Port, and they have been preserved in the aptly named 'Jardin des Vestiges', but they are unimpressive and give no sense of what was once here.

At the centre of the Vieux Port is a small bronze plaque on the pavement, which was installed in 1952 on the orders of the corrupt Socialist mayor Gaston Defferre, who nonetheless truly loved Marseille. It reads: 'Here, in the year 600 BC, Greek sailors landed coming from the city of Phocaea,/ They founded Marseille,/ Whence civilisation shone in the West.' But it can be hard to make out the plaque under the feet of rushing pedestrians, or hidden by parked cars or delivery vans to the market or local restaurants. There are no ruined temples, wrecked arenas, lost cemeteries. It is as if the life of the Greek *polis* has simply melted into air.

However, myths sometimes persist in the oddest places. One early evening a few years ago, hungry and thirsty, I wandered into a kebab shop on the rue des Feuillants, a five-minute walk from the Vieux Port, which had the unusual and even slightly surreal name of 'En Suisse, le palais du roi' ('In Switzerland, the King's Palace'; I have still no idea what this means or where it comes from). Waiting for my grilled lamb and Orangina – a drink invented in Algeria, the serving staff told me unprompted – I noticed that all four sides of the room were made up of a fresco of an imagined classical Marseille. On closer inspection, I could see that it actually depicted the marriage of Gyptis and Protis in the soft setting of the Phocaean city. The Franco-Egyptian owner of the kebab shop did not know who had painted the fresco or why it was there, but he agreed that it was quite beautiful.

Later, I did some research and found out that the kebab shop had once been part of a bank and then an elegant cafe. The fresco was signed '*Gilardoni fils et cie, Céramiste JB Pons et cie*' and dated 1895. It turned out that I was not the only one who had stumbled upon this hidden treasure. There was a Facebook page dedicated to the fresco, and it was mentioned in some Marseille tourist information. The brilliant Spanish artist and photographer Marie Bovo, who lives in Marseille, has also taken some photographs which show how strange and exquisite the fresco is. In one image, she placed a can of Coke and a *barquette de frites* against the bucolic seascape, perfectly capturing the interplay between past and present. More than this, Bovo said that she wanted to reveal in her images how Marseille was a continuum – that the kebab shop, with its buzzing crowd of customers, strays, drunks, dealers and local families, was all part of the deep historical texture of the city. The Levantine origins of Marseille still lived on in the pan-Mediterranean make-up of its people. 'The whole of the Mediterranean, migrants, travellers, multiple voices, are all in the room,' she said.

Sadly, despite protestations from the *mairie*, the fresco has been covered up by the new owner of the shop, who has given the place a makeover and the generic name of Istanbul City. The memory of the antique past is still there, however, just below the surface of the newly painted shop, waiting to be uncovered and discovered again. For this reason, Marie Bovo has called the now-hidden fresco 'a new, forgotten ruin'.

When I recounted the story of the fresco in the kebab shop to the writer, journalist and historian François Thomazeau, he smiled and said that this was typical of the Marseillais indifference to the past. 'This is not Paris or Lyon,' he said. 'In both of those cities, which I love, the past is revered and celebrated in monuments, great buildings and statues, and the city's past is as important as the present, sometimes more important. That's just not the case in Marseille. It never has been. Life here has always been so intense, and maybe so difficult for the people who have come here or already live here that we have always only been able to focus on the present.' This made sense to me. In a city of permanent flux, of an endless flow of transient people and populations, it would be impossible to fix on any of the points in its history which singularly define the place.

I met up with Thomazeau in the Café de La Banque on the boulevard Paul Peytral on a bright afternoon in late October 2023. The cafe is a traditional brasserie, founded in 1898, quietly elegant and a long-established classic in the literary, business and political life of Marseille. We were sitting at the back, both sipping a *pac à l'eau*, a fiendishly sweet mixture of water and lemon juice which looks like a glass of *pastis*.

I had never heard of this drink, but it was Thomazeau's idea, a bit of a joke. As he explained, this was a favoured drink of the southern working classes and was considered to be '*vulgaire*' and even '*ringard*' – meaning 'chavvy' or 'naff' – by the posher classes. 'The working classes of the north of France and the south of France are not the same. In the south, we are less angry or depressed,' Thomazeau said. 'I was born in the north but I am a Marseillais, and we like to enjoy ourselves and are proud of who we are, even if we are *ringard*.' Drinking a *pac à l'eau* in a snooty bar like the Café de la Banque was, he said with a mischievous wink, an act of working-class solidarity and an act of defiance. The waiter who served us seemed to be in on the joke.

Thomazeau was not at all what I had expected. I had read his histories of Marseille, which were witty and clever, and knew of his excellent reputation as a journalist (especially on the Tour de France) and novelist (especially his crime novels). But I was most interested in him as an expert on the many cultures of Marseille, where he had grown up (his family had moved there from Lille when he was a child). I did not expect, however, his near-perfect English to be northern-inflected nor for him to have such a knowledge of and love for English working-class culture, which, he said, matched the Marseille he had grown up in. He had first-hand experience of northern working-class English life in his early twenties, when he worked as a student teacher in Doncaster.

He was also a lover of Northern Soul music and had DJed at gigs across the north of England. Now in his sixties, Thomazeau still dressed like a mod – Harrington jacket and Fred Perry polo shirt with piping. When I pointed out to him that this could have been the uniform of the present-day young Fascists I had met in Lyon, he replied that the Fascists did not understand the English mod style, its philosophy or its politics. They were ugly and ignorant parodies of what mods were about. Mods were about working-class pride, Thomazeau said, about style and beautiful clothes, and not about hate. The best way to be subversive, he added, was to dress better than your class enemy.

Thomazeau told me about growing up in Marseille in the 1960s and 1970s. 'Marseille was very poor then,' he told me, 'much poorer than it is now. During that time, the rest of France just turned its back on the city. Marseille was crime, unemployment, poverty, immigrants and football, all things that are despised by the French middle classes. So when I went to the north of England, which was poor then, too, and was looked down on by the southern English for some of the same reasons that the French looked down on Marseille, I felt at home. For one thing, I understood the football culture, even if it was violent. In Marseille, we all thought that supporting OM was to be in a kind of resistance movement against the French, who treated us as non-people.'

I wondered silently whether Thomazeau had inherited this spirit from his father, Marcel Thomazeau. Marcel was an extraordinary man who lived a historic life. He was born in 1922 in Saint-Lumine-de-Coutais, a small *commune* in the Loire-Atlantique, and spent his early years learning to be a printer. When the war came he joined the Resistance as a Communist. He was arrested by the Germans in Nantes in 1942. At the same time, his brother, also a *résistant*, was sentenced to death and shot by a firing squad. Marcel was sent to the concentration camp in Mauthausen in northern Austria, and when he was released at the liberation he weighed only thirty kilogrammes and was suffering from tuberculosis. He then stormed into a media career, more than ever a committed Communist.

Marcel Thomazeau became director of *L'Echo du Centre* in Limoges, then *Liberté* in Lille, and then finally the Communist newspaper *La Marseillaise*, where he stayed for twenty years and fell in love with the proletarian life of Marseille. Even in his old age, he would go down to the Vieux Port every morning to get his daily copy of *La Marseillaise*, reading everything from *les faits divers* to the football results. When he died at the age of 101, he was celebrated across the French media as a great *résistant* in every aspect of his life. I would have liked to have met Marcel, and I liked to imagine that it was his Luciferian energy, a passionate desire to create the world in words, which drove on his son François, with his non-stop output of novels, articles and histories.

The OM football team, François told me, is a fundamental part of the Marseillais identity, but the key to understanding the sense of defiance which marks that identity is the team's motto, '*On craint dégun*' – 'We fear no one'. 'The Marseillais mentality is to be against the rest of the world. Marseille was very violent in the 1980s and had lots of aggressive youth cultures: punks, skins, hard rockers, rockabillies.'

Thomazeau continued: 'That violence is also an energy. I'm still nostalgic for my own younger years, when my friends and I listened to two-tone music, soul music. There were mod groups in Marseille – the Papillons Noirs and the Imposters (who played in front of a Union Jack flag). It was a small scene, cool but not aggressive like some of the other groups. Marseille is a great city to be young in. It's an old city that has never become grand or distinguished. Instead, it feels not quite grown-up. It's always had that kind of adolescent edginess and energy.'

We had met specifically to talk about his remarkable book *Marseille: une biographie* (Marseille: A Biography), published in 2013. This book takes the form of an elaborate shaggy-dog tale, pitched almost as a detective novel and constructed out of elements of real life in the city. Thomazeau acknowledged freely that he had borrowed the title and the technique of the book from Peter Ackroyd and his magisterial *London: The Biography*. Like Ackroyd, Thomazeau believes that a city has a personality that is expressed in its history, food, architecture, politics, language. He also believes that this 'personality' is more than the sum of these distinctive characteristics, that the city is a singular living entity, hence the need for a 'biography', or indeed a psychological portrait, rather than a strictly chronological history.

It is also important how you tell the tale. Specifically, the Marseillais are notorious for their exaggerations. In 1914, Guillaume Apollinaire joked about the origins of Massalia in his book *La Fin de Babylone*. He describes the marriage of Gyptis, a local girl, and Protis, a Phocaean mariner – supposed to be the real founding moment of Massalia – as a drunken mistake, confirming the suspicion of the Marseillais and their tall stories. These exaggerations, or *galéjades* (the local term for a tall story, derived from the Provençal *galejado*), can be art forms in themselves, and the Marseillais will often take pleasure and pride in bending the truth as far as it can be bent, goading the non-Marseillais audience to disagree. Thomazeau said that he was proud of this tradition, which was a form of artful lying and an authentic literary method.

'The *galéjade* is a different way of looking at the world,' he said. 'It is a heightened perspective. When a Marseillais begins a *galéjade*, he starts to almost sing – the accent is stronger, the lilt of the voice more musical. It's like he's preparing his audience for the poetry, lies or nonsense to come. I love that you can hear the noise of the old language of Provence when this happens. Then, the Marseillais is transformed into a Gaulish bard or an African *griot* – a storyteller who finds the world more beautiful, or more ugly, than it really is. There are rappers in Marseille who still do this all the time.'

I told Thomazeau that I thought *Marseille: une biographie* was a *galéjade*. 'I take that as a compliment,' he said. 'My aim in this book was to try to understand the charisma of Marseille. Not all cities have that. But there is a singular atmosphere here that seems to cast a spell over people in a way they can't easily explain. It's like a form of magnetism. All Marseillais think that their city is special and unique, but no one can explain why. This is a city without monuments, with apparently no memory or at least no interest in the past, but I think that, actually, memories are all around us. And it's just a question of finding them. And for that, you need a technique. You need the *galéjade*. What better way to tell the story of Marseille?'

As a lifelong committed mod, Thomazeau has a self-declared fetish for detail – the right button or perfectly executed tie knot. (He can't help but tell the reader, for example, that during one of his sorties in *Marseille: une biographie*, he is wearing a Ben Sherman shirt, which marks him out for attention from the local '*minots*' from a nearby *cité*. '*Minot*', by the way, is an old Marseillais word meaning 'urchin', now used to describe kids in the *cités*: another detail.)

With a copy of Thomazeau's *Marseille* in hand, I explored the *quartier* of Saint-Marcel in the 11th arrondissement, where he was brought up, and which, he says, is a microcosm of the city's life and history. This *quartier* is eight kilometres inland of the Vieux Port, sheltered by the *massifs* of L'Etoile and Saint-Cyr, which form a frontier between Marseille and the rest of Provence. I found a relatively mixed population in terms of social class and ethnicity. Architecturally, it is composed of homely villas and *bastides*, as well as the mid- and high-rise blocks that make up the *cités*. The 11th is not nearly as dangerous as some other parts of Marseille, but the *cité* of Air-Bel is particularly well known for the occasional shooting and as a handy drugs supermarket for well-heeled citizens who don't fancy a trip to the more threatening *quartiers nord*.

The rest of the arrondissement is, however, a busy residential area, and in the more villagey parts are single-storey nineteenth-century villas with views of the sea from their living rooms and gardens which flank the roads. In his own walks around the 11th, Thomazeau is enchanted by the proximity of the busy workaday life and the totems of the city's history and civilization. These include the training ground of OM (not far from the Nike factory), a medieval castle, a mysterious chapel, the ruins of a great factory from the golden age of the Industrial Revolution, the Château de Forbin (once the seat of the noblest family in Provence and the burial site of Claude Forbin, who in the late seventeenth century was an admiral and a general to the King of Siam and probably the most venerated mariner in French history), a Vietnamese pagoda and run-down, crime-infested *cités*.

The place that fascinates Thomazeau most, however, is

l'Oppidum des Baou de Saint-Marcel, the ruins of an ancient Gaulish settlement dating back to before even the Phocaeans came here. Fantastically, he imagines Gaulish warriors and bards gazing over the training of OM, and all of this as part of a continuum, the long history of Marseille. Describing this image to me, he kept using the word 'telluric' – he explained that he imagines an electric current close to the surface of the earth which gives Marseille its magnetic power. 'This is, of course, all in my imagination,' he says. 'But that doesn't mean it's not true, at least for me.'

The Oppidum was once the home of a Celto-Ligurian tribe called the Segobrigii, mentioned by Aristotle and in the chronicles of the Gallo-Roman historian Pompeius Trogus. These were the people who, having turned their back on the sea, met and traded with the Phocaeans and sealed the marriage of Gyptis and Protis. The word '*baou*' ('*baus*' in Provençal) means a cliff or steep escarpment, and for the Segobrigii the *baou* was the perfect vantage point. If you can make the unpaved eight-hundred-metre climb to the top of the ridge, the view is a revelation. All of Marseille is at your feet.

The only other view that matches this in Marseille is the panorama from the esplanade of Notre-Dame de La Garde. Marseille is a huge, sprawling conurbation and is famously confusing to navigate. From this esplanade, however, it looks as if it all might make sense. On a clear day from this height, you can make out the mountains that ring the north, east and south of the city. You can make out, too, how its layout has been shaped around the Mediterranean, from the elegant Corniche to the Vieux Port.

At ground level, this world is confusing. Graffiti is everywhere in Marseille, not only in the tougher neighbourhoods but also in the well-heeled parts of town, and this sometimes makes it hard to work out exactly where you are. Recently, many of the younger inhabitants of 'Planète Mars' – the newish local nickname for the city coined by its fashionable youth, who call themselves Marsiens – have claimed that they thrive on the chaos, in this environment where nothing seems to have been properly planned.

For Thomazeau, this is one of the ways in which the city is able to guard its secrets. 'Marseille does not give its mysteries away easily,' he said. 'There are lots of invisible frontiers here. Everybody who lives here knows exactly where they are. For the outsider, it can be difficult.'

It can feel intimidating, too. I suggested that there were good reasons why some parts of the city, particularly the *quartiers nord*, were more feared than others. The current dangers in Marseille, Thomazeau pointed out, were down to the fact that the nature of crime had changed in the city. 'One of the problems is that Marseille has always been half in love with its criminal past,' he said. 'And this has blinded us to the new reality of the *quartiers nord* and what happens there.' In his biography of the city, Thomazeau speaks to a law-enforcement veteran he calls the 'Inspector', who concedes that even the twenty-first-century police have a nostalgic vision of the 'golden age' of the city's old-style mafias. In the nineteenth century, territory in Le Panier was fought over by rival gangs of '*nervis*'– a '*nervi*' (a Provençal word for 'muscle') being the Marseille equivalent of the Parisian '*apache*', a street thug with a swagger. Organized crime took over the city in the 1920s with the waves of Corsican and Italian immigration, along with the formation of '*clans*' according to where you came from and who you knew.

The big names were the Corsican Paul Carbone and the Italian François Spirito, who were in league with the corrupt and powerful politician Simon Sabiani, and their main activities were white slavery, prostitution, protection and the refinement of opium into heroin. These gangs also took over the territories of Montmartre and rue du Faubourg Montmartre in Paris, but their home turf was Marseille and the famous '*quartier réservé*' (sometimes called 'the Sinister Quarter' in English), which was to the north of the Vieux Port. (In Evelyn Waugh's *Decline and Fall*, this is where the unlucky Paul Pennyfeather has his hat stolen by a prostitute – this was actually a common occurrence in the *quartier réservé*, a way of luring unwary punters into a back room, where they could be drugged and robbed. In his diaries, Waugh called the rue Ventomargy, where he sets this scene, 'the toughest street in Europe'.) With their vendettas and Wild West shoot-outs in the bars of the Vieux Port, La Canebière and around the *opéra*, the gangs were famous and quickly became part of Marseille folklore, even as they continued to wield control while surviving successive dynasties and power struggles.

This all changed in the 1980s, when the economic infrastructure began to disintegrate and the large gangs broke up into factions and new constellations of rivalries. These are now mainly (but not exclusively) Algerian and Moroccan, or based on the geography of the *quartiers nord*, which have emerged as the new nexus of crime, almost entirely based on drugs. Now the *quartiers nord* are the fiefdom of drug lords, many from North Africa, who spend their money outside France on luxury villas in Morocco, Spain and Switzerland, leaving the city to their feuding foot soldiers. The police, blighted by corruption, are unable to reach the ringleaders, nor can they stop the internecine mini-wars breaking out between the gangs. Nothing seems able to break the dismal cycle. The situation has got even worse, Thomazeau explained, since newer and younger gangs had been challenging the established authority of the drug lords. These new gangs had no code or rules.

In recent years, the police have effectively been nothing more than bystanders to these gang wars. Worse still, for a long time, they have been exhausted and under-resourced, increasingly relying on counter-insurgency tactics, using assault rifles and stun grenades to deal with the gangs – but to little effect. The deputy mayor of Marseille, Samia Ghali, has repeatedly called for the army to be brought into the *quartiers nord*.

Thomazeau's rendezvous with the 'Inspector' often took place in the restaurant of Le Cercle des Nageurs, the private club which overlooks the Plage des Catalans. This has long been a meeting place for Marseille's literary and political elites, but is equally well known as a neutral zone where cops, ex-cops and criminals could meet, drink and eat together, and share information and gossip. The 'Inspector' also advised and helped Thomazeau with his crime novels ('*polars*' in French) about the Marseille underworld.

Thomazeau has been publishing these novels since the mid-1990s and is considered a leading light in the movement called '*polar marseillais*', perhaps second only to Jean-Claude Izzo (who died in 2000 at the age of fifty-four). Izzo's finest work is the so-called *Marseille Trilogy*, a cycle of novels that, reminiscent of James Ellroy's depiction of Los Angeles, document in detail the social and economic catastrophe of Marseille in the 1980s and 1990s, setting this disaster against the backdrop of its long and great history. The main character in his books is Fabio Montale, a son of Italian immigrants, who was brought up in Le Panier, moved to Belle de Mai (Thomazeau territory) and then lived in a *cabanon* (shack) by the sea in Les Goudes. Montale is, above all, a lover of Marseille, which he sees dying in front of his eyes. For this reason, Izzo's work has been called an 'urban tragedy'.

Thomazeau is less pessimistic about Marseille than Izzo. Then again, although they are roughly of the same generation, Thomazeau has lived on to see the city reinvent itself in the twenty-first century. This does not mean, however, for all the talk of a cultural and economic renaissance, that things have got better. They are just different now, he says.

This can be seen most clearly in the wildernesses of the *quartiers nord*, places which Thomazeau says have become alien to the old-style Marseille writer of *polars*. 'The crime that is happening there now is of a different magnitude to the old banditism,' he says. 'It is closer to warfare than anything else. To write about it now, you have to be more of a war correspondent, not just a writer. Not even a crime writer can make sense of it all.'

The areas known as the *quartiers nord* are the 13th, 14th, 15th and 16th arrondissements and sometimes parts of the 3rd arrondissement. They are an agglomeration of cheap concrete tower blocks built to house immigrants in the 1960s and 1970s and stand starkly out of place, wedged between the Mediterranean and the hills of Provence. The *quartiers nord* make up almost a third of the metropolitan space of Marseille and are considered one of the most dangerous and lawless parts of France. This is where Amine Kessaci, who is now twenty-one years old, has spent his whole life, knowing little else beyond school and gangs.

Amine was born and brought up in the *cité* of Frais-Vallon in the 13th arrondissement, one of the most notorious *cités* in the *quartiers nord*. At 5 a.m. on 29 December 2020, his life was 'blown apart', as he put it to me, when his brother Brahim, who was twenty-two years old, was found dead in the boot of a car in a side road near Pennes-Mirabeau, just off the Autoroute 55 to the north of Marseille. The car had been set on fire, and his remains were burned to a cinder. All that was left were charred bones and ashes. Brahim, who was a small-time drug dealer, had fallen victim to the latest fashionable method of execution in the drug wars – dismembering and then setting fire to victims. These blackened pieces of what was once a human being, now unidentifiable to the police, have sometimes been sent to the victim's family. This is known locally, with vicious black humour, as a '*barbecue*'.

The vogue for this form of execution began in 1999, when a *caïd* (Arabic slang for a gang leader) called Farid Berrahma decided to up the stakes in criminal sadism and killed twelve rivals in this way over the next few years. This soon earned him the grim nickname '*Le rôtisseur*' – 'the roaster'. By 2000, Berrahma was effectively in charge of every drug transaction that took place in the *quartiers nord*. He was shot dead in 2006 in a bar in the 13th arrondissement while watching a football match between Lyon and Milan. His legacy lives on, however, in the killing technique which he invented and has now become a grotesque speciality in the criminal underworld of Marseille.

The Kessaci family were devastated by their son's murder and his 'roasted' remains. Brahim was a rogue and criminal, but they were a respectable family – Amine's mother was a cleaner and his father a car mechanic – with no other links to criminality, as was the norm rather than the exception in their *cité* of Frais-Vallon. Despite the notorious violence of their *cité*, no one, Amine says, could have guessed that this would happen.

With his slightly chubby fresh-faced features, Amine Kessaci looks a good few years younger than his twenty-one years. When he speaks, he has an earnest and guileless manner, and in spite of the destruction he has seen and experienced in his young life, he even seems innocent, although perhaps this is shell shock. At school he had been hard-working and a lively and outspoken class delegate, often leading class protests at perceived injustices. He was also developing a political conscience and had marched with his father on demonstrations in support of '*sans-papiers*' – immigrants without papers. In the wake of his brother's death, he was determined to find a practical way out of his inner chaos and despair, and he threw all his energies into his organization, Conscience.

Amine set up this organization in July 2020 with a group of friends from the *quartiers nord*. They had no money, but with the help of local associations, they were able to finance a modest office in the 16th arrondissement, not far from where Brahim had been killed. The mission was simple: to provide support for ordinary local families whose sons and daughters had been caught up in the drug wars, and to point out relentlessly to everyone that they could be such families, and that all the inhabitants of the *quartiers nord* were victims of the casual everyday horrors of a part of France where republican order did not apply and which had been abandoned by the French state.

I first spoke to Amine Kessaci in the spring of 2023, when the drug wars were spinning wildly out of control, making national and international news. Already by May, eighteen people had been killed in *'règlements de compte'* ('settling of scores'). Worse still, the victims, and the perpetrators of the killings, were getting younger. In April, an eighteen-year-old had been charged with the murder of a fifteen-year-old and the attempted murder of two other teenagers, aged thirteen and fifteen. The violence was also spilling over into the city centre. In early April, a teenager had been shot dead in a fast-food restaurant on the rue Vincent Leblanc in the La Joliette district of Marseille. By the end of 2023, forty-nine people had been killed and 118 injured in gun violence. For the media, the really big, ongoing story was whether Marseille was about to become France's, or Europe's, first 'narco-city' – a city controlled by gangs and not the government.

Kessaci was dismissive of this headline and was more concerned with the way that the media persistently dehumanized the people of the *quartiers nord*. Obviously, there was a personal edge to this. He insisted that he could not accept the language used in the media to describe his brother's execution or the killing of others. These were not, he said, just *règlements de compte*, which could be explained away by the police and the press, giving a kind of dark glamour to the bandits, outlaws and murderers.

'My brother was assassinated,' Kessaci said to me, displaying a cold anger. 'I read in *La Provence* (the local newspaper) that what had happened was a "*barbecue* at Pennes Mirabeau",' he went on, 'but how can these journalists forget that we are human beings? That even my dead brother needs respect? We are not just a folkloric story. If you live in the *quartiers nord*, this is how you are treated. We are nothing but gangsters and drugs, the "homicide barbecue", and then easily washed away. They forget that we are real human beings and we suffer.'

Kessaci's campaign soon captured the imagination of Marseillais politicians and media outlets, and by September 2021 he was enough of a minor celebrity to be presented to President Emmanuel Macron when he made a two-hour visit to the *cité* of Bassens in the *quartiers nord*. That same year, Macron announced that he was sending in three hundred police officers from the Compagnies Républicaines de Sécurité – an elite force usually deployed for security and riot control – as reinforcements. Five hundred cameras were installed in the *cités* as part of a 150 million euro package to assist the local police. Macron claimed that helping Marseille was 'a duty of the nation'. Macron has long had a deep affection for Marseille. He is a passionate supporter of OM and is often seen wearing their colours. He claims to love the literature of the city, especially the writings of Jean Giono and Marcel Pagnol. Before taking power, when he was still Minister for the Economy, Macron said to a journalist from *Le Figaro* that his dream job was to be mayor of Marseille. 'I'm in love with Marseille,' he said, 'because I am in love with tragic Mediterranean cities. Everything is at the same time complex but possible.' When he became president in 2017, he spent his first holiday in Marseille, rather than at the official state residence at Brégançon. Macron's love for Marseille has not so far been reciprocated, however. At best, the local politicians treat him as an amateur from the north of France, a romantic who has become intoxicated with the southern sun but who can never understand the Mediterranean way of politics. At worst, he is yet another interfering Parisian, trying to control the uncontrollable.

During his visit to Bassens, Macron was booed and whistled at, but also applauded by the families who had lost their children to violence. Kessaci was their spokesman in a tactile exchange with the president, pleading with him to bring them back into the Republic. Amine told me that this was one of the great moments of his life. It gave him even greater faith in his mission, and in his many media appearances thereafter, Amine always appeared confident, assured and sure about his cause.

I tried to meet up with Kessaci again in the spring of 2024. By now, it was clear that Macron's initiative had not worked. The killings in the *quartiers nord* had intensified – there had been another four *barbecue*s by April, one of them of a twenty-six-year-old woman, whose 'roasted' corpse had been found in an abandoned building in the *cité* of Parc Corot. The apparently uncontrollable crisis in Marseille was now more than ever a national problem.

Kessaci was hard to get hold of. Sometimes he wouldn't answer the phone or texts, and then would send me a flurry of apologies, or he would get someone else to explain his unexplained disappearances. I had originally suggested that we meet his colleagues at the offices of Conscience and walk around the *cité* of Frais-Vallon. I told him that I had already visited the area and wanted to understand through his eyes the lives that people led there. I wanted to describe the quiet dignity with which they went about going to work, raising families, being ordinary.

He had agreed to this, then suddenly changed his mind at the last minute. He suggested meeting at Les Réformés, a chic rooftop cafe overlooking La Canebière and popular with the arty youth of Marseille. We arranged to meet at midday, but he didn't show up. This was the second time this had happened, and I was irritated. Later that day, I received an anonymous text telling me that he had been called to Nice and didn't know when he would be back. There would be no further explanation.

That evening, over a *pastis* in the Bar de la Paix, a tiny, homely place on the rue du Rouet, I expressed my frustration to a colleague who knew Kessaci quite well. As we talked and drank on the *terrasse*, a card game was setting up inside, led by a large, raucous middle-aged blonde woman in a green dress hitched up too high. The other players were all smoking and joking and talking football. My friend was a journalist whose speciality was French-speaking Africa and also knew the gang politics of the *quartiers nord*. I needed to hear her advice.

She told me to calm down. I wasn't the only journalist who was unable to pin Kessaci down. The likelihood was that he was under pressure. After the meeting with Macron, and all the publicity, he had started to voice big political ambitions, even joining the Green Party and putting himself forward as a candidate for the European Parliament. For this, Kessaci had been threatened with execution by the gangs, who thought he was bringing them trouble. His family were pariahs in Frais-Vallon – snitches, *harkis* and crybabies. Kessaci was out of his depth and frightened.

Even those who weren't part of the gang culture in Frais-Vallon were sick of him. He was seen in the *cité* as a '*profiteur du malheur*', someone who was making career capital out of misery. It all made sense now. To be seen with me, quite visibly an outsider and some kind of spy, would have been a provocation too far for the gangs. 'He is in much more danger in Frais-Vallon,' she said. She then explained: 'No one will kill a journalist, especially a foreign journalist, in the *quartiers nord*. That is as bad as, or worse than, killing a cop. The political scandal would be massive. The killer would never get out of prison, and his life inside would be hell – constant beatings, solitary confinement and other stuff. No gang would protect him.'

'It is actually *you* who are creating the danger for Amine,' she said, letting the accusation hang in the air. I suddenly now felt quite guilty about my own pursuit of this young, idealistic and dangerously naive young man.

I had been half-planning to go back to Frais-Vallon the next day. I hesitated for a moment, though, when my friend added, '*You* will not be murdered in the *quartiers nord*. On the other hand, if you carry on, you will probably be harmed. It'll either be a scooter accident or a bullet in the leg. Either way, you'll know straight away the moment when you're not welcome.'

Getting to the *quartiers nord* is easy – you can go there by bus, metro or taxi or on foot from the city centre in ten minutes. There is nothing of the physical separation between *centre-ville* and *banlieues*, with difficult transport and complicated road systems, that you find in other big French cities, particularly Paris and Lyon. When you are there, however, it takes time and patience to properly understand where you are at any given point and, probably most importantly, your assigned place in the complicated social ecosystem.

The first thing to know is that the various arrondissements of the *quartiers nord* are not all the same. The 13th arrondissement is, for example, a mixture of social housing from the 1960s and older, semi-rural 'villages' dating back to the nineteenth century. The roundabout of Bachaga-Boualem functions as a kind of checkpoint between the two styles of architecture – brutalist modern *cités* alongside quaint *résidences*, villas with gardens, churches – and two very different ways of life. North of the roundabout is in fact a quite desirable area with some high property prices and a mixed population of older inhabitants and newer incomers working in the media, academia or IT start-ups. To the south are the forbidding slabs of the *cités* of Malpassé, les Olives, La Croix-Rouge and Frais-Vallon, with all their poverty, unemployment and crime.

The 14th arrondissement is built upon the ruins of what was once a busy industrial district, where whatever vestiges of the Provençal countryside were swept aside by business and then immigration. This was most marked in the 1960s, when waves of Algerian Muslim immigrants came to Marseille after the Algerian War of Independence. There was at first nowhere to house these many thousands of people, and for years the area was dominated by massive shanty towns. Now the descendants of these first immigrants live in the housing estates of Les Flamants, La Busserine and Les Rosiers with newer incomers from the Antilles and sub-Saharan Africa. There has always been a strong, militant political presence here, an inheritance from the days when this was a Communist stronghold in the early twentieth century. These days, the politics is pluralist and postcolonial, finding its form in Radio Gazelle, the radio station which broadcasts exclusively about and for the *quartiers nord*, or Mam'Ega, a collective which tries to promote literacy and education, or the association Schebba, which with government support tries to promote jobs and businesses in the local area.

The 15th and 16th arrondissements both used to be part of the industrial complex and the fishing port of Marseille, but have now spread inland from the sea. They have a mixed population of North Africans, sub-Saharan Africans and what is left of the Italian, Corsican, Armenian, Spanish and Greek populations who came over the past hundred years or so. One of the particularities of the 16th arrondissement is the history of the shanty town of Campagne Fenouil, which was founded in the 1960s and 1970s by Roma families from Oran and Algiers. This population lived apart from their immigrant neighbours in terrible conditions and were outsiders in a city of outsiders, neglected by the city authorities and ignored by everyone else. The last shanty town, the encampment of Les Plombières, was cleared out by the police in 2014, but there are Roma families still here, living on the street or in improvised shelters that look like refugee camps in the Middle East – all of which should be a source of shame to a major European city.

For many of my visits to the *quartiers nord*, I had a local show me around, but sometimes I wanted to take in the place unmediated by the political opinions of my well-meaning guides. Even with some basic cultural knowledge of the area, it wasn't always easy to travel alone there. I tended to adopt habits I had learned on trips to the Shia-held *banlieue sud* of Beirut or the wilder suburbs of Algiers, two other fringes of a French-speaking metropolis. I would take a bus or taxi to a fixed destination and start walking. Keep moving, look as if you know where you're going, and show no curiosity about whatever you might see on the way.

Mostly, I saw ordinary people living ordinary lives. The *quartiers nord* are not a monolith. Rather, they are a patchwork of dozens of micro-societies which are not just defined by ethnicities – Algerian, Comorian, Moroccan, Senegalese and so on – but also bound together by roots in a village, region or language. Sometimes they collide, sometimes they interact, but a lot of the time they just ignore each other. This is partly a survival technique. Whatever trauma they have known, seen or lived through has to be buried as they go about their day. But the potential for trouble and the daily reality of the drugs trade are apparent everywhere. Sometimes I was watched by *choufs*, who were easily identifiable, either perched on high balconies or loafing at the foot of a building, seated on a deckchair shaded by a sun umbrella – a grim parody of the French Riviera lifestyle – smoking dope and listening to music. I stayed away from the tower block fortresses, where 'business' was taking place. Sometimes I would come across obvious signs of the drugs trade in the streets – a group of dealers loitering, flanked by their emissaries on bikes and on scooters, or a gaudily scribbled 'menu' posted on a wall or cafe window offering hash or cocaine at competitive prices (beginning with '*shit*' and '*beuh*', varieties of hash, at 50 euros, going up to 80 or 150 euros for a taste of cocaine).

The criminal world of the *quartiers nord* is a model of successful capitalist economics. Over the past few decades, the drugs trade in Marseille has grown far bigger than anyone could have guessed or predicted, even the most ambitious drug lord. This is partly due to the globalization of the trade – like any other capitalist commodity in the twenty-first century, drugs know no national borders and are drawn to the largest markets. Marseille is a hub because it is a gateway not only to France but to the whole of Europe, and a confluence of geopolitical factors has made Marseille a trading centre for drugs from countries like Pakistan, Iran and Afghanistan, as well as the more traditional territories of the Eastern Mediterranean. In the *quartiers nord*, there are at any time roughly 130 different gangs fighting over these markets at ground level. This is capitalism in its purest form – a series of forever wars against your competitors and enemies.

Quite aside from the horror of the individual murders and the impact on their families and the community, this was a far cry from the image of Marseille the authorities wanted to convey. Since 2013, when it was crowned as a European Capital of Culture, Marseille has been on a mission to rebrand itself as the 'Barcelona of France', a second city with its own unique and vibrant culture centred on art, football, tourism and good weather. La Joliette, the former docklands of Marseille, was one of the flagships of this mission, redesigned as a new arts and business area at an estimated cost of nine billion euros. It was a commercial and architectural statement intended to show a new side to the city, that it could shed its crime-soaked reputation of the past.

Over ten years ago, in April 2012, I had met Julie Chénot, the woman who had the daunting job as overall leader of the 2013 Year of Culture. On a lovely bright afternoon, we drank coffee in her office in the Maison Diamantée, the beautifully restored mansion from the sixteenth century overlooking the Vieux Port, and talked about the challenges she faced. She was brittle and fidgety, but open and realistic about what could really be achieved.

'Marseille is unique,' she said, 'but not always in a good way. We are promoting the city's culture, but the problem is that crime has always been part of the culture here, and we cannot deny that. We are not the police, so we can't control the crime here either. All we can do is hope that one day, Marseille will be known for other things that are good here – the food, the mix of people, the sea. But we can't pretend that it's perfect, or that we don't know how bad it can be.'

This seemed to me to be an unusually gloomy perspective from someone who was supposed to be the city's chief cheerleader. But then Julie lived in Paris and only commuted here for the job. I also sensed from her glum demeanour that she didn't like Marseille very much and that this was a job being done in bad faith. This has traditionally been one of the political stumbling blocks for Parisians who are sent to Marseille, whether in civic administration, business or law-keeping. Not only do they often lack a feel for the city, but deep down they actually don't like it. And if you don't like Marseille, or can't understand it because you are an outsider, you are always going to feel that whatever you do is hopeless.

By many criteria, Marseille's year as a European Capital of Culture was a success. There were events and exhibitions, the Mucem was unveiled, tourism and investment flowed back into the city. But there were dissidents from the official line. Notably, the inhabitants of the poorer districts, including the *quartiers nord*, felt pushed out of the celebrations and ignored. The culture on show was mainly high culture – there were few rap performances, for example, despite the city's massive scene – and little or no acknowledgement of Marseille's status as the unofficial capital of the French working class. Yet again, many Marseillais argued that the dead centralizing control of Paris was neutering the real life of Marseille. There were two versions of the city facing in opposite directions: the *bourgeois* fantasy of Marseille as a chic, Mediterranean destination like any other on the south coast, and the reality of a criminal microsociety which was not only riven with its own civil wars, but seemingly also at war with France and the rules and norms of civilized European society.

Looking back now, the 2013 Year of Culture was a chimera. Marseille is now tougher than ever. On my most recent visit to the *quartiers nord* in spring 2024, I was reliably informed that the price of a Kalashnikov – known as *'un kala'* – imported from the Balkans was 350 euros, and 500 euros ready-loaded with ammunition. The same source – a young lad from the 13th arrondissement who drove me around his home area in his taxi, cheerfully pointing out which gangs control which *cité* – told me that one reason why the *quartiers nord* were relatively quiet during the summer riots of 2023, which had convulsed many other parts of France, was because the drug gangs had no interest in stirring up trouble and disturbing business. They were not political in any way. But he went on to say that there were so many weapons in the *quartiers nord* that if the gangs had wanted to launch a real war against the police, they would have won it. 'The police are outgunned and they know that.' The gangs also kept the Islamists in line, which also explained why Marseille has seen so little of the Islamist radicalism present elsewhere in France. 'The *intégristes* (Islamists) don't dare fuck with the gangs,' he said. 'They know who is in control.'

That spring, I walked deep into the *quartier* called Saint-Mauront, wandering in zigzag fashion between Gare Saint-Charles and the sea. This is a historic district and from the 1860s onwards was the home of successive waves of Italian immigrants employed in the local tobacco factories. You can sense this history in the street names – rue François Barbini, rue Spinelli. When the Italians moved on, North Africans moved in. Now the neighbourhood has a large African population from the sub-Saharan countries, and it is officially one of the poorest parts of France.

According to propaganda from the *mairie* de Marseille, the area is gentrifying and the worst habitations are being destroyed or renovated. But you can still feel the poverty, see it in the broken pavements and smell it in the dank corridors between apartment blocks. The public services are abysmal. As I walked around, the streets stank of uncollected rubbish in the high heat of a May afternoon. I had heard on the radio that the local schools were infested with rats and cockroaches. At the end of April, just before I had arrived in Marseille, it was reported in *La Provence* that one tower block had no running water for five days. The real danger here is not so much from crime as from circumstance: being stuck, as an immigrant or unemployed or just poor, in a bad life that you can't get out of.

On another blazing afternoon, I met with Philippe Pujol, a slim and bearded forty-nine-year-old writer, journalist and film-maker, in the Café Saint-Victor, where he is a regular. The cafe is a homely place in the 7th arrondissement of Marseille, near where he lives. He likes the area because it has a mix of Italian and Corsican immigrants. He is proud of being half-Corsican (and half-Catalan) and told me that the informal name for this *quartier* is 'Endoume', which in Corsican means 'Chez Dominique', in other words, to be at home. (This isn't strictly true: 'Endoume' is in fact Provençal and has been since the twelfth century, a reference to the domed architecture of the port. I put it down as another Marseillais *galéjade*.)

One way or another, Pujol has been involved with the *quartiers nord* for all of his life. He was brought up in Saint-Mauront in the rue de Crimée in the 3rd arrondissement and was intimate as a child and then a young adult with the secretive underground criminality of the place. Pujol worked hard as a student, finally obtaining a master's degree in biology, planning a career in eco-studies. He discovered his true vocation, however, when he went to work as a trainee for *La Marseillaise* newspaper. He was originally assigned to cover *les faits divers*, and very quickly he found himself drawn to the *quartiers nord*, where most of the crime in the city was happening. His work brought him into contact with the police, and his local knowledge earned him the trust of the gangs, so with his feet in two very separate camps, he soon developed a sense of what was really happening in Marseille. Eventually, some of his articles were published in Le Monde as a series called '*les quartiers shit*'. This series stunned French readers, uncovering a France which they either did not know existed or struggled to understand beyond the televisual clichés of hoodies, rappers, gangs and guns. (Bracingly, Pujol tells me he detests rap music for selling the *banlieue*'s worst clichés back to itself.)

That day, Pujol was crackling with nervous energy. Over Diet Coke and coffee, he talked almost non-stop for four hours, one story crashing into another – they were alternately very funny or horrifying – and falling over himself as he changed his analysis of a given situation. He was also very good at telling stories against himself.

He told me how once, while he'd been waiting to meet the boss of a gang who was late, he'd been mistaken by a gang of fifteen or so armed youths in the *quartier* of Félix-Pyat for the boss of another gang. Scared to tell them who he really was, he fronted it out for ten hard minutes as they surrounded him in the wrecked lobby of a tower block. The gang were suspicious and Pujol was getting tenser every second as his tough-guy acting skills were put to the test. When the real boss arrived, Pujol swaggered towards him, swearing fluently in the slang of the *cités*, still playing his role. The boss looked at him, puzzled: 'So you're a real gangster now?' he said. 'I thought you were just an asshole.' Suddenly, laughter broke the tension. Pujol said that he'd been sweating, his heart beating, and he'd felt like fainting. That was the most terrified he'd ever been in the *quartiers nord*.

Pujol spoke so fast because he had witnessed so much, and knew so much, that he simply could not contain it all. Trauma can do this to people, but he said that trauma had not touched him, and I thought that this was true. None of the stories he told seemed to trouble him. It struck me that in another life he would have made a good professional soldier – detached, emotionless, there to do a job. 'I cannot let what I have seen and what I know in the *quartiers nord* affect me,' he said. 'I feel that I have sometimes voyaged outside civilization. I am like an explorer in unknown lands. But it's not for me to make judgements about how people live there. I can return to my wife and family and value the beauty of ordinary life. This is because I have so often seen its opposite.

'You have to remember,' he said, 'that, like me, the *voyou* (gangster) lives in two realities. On the one hand, he is a hard man, or has to pretend to be to his comrades. So he is callous, indifferent to human life, cruel, sadistic. This is what the baby gangsters see and what they try to imitate, so that is why they are now shooting each other instead of just fighting it out. But most of them are not psychopaths. They are husbands, boyfriends, sons, brothers, fathers. That's how I manage to communicate with them. I always focus on the individual. I think that's something I learned by working for a Communist newspaper. The ethic there was always that these people are part of the class system, even if they are criminals. There is no great psychology. You just have to understand that the gangsters are working in a bigger social and historical context. They are victims, too. They are not in control, although they always think they are. This is how you can usually find some humanity even in the toughest characters.'

Pujol gave the example of Farid Berrahma, the sadist who had invented the 'homicide *barbecue*'. 'Berrahma was bad, there is no doubt about it,' Pujol said. 'He did evil things. But he was also very scared. He had been diagnosed with cancer at the age of seventeen and was convinced that he would die at any moment. He didn't want to die. One way of conquering this fear was the adrenaline rush that came with running a gang, fooling the police, and then taking it to the next level by killing his enemies in the most atrocious way. It's perverted, but there is a logic there. Most of the gangsters I know, especially the most powerful ones, are very logical.'

I asked Pujol how he coped with the dangers of his work. 'I don't know,' he replied, 'except that I understand how the *voyous* work and how they communicate with you. They are always very direct with their messages. Very black and white. One of my most difficult moments was when a *caïd* had decided that I had given too much detail about what he looked like in my description of a drug deal, and that this was why he had been picked up by the police. So I got the phone call – "I see you've got children. Children are very important." And that was it! I had a police guard on my house for a month. This is not a good thing because it makes the gangs think that you are in league with the police, that you can't be trusted. But I had to do it. I wasn't personally scared, but with your family it's different. A month or so later, I heard that the guy had been shot dead. I don't take pleasure in anyone's death but I admit I was relieved, actually yes, I was pleased. So where does that leave me morally? Am I as bad as them?'

This was not the gritty glamour of *The French Connection* but rather a description of a secular hell, a Hobbesian world of endless conflict, struggle, brutality, disorder, with everyone pitted against everyone else and with no way out other than prison or death. For this reason, Pujol seemed to be a very moral writer describing an amoral world.

He seemed pleased with this. 'Like George Orwell, I just try and describe the way things are as plainly and as accurately as I can,' he said. 'I am not trying to make a case for social justice. That is for other people. Anyway, I am not sure that the problems of the *quartiers nord* can be explained away by a simple lack of resources or money. There are bigger forces here, a globalized drugs trade and so on. There is plenty of money here, of course, but it is all in the hands of the wrong people: the *voyous* and their bosses.'

His other literary model was Louis-Ferdinand Céline, whom he admires for his deeply sympathetic writing about the poor. Céline is a writer whose reputation has been understandably tarnished by having been pro-Hitler, pro-Nazi and deliriously antisemitic. He also hated Marseille. Céline passed through the city for the first time on his way to a colonial posting in Cameroon. In a 1942 letter to his friend Henri Poulain, he complained bitterly about Marseille's many Africans and Arabs, and especially about the Jews. For all of his hatred, Céline, who had been a doctor working in the most wretched slums of northern Paris, could be a strangely compassionate writer. He despised French colonialism and wrote with sympathy for France's colonial subjects. He also hated capitalism – an 'Anglo-Saxon' and Jewish invention – and had a deep feeling for the poor and damaged lives of his patients and the way they suffered at the substratum of the French class hierarchy. His two great novels of the 1930s, *Voyage au bout de la nuit* (*Journey to the End of the Night*) and *Mort à crédit* (*Death on the Installment Plan*), described how it was to live at the very bottom of French society. Céline also turned the voices of these abject lives into poetry, creating a new literary vernacular born out of the authentic language of the French sub-proletariat.

'Céline understood the two meanings of the word "*misère*" [literally "misery" in French],' said Pujol. 'First of all, it means poverty in the fiscal sense. It means to have nothing. But it also has a religious sense. We learn in school about what Pascal calls "*La misère de l'homme sans Dieu*" ["The wretchedness of man without God"]. This is to live without meaning or morality, and this is a kind of hell. It is also a condition that allows men to be evil, to perform evil acts. That is what I have seen in the *quartiers nord*. It goes beyond politics.'

Whether it is a political or a moral problem, Pujol argued that Marseille cannot be understood in isolation from the rest of France. For all that the Marseillais like to think of themselves as unique and separate, the problems of the *quartiers nord* are part of a national picture. In his book *La fabrique du monstre*, Pujol wrote that the badlands of Marseille function as 'a kind of safety valve to release the dangerous pressure of the repressed problems of France as a whole'. For all the rhetoric that blames the non-French, outsiders or immigrants for the present chaos, this is a home-grown 'Frankenstein's monster'. The *quartiers nord* may magnify its social divisions, making them grotesque and frightening, but they are nonetheless rooted in the fundamental contradictions of a society which aspires to a totalizing civilization but contains within itself the uncontrollable forces of anti-civilization. These places have been made by French history; they are part of Marseille's long colonial history. As Emmanuel Macron pointed out when he spoke of 'a duty to the nation', the French government cannot turn its back on the *quartiers nord*. France has a responsibility not only to the people who live there, but to mainstream society, who feel threatened by their existence. How can a 'concordance' be found between these two worlds? Maybe it is impossible, and this is part of the 'tragic' nature of Marseille in the twenty-first century.

Wearily, at the end of *La fabrique du monstre*, Pujol writes: 'The prettiest city in France does not hide its wounds. It is sincere. That's all. This city is merely the visible illustration of the defects of the French Republic.'[5]

There are parts of Marseille which are not just 'pretty', as Philippe Pujol puts it, but which are in fact quite beautiful, sometimes magnificently so. One of my favourite journeys in Marseille, or indeed anywhere in the world, is to take the 83 bus from the Vieux Port to the Plages du Prado. The bus, first of all, heaves you along the boulevard Charles Livon to the Pharo Palace, leaving as a backdrop the basin of the Vieux Port, crowded with small boats and jetties and which looks all the more like a stage set as you rise towards the Corniche. The bus turns left at the Plage des Catalans, which is where you will first see the now wide expanse of sea. This is where you will also glimpse the first islands which pepper the coastline – Frioul, Riou and the island fortress of Le Château d'If, where Dumas's hero Edmond Dantès was cruelly imprisoned and learned to become 'the Count of Monte Cristo'.

The Plage des Catalans is always lively, and it's worth getting off here for a half hour to sit at the *terrasse* of the Café Bikini, drink an Orangina, beer or *pastis*, and catch the movement and life of the *plage*, which begins with the early swimmers at first light. If you want to get away from the crowds on the beach, you can slink off to an adjacent mini-cove of rock and concrete, separate from the beach, where there is no irritating volleyball with its noisy crashes, smacks and grunts. This is where young North African men loll and smoke dope, staring wordlessly out at the crashing waves.

Philippe Pujol told me of a thought experiment he once did with these stoned young men. Smoking with them, he asked what visions they had and what they saw when they looked out at the waves, the islands and the clouds, offering up to them that his own thoughts turned to landscapes, hills, mountains and nature. Unanimously, the young men, apparently lost in a *beuh*-irrigated reverie, saw only '*kalas*', naked girls and their breasts and behinds. 'Guns, tits and ass, that's all they saw,' he said to me, laughing. 'I suppose that's what the *quartiers nord* do to you. Life is always reduced to its bare essentials.'

If you stay on the bus, you will follow the Corniche, which is one of the most elegant roads in France and has some of its most expensive properties. There are ordinary dwellings here too – *cabanons* in the inlets, a mixture of houses and apartments in all architectural styles. Each *anse* (cove) or *vallon* (narrow valley) has a bus stop and, with its fishing boats and gaily painted cottages giving directly onto the sea, is a mini-neighbourhood separate from the rest of the city. This is where

Izzo's Fabio Montale had a *cabanon* halfway to Cassis, the ideal hideaway for a melancholy policeman who needs to escape human wickedness and reconnect with nature. Most impressive, however, are the grand villas and their gardens on your left-hand side, most dating back to the nineteenth century. Every time I pass this way I try to imagine what it must be like to wake up every day to one of the most glorious views in Europe, to gardens of elegantly trimmed flora – peach trees, bougainvillea, lavender, cycads, papyrus, laurels, olive groves and palm trees – all guarded by the grey, green and white *massif* of the Marseilleveyre, the small steep mountain which announces Corsica and Italy, and then the azure sea glittering all the way to the horizon.

And yet, not far from the Corniche, twenty minutes by bus and in the commercial centre of Marseille, there are buildings so rotten they are unsafe to live in. On 8 April 2023, two apartment buildings exploded and a third crumbled in flames on the rue de Tivoli in the 5th arrondissement, a pleasant part of the city with a large student population. Eight people were killed. The leading theory is that it was a gas explosion, but the actual cause is still unexplained. There were rumours of deliberate avoidance of housing regulations, neglect of basic safety protocols, wretchedly antique plumbing and electrical systems, backhanders to the city authorities, even simply greedy landlords wanting to get rid of tenants they didn't like by murdering them.

This wasn't the first such incident. On 5 November 2018 on the rue d'Aubagne in Noailles, another neighbourhood in the city centre, two buildings collapsed without warning. Eight people were killed here too, and over the months that followed, nearly five thousand people in the surrounding area were evacuated from buildings thought to be at risk of falling down. Some locals called it Marseille's Grenfell Tower moment – a reference to the terrible fire at the London tower block in 2017, when residents mainly from immigrant backgrounds perished as a result of poor construction and civic neglect in full view of the rest of society.

Noailles is the kind of place where it's hard to avoid falling into conversation when you sit at a cafe *terrasse*. One afternoon at the Café la Muse, I spoke to Ibrahim, a fifty-something local Senegalese who had been here on the day the buildings collapsed. 'It was terrifying,' he said. 'I thought it was an earthquake. We didn't know what was happening.' Ibrahim has lived and worked in this district for most of his life and loves it, but he knows it is falling apart. He puts it down to corruption and, perhaps, racism on the part of the town hall. 'The people who live here are poor. Some of them are immigrants who have no papers. They don't officially exist. Why should the government care?' Ibrahim had been in France for thirty years or so but was still dubious and unclear about his official status. This was not something I intended to pursue – I didn't want to make him nervous or think that I was a cop – but he himself brought it up when he said, 'It's easy to forget us, to forget whether we live or die.'

The *quartier* of Noailles is one of the oldest in Marseille, dating back to the seventeenth century, when it was inhabited by wealthy *bourgeoisie*, who funded the building of grand *hôtel particuliers*, some of which are still here but now decrepit. However, most of the architecture dates back to the nineteenth century, when the area was busy with banks, traders, import–exporters, a labour exchange and a huge food market, which served as *le ventre de Marseille* (the stomach of Marseille), all connected with a new train station at the Gare de Noailles. Visitors to the Grand Hôtel de Noailles included Richard Wagner, Guy de Maupassant and the Duke of Edinburgh.

The pioneering investigative journalist Albert Londres (a hero of François Thomazeau) was here in the 1920s as Noailles became a *quartier* of immigrants from all corners of the French Empire. Londres's style was to hand over journalistic authority to his subjects whenever he could, always favouring the oppressed or dispossessed. Well ahead of his time, Londres's writing about Marseille makes the reader sense the savage, chaotic and poetic life of the city and why it stands apart from the rest of France. In an essay called 'The Hundred Faces of Marseille', he takes the reader's elbow, leading them on a detour to the rue des Chapeliers at the bottom end of Noailles. 'This is the perfume of the Orient,' writes Londres, 'the odour of an old candle frying and melting on a stove. There you'll find sheep hanging with old buttocks and strung up by their heels. The *sidis* coming back to the casbah from work at the port. Give way and don't speak to the women if you don't want a fight. This is Arab territory. You're in Sfax, Rabat or the ghetto of Oran. There's nothing missing: the Turkish coffee brewing on the stove, candles hanging from the ceilings, the unhealthy but alluring penumbra of Mediterranean cities. And their fleas! If the government, for once properly understanding the needs of the homeland, made me the governor of Algeria, I would not go to Algiers, but settle here in rue des Chapeliers.'[6]

The poetic landscape that Londres describes persists, if you want it to, and it explains why Noailles is such a compelling destination. Turning away from La Canebière into Noailles at the rue du Marché des Capucins is like leaving France. The scene is mostly a North African *souk*, although there is also a strong West African presence, interlaced with the cafe *terrasses* and boulangeries of a traditional French *quartier populaire*. This is surely what colonial Algiers, with its intermingled working-class *pied-noir* and Muslim populations, must have looked like in the 1930s, when Europeans and Muslims mixed in the city. This is the world captured in the opening scenes of Julien Duvivier's 1937 film *Pépé le Moko*, which famously begins with a montage of the Mediterranean races raffishly at home in the cramped streets of the casbah. You can leave France in just the same way in the *quartiers* of Barbès in Paris or La Guillotière in Lyon, but it makes more sense here. You are already a long way south, and Africa is less than a day away by ferry.

Noailles may be picturesque but it is also impoverished. Philippe Pujol does not know exactly when what he calls the 'pauperization' of Noailles began, but he told me he has never known Noailles as anything other than a slum. In his 2019 book, *La chute du Monstre*, he evokes the bleak daily lives of those who wash up here, often fleeing dreadful conditions back home, and sees only *la misère* (misery and poverty). He writes with 'anger, even rage' about the horror of the collapsing houses and those who lost their lives, and points the finger of blame directly at the city government. It could have been avoided a long time ago, he says. But it wasn't and it was therefore bound to happen. Everybody now is just waiting for the next time.

Professor Kenneth L. Brown, who is eighty-eight years old and a renowned scholar of the Mediterranean, has lived at 47 rue d'Aubagne for the best part of a decade. On the day that his street collapsed, he was at the local airport of Marignane, returning from a trip to England. He was told of the unfolding disaster by an official at the airport, a friend, and rushed home perplexed and in a panic. 'I didn't know what to expect,' he said. 'I was in shock. When I got back here, it was devastating. A scene from a nightmare.' Ken didn't yet know that people had been killed. When the news came through a few hours later, it was a double blow. 'My own house was safe,' he said, 'and I wasn't scared. But my neighbours were dead. I still can't register that.'

Ken told me all of this on the back *terrasse* of his own apartment, his favoured spot for tea, dinners and long, fierce and convoluted conversations. 'Just like Naples, huh?' Ken growled in welcome, as I sat down at a long table overlooking a mini-panorama of back alleys, the faded rear ends of buildings, and washing hung out to dry. Yes, it is exactly like that, I thought, with all the bad-dream-like dread and claustrophobia I always associate with the back alleys of Naples.

'Living here is like living next to Vesuvius,' Ken said, which is what he really meant by the reference to Naples. 'We can't know from one day to the next whether we will survive the environment. The difference, though, is that Vesuvius was made by God or nature. This place was made by capitalists, and they are the ones who really couldn't care less about human beings.'

This was only the second time I had met Ken Brown, having been introduced in late October 2023 at a *soirée* organized by my friend Mary Fitzgerald, a former correspondent for the Middle East, who has an old but stylish apartment near the Vieux Port, where she loves to entertain *'le tout Marseille'*: writers, publishers, artists, journalists, politicians and diplomats. When I arrived, she told me she had invited Ken Brown, describing him as 'a salty sea-dog Hemingway character'. I had heard of him while still an undergraduate in the mid-1980s and I became an avid reader of his journal *Mediterraneans*, an intellectually ambitious project in which he commissioned work from Orhan Pamuk, Edmund White and John Berger among others. I told him that I had been a fan of his work for the past forty years. He wasn't bothered but gruffly agreed to meet me on my next trip to Marseille to discuss my work and his. This was how I ended up in mid-April 2024, seated at the long table on the *terrasse* of his apartment. Inside, there were books in several languages and alphabets everywhere. These were punctuated by mementoes of Ken's travels: pottery, small statues and figurines, postcards and photos. There was a large vinyl collection, and in the centre of the living room, a large table supported two computers, both switched on, in action and surrounded by notebooks and scribbled manuscripts. This was evidently the intellectual engine room of the apartment, still busy and humming away. One of Ken's friends, the sociologist William Kornblum, described Ken as the 'scholar-poet of the rue d'Aubagne'.[7] I also thought there was something of Walt

Whitman about him – not just that he was fiercely bearded and with a steely glint in his eye, but also that he embraced without question the totality and complexity of the world.

Ken is blunt and crafty in conversation, and unforgiving in argument. I didn't agree with much that he said, and I preferred to let him talk. We spoke about his upbringing in a secular Jewish family, his engagement with Islamic studies, and then his long and very politicized odyssey through the Arab world, beginning in the Palestinian territories, then through Egypt, Libya, Tunisia, Algeria, to Morocco: first to Tangier, where he mixed with Paul Bowles and William Burroughs ('typical American assholes'), before settling for a while in the hills above Agadir, where he learned Berber (properly called 'Amazight') and translated Berber poetry into English at a time when the Berber language was still banned in Morocco.

We talked about Marseille. For Ken, the city was the logical end point of his travels through the Arab world, although he insisted that he had no intention of checking out in the near future. 'I'm not going anywhere,' he said with an ironic grin, 'and I ain't leaving this place soon either.' All of the Arab world was in Marseille, from the Eastern Mediterranean to the western tip of the Mahgreb ('the West' in Arabic). Ken had spent his life as a student of the Arab mind, and here in Noailles he had found the perfect distillation of its Arabic essence, a blend of Muslim cultures which lived together if not always in harmony then in reasonable tranquillity. 'Marseille is a rare place,' he said. 'It is part of France, always was and always will be, but there is also something else here. You don't have to be in France if you don't want to be, or if you don't feel you belong there. In Marseille, you can live any way you want and the city is still yours.'

I wondered if, in the story of the shattered houses of the rue d'Aubagne, there might be some kind of useful metaphor for the splintered state of French society in the twenty-first century. This was, after all, literally France in fragments, structures left to rot and collapsing from within. People like Alain Finkielkraut took this one step further and talked of the 'Lebanonization' of France, a society disintegrating into warring factions with no common interest. Ken winced. He was having none of this. 'That's too easy to say,' he said. 'What happened here in the rue d'Aubagne was straightforward. The money people who own the place, who own Marseille, don't care who lives here. And they don't care if they die, or how they die, as long as they don't have to see it. It's like any poor shithole with poor people in the Middle East or Africa, except it's in France, in Marseille. Nothing to do with any social theory. It's just about people.'

Ken chastised me for my interest in the *quartiers nord*. 'You and that guy – what's his name? Pujol? – you're both way off beam with all that stuff. That's just gangsters. Why are they so interesting?' I tried to point out that it was more than that, that the *quartiers nord* were like a state within a state and that this was a danger to France. Ken had never been to the *quartiers nord*. Why should he? Drugs and gangs were problems for Western culture, created by Western civilization. This was of no interest to Ken, whose lifelong passion was the study of the East.

Ken scorned 'orientalists' (I suspected that he thought that I was one). He used the term with contempt and was faithful to Edward Said's definition of an 'orientalist' as a kind of vampire, draining the 'Orient' of its lifeblood and reducing it to a weak, powerless fantasy or parody of its real life and, as such, easily controlled and dominated by Western colonial forces. This is, however, only a recent and very reductive definition of the 'orientalist'. More to the point, this is to ignore the long tradition of Western scholars of the Orient, dating back to antiquity, who have sought only knowledge from the East, albeit in refracted or partial form.

Whether he likes it or not, Ken Brown is very much in this older tradition. William Kornblum has compared him to Nicolas-Claude Fabri de Peiresc, the seventeenth-century geographer, astronomer, man of letters, and collector. Merchants and diplomats looked to Peiresc for information about trade routes, wars and piracy across the Mediterranean world. Without leaving Provence, Peiresc established a network that brought him gossip, rumours and news from sailors, traders, missionaries and sometimes philosophers and alchemists. For Peiresc, Marseille was a place where you could travel a long way without ever leaving the city. From his lair in the rue d'Aubagne, via the miracle of the internet, Professor Ken Brown operates in much the same way: an exile, outsider and expatriate in France, but in Marseille an invisible spectator of a wider and deeper Oriental world.

The evening after my chat with Ken, I wandered around Noailles, as I had so often done before, looking for a decent restaurant. I finally settled at a Moroccan place called La Fabrique on the Place Jules Verne. The meal was simple: grilled, herby *koftes*, long strips of spiced sweet potato, a crunchy salad, and a home-baked baguette in the old-fashioned style, which seems to have faded out in France about twenty years ago. (The old-style baguette has been replaced by the fashionable '*traditionelle*', which is supposed to be 'artisanal' but is most often chewy and tasteless. I don't know why French people don't complain about this more.)

This was the best meal I had eaten in Marseille for a long time. The city is famous, of course, for its fish soup, *bouillabaisse*, which I have always found to be a sour and venomous dish made out of spiky or slimy monsters of the deep. I reserve for '*pieds et paquets*', the other totemic meal of Marseille, the same disgust I have for *andouillette*. It is basically slow-cooked sheep's feet and tripe, and tastes how you might imagine that to taste. At La Fabrique, I devoured my uncomplicated meal and surveyed the scene from the cafe *terrasse*.

There were clearly two visible realities in Noailles. One was the homely, busy life of the cafe owners, shopkeepers, shoppers, even the dealers in *trabendo* (illegal contraband, usually cigarettes or other stolen stuff) at the street corners. This was a mini-society with its own hierarchies and structures, solid and reassuring, and I could see how Ken Brown could feel at home here. But there was also severe poverty and neglect and accumulated street filth. Just above the Place Jules Verne, heading to Place 9 Novembre, the smell of shit is met by the stench of cheap spirits and the sour beers with eleven per cent strength of the local street drinkers, sprawled out in cosy enclaves against the bins and trash. Here, the low-level street dealers are jumpy and twitchy, as if plugged into some invisible voltage.

These two realities do not quite meet each other, which creates a tension. This, I reflected at La Fabrique, is perhaps one of the factors that helps give Marseille its electricity, created out of its impossible contradictions – the endless interplay between beauty and brutality. Walter Benjamin, under the influence of hashish in Marseille, remarked that the city provoked in him a sense of 'primitive sharpness' not to be found in Paris.[8] This feeling is real and one of the reasons that those who love the city, as I do, appreciate it so much.

For others who actively dislike Marseille, these contradictions are a permanent irritant at best, and at worst insurmountable obstacles to social and economic development. Most of all, for the city's enemies, Marseille is too full of proles, immigrants and crime. Corruption is everywhere and as corrosive as it is all-pervasive: it is both physical – Marseille has always had a problem with its '*ordures*' and its detritus, and is regularly described as 'the filthiest city in France' – and moral. At every turn in the city, at the most visible level of the street, order is always undercut by disorder. It is easy to see why Marseille has earned itself the sobriquet of 'Wicked City'.

This description first properly entered the popular imagination in 1949, when it was used as the English-language title of a film known in French as *Hans le Marin*, based on the 1929 novel of the same name by Edouard Peisson. Both the film and the novel tell the story of Hans Muller, a marooned American sailor who falls in with a prostitute, Marcelle, who tricks him into getting beaten up and robbed. After various adventures among the lowest of the low life in Marseille, Hans finds her, kills her in revenge, and sets off for Paris. It is the perfect Marseillais fable of how the corrupt city will finally corrupt anyone.

The same theme persists today in the music, art and literature of Marseille. One recent example is the 1990s Raï music hit '*Seknet Marseille*' ('Marseille, the Siren') by Chaba Zohra, which tells of a young Algerian woman fatally seduced by the 'mad city'. A more recent example is the hit Netflix series *Marseille*, starring Gérard Depardieu, who travels between the high life of the Corniche, the rotten world of town hall politics and the vicious gangster subculture, with equal amounts of betrayal and ruthlessness in all quarters. The best part of the series is the opening scene, a beautiful montage of shots of Marseille at its most glorious accompanied by a lovely lilting Arabic jazz refrain of bruised melancholy called '*Ya Sidi*' ('Master').

To generations of English-speaking visitors, Marseille was always an exotic spectacle, the nearest thing to the Orient. Lying in convalescence in a suburb of Marseille, Robert Louis Stevenson wrote a poem to 'Marseille, the many-masted'. For Stevenson, it was a city of 'Algerian airs through all the place', the home of the 'thief, prostitute, and banker'. Charles Dickens, a devotee of Murray's *Handbook for Travellers to France*, found the city to be 'a fact to be strongly smelt and tasted ... dirty and disagreeable'. But it still was compelling enough for him to depict Marseille in the opening pages of *Little Dorrit* as a shifting people-scape: 'Hindoos, Russians, Chinese, Spaniards, Portuguese, Englishmen, Frenchmen, Genoese, Neapolitans, Venetians, Greeks, Turks, descendants from all the builders of Babel, come to trade at Marseille.'

Arthur Young was unimpressed by Marseille, describing the Vieux Port as 'no more than a horse-pond' and spending his few days there catching up on the latest Parisian newspapers in the Café d'Acajon. For Young, Marseille was very much not Paris. And this is definitely the case for the Marseillais today.[9]

This is not, as it is with other regional capitals in France, simply a question of good-natured rivalry – the provinces versus Paris – but most often a bitter conflict over who owns the city, and who owns its destiny. This is another conflict which dates almost as far back as the city has existed, with power almost always being resolved in the capital, but latterly, this conflict has intensified as Marseille has been seen as a rogue and dangerous city.

In recent years, Marseille also seems to have set its face against the rest of France. This is not in the form of an independence movement, such as to be found in Barcelona, Marseille's closest sister Mediterranean city, but rather in a violent nihilism. I caught a glimpse of this one afternoon in late October 2023 as I was finishing an open-air lunch at Le David Brasserie at the Plages du Prado. I was surrounded by football fans wearing the pale sky-blue shirts of OM, who would soon be heading off to the *vélodrome* for that evening's match against Olympique Lyonnais. As I was drinking my coffee, I heard the beginnings of a murmur stirring among the fans, all men and mainly middle-aged, crowded at the wide tables of the large *terrasse*. People were starting to get agitated, standing up, even getting onto tables, and then the murmur turned into a roar. I could now make out the reason for the nervous excitement, which soon broke out into a frenzy: the coach carrying the players of Olympique Lyonnais was turning the corner to head up the avenue du Prado to the stadium.

From the restaurant and beyond, OM fans ran to harry the bus, waving flags, throwing flares, fireworks, stones and other missiles. OM fans have long been proud of their capacity to intimidate visitors, whether fans or players, but here there was a hard and nasty edge to the intimidation, passing very quickly from frenzy to rage. I have seen plenty of football violence across Europe in France, Spain, England and Italy. But I had never seen fans rush the coach of an opposing team like this, like a small army, bent on pure destruction. This was not local patriotism but a will to mayhem. Windows were smashed, on the coach and in local premises, more flares were thrown, and the more vicious OM fans managed to get close enough to throw missiles at the Lyon players. The head coach of Lyon, Fabio Grosso, and his assistant Raffaele Longo were cut by splinters of shattered glass, drawing blood from their faces. Another coach carrying Lyon supporters was nearly overturned, and inside I could see that everyone was very scared; there was no *braggadacio* or banter from the Lyon fans or supporters, simply the fear of the mob. The match was cancelled, a rare event in the French football league.

When I spoke to OM fans the next day at a cafe in Saint-Victor, they were nonchalant. The match would be replayed anyway. Lyon had it coming, I was told. Nobody disagreed with this, not even the older, apparently more level-headed guys drinking at the bar. 'This was about honour,' said Yassine, who lived in the area. 'They can't just insult us and think that they can come here, into our territory. We have to defend ourselves.'

The background to this incident had very little to do with football. *Les Gones*, as the Lyon fans called themselves, have traditionally been made up of many of the city's young Fascists. OM's visits had for a long time provoked incidents in Lyon, in the city centre, in Vieux Lyon, as well as at the stadium in the *banlieue* of Décines. The last meeting between OM and Lyon had resulted in a series of running battles, with the mainly white Lyon fans taunting the OM fans with a variety of racial insults, calling them Arabs, foreigners, outsiders to France. A favoured insult was '*bicot*' – now pretty much an archaic term in France but which for a while was the favoured equivalent of 'nigger' in

Algérie Française, digging deep into painful memory. The assault in Marseille on the football team of Lyon was not about rivalry between two teams: it was about revenge, about postcolonial hurt and humiliation. It was another way of living up to, and giving new meaning to, the OM motto of *On craint dégun!*

This statement is not just poetic rhetoric but also a statement of political fact in Marseille. This found one of its latest expressions on the streets of the city in the spring of 2023, when Emmanuel Macron's authority was being tested as strikes, demonstrations and riots over his policy of raising the age of retirement swept across the country. Inevitably, given the high levels of poverty in the city, Marseille was the setting for some of the most violent demonstrations. The unrest peaked on the night of 16 March as masked youths rampaged down the swish rue Saint-Ferréol, looting everything they could, chanting '*Fuck la bourgeoisie!*'

In the wake of this riot, a scrawling graffitied slogan, written in the half French, half Arabic slang of the *quartiers nord*, could be seen on walls all over Marseille. It read '*Qui sème la hess, récolte le zbeul!*' – 'Whoever sows misery ('*la hess*' is street Arabic for '*misère*') reaps a fuck up!'

I first saw this slogan one rainy spring morning as I walked up the rue Bernard du Bois, a faded seventeenth-century urban corridor in Belsunce, heading for the Gare Saint-Charles and then to Paris. I couldn't quite decide whether it was a warning or a threat.

Epilogue

10

The View from Pernety

Everyday life in the quartier

At about 3 a.m. on Friday 30 June 2023, I was woken up by what sounded like gunfire. I wasn't far wrong. From the back windows of my apartment in southern Paris, I could make out fireworks being hurled at the police and hear the immediate response with 'Flash-Balls', the 'less than lethal' weapons used by French police for riot control.

The news that evening had been dominated by one story: that

riots were breaking out spontaneously all over France. There were familiar images of cars and buildings on fire and heavily armed police lines – familiar at least to anyone who has lived through the past few years of angry protest in France. But what was most disturbing about these riots was the sheer scale of it all: the violence was not just contained to the *banlieues* of the big cities but was everywhere. This included picturesque towns such as Montargis in the Loiret, a quiet, charming town known for its bridges and canals and sometimes called 'the Venice of the Gâtinais', Gâtinais being the old name for the oldest county of the Loire, where two hundred rioters looted eighty shops, and two houses were wrecked. After the news and then the Flash-Balls, I slept badly that Friday night with an uneasy feeling that this was all about to get worse.

My instincts proved true. The following Saturday night, in the small sedate town of L'Haÿ-les-Roses in the Val-de-Marne, south of Paris, a burning car was driven into the garden of its mayor, Vincent Jeanbrun, a member of the centre-right Republican party. Jeanbrun was not at home when it happened, but his wife and two children were forced to flee as the car burst into flames a few metres away from the front door. Jeanbrun's wife, Mélanie, fractured her tibia as she tried to escape from the house. The regional prosecutor Stéphane Hardouin declared that he would be opening an investigation into an 'attempted assassination'. Local politicians across the country reported that they had seen graffiti in their towns which read, 'We know where you live. We are coming to burn you!'

The attack on Jeanbrun's residence and the threats to other politicians raised the already chaotic situation to a new level of tension. During the first days of rioting and looting there had been assaults on post offices, schools, crèches, tax offices, public transport – anything representing the French government. But these attacks were purely symbolic, targeting the institutions of the Republic, not real people. What happened in

L'Haÿ-les-Roses was the first, alleged, attempt on a politician's life. A revolt that began as angry protests against police brutality had been elevated to rage towards the whole French state.

The next day, I walked around my neighbourhood, the *quartier* of Pernety, inspecting the wreckage from the night before – burned-out cars, motorcycles and rubbish bins, a *café-tabac* which had been raided for cigarettes, and a Chinese restaurant smashed up for no particular reason. At the corner of the rue Vercingétorix and rue Alain, I spoke to two police officers, who were part of a team patrolling the area on bikes. They were friendly enough, one of them black and the other white, but edgy. I asked them about the incident that had triggered the riots – the shooting or 'execution' of seventeen-year-old Nahel Merzouk at a traffic stop in the Paris suburb of Nanterre last Tuesday. They said that it was bad, but added that sooner or later something like this was bound to happen. 'You have to understand that when you go into some of these *banlieues*,' one said, 'you have to be constantly tense and alert, ready to be attacked at any time. It feels like a war zone.'

The *quartier* of Pernety in the 14th arrondissement of Paris is at quite some remove from 'peripheral France' but is not quite yet part of what Christophe Guilluy calls a 'new citadel'. It is busy, well connected, mildly prosperous, but also fiercely independent, with most of its long-term residents setting their faces against 'Paris', a near but alien place of power, money and vice. It is also where I have lived for the past two decades, longer than anywhere else I have lived, including my childhood home of Liverpool.

Historically, Pernety has always been resolutely working class, settled originally by migrants from Brittany in the mid-nineteenth century, and always at a remove from the far and distant world of central Paris. In the early twentieth century, historians of the French language recorded the local dialect for posterity, concluding that it had more in common with the rhythms and cadences of spoken Breton, with some southern inflections provided by waves of Catalan and Portuguese migrants.

The architectural historian Ian Nairn called Pernety 'the grey backside of Montparnasse', which was not necessarily an insult (Nairn always favoured the out-of-place or uncommon aspects of city life), and he came here specifically to admire the church of Notre-Dame de Travail, a long way from the classic sights of Paris. The church, built at the end of the nineteenth century, delighted him because it was so modern, with no trace of the Gothic style then in vogue. For this reason, Nairn called it 'the gayest of all the iron churches in Paris'.

When Nairn was here in the mid-sixties, the area was low rent, dilapidated, messy and unloved, and waiting to be developed into a shiny new autoroute. This never happened, and ignored and neglected by the city authorities, an independent working-class culture thrived here. In the 1980s, the area was again marked for redevelopment, and municipal wrecking balls arrived to knock down the most slum-like and fragile nineteenth-century buildings. The transformations were beautifully documented by the local photographer Daniel Chenot, who knew that a world was disappearing and so captured it forever in his photographs of cafes (including a much-loved cafe called Le Cadran), the *habitués* of the cafes, or just neighbours gossiping in the streets.

Pernety has its rough edges. There is a *café-tabac* on one corner which has long been a den of roguery, dense with smoke and the intrigues of small-time gangsters. There are also long-simmering hatreds between rival communities here, which can occasionally turn deadly. In 2011, two men were shot dead and one critically injured as they sat at a cafe terrace near rue de Plaisance. They were all Roma and part of a family at war with Algerian drug dealers.

There are also political undercurrents. For a long time, there were rumours of a secret Salafist mosque near the rue Niépce.

An Islamist cell, primed for operations with weapons and explosives, was discovered and raided on the rue Pernety almost directly opposite my office. Although the RN has no real presence in the area, public signs have been plastered with 'White Power' stickers – an image of a Doc Martens boot smashing into a brown-looking face. The plaque on the infant school on the rue Hippolyte Maindron, which remembers the deportation of Jewish children to the death camps, is regularly defaced with swastikas and the Star of David.

Almost a year after the riots, tensions came to a head in Pernety in the summer of 2024, when it looked briefly as if the RN might finally gain real power as Emmanuel Macron gambled his fast-ebbing popularity on a snap parliamentary election. Sitting at a cafe terrace, it was impossible not to silently wonder who had voted for whom. A few weeks after the RN had stormed into its daunting lead in the first round of the French election, a menacing graffito appeared on a busy street corner between the local boulangerie and the wine shop. Written in black, in a clear and steady hand, it read *'Les nerfs sont tendus, les Fachos seront pendus'* – 'Nerves are being stretched, the Fascists will be hung'.

Certainly, that summer the extremes were now dangerously far apart. This much was demonstrated with the vying viral popularity of two music anthems from the Right and the Left. The song *'Je partira pas'* ('I ain't going' in bad French) has now been banned from TikTok but it was still a massive hit with the right-wing Gen Z youth. It begins with the voice of an immigrant being deported before crashing into a bouncing Europop refrain with the catchy chorus ('oh yes, you're going' in correct French), taunting the deported immigrant to pack his djellaba and go home.

The anti-RN rap opposition was not heartening. It was a track called *'No pasarán'*, concocted by DJ Koré and a rap collective. It took aim at the RN but along the way was loaded with misogyny, death threats, conspiracy theories, Islamism and antisemitism. As such, it may well have been an accurate reflection of political nihilism in the *banlieues*, but it was hardly a rallying cry. Rather, it affirmed every easy prejudice that RN supporters and others have about the culture of the *banlieues*. The track was, however, the sound of 'nerves being stretched', as the graffito said.

From this point on the tensions in France grew ever sharper and more needling, the fractures ever more clearly visible. President Emmanuel Macron hung on to power with deft, last-ditch manipulations and the support of a left-wing coalition led by the radical leftist Jean-Luc Mélenchon. Le Pen's supporters felt that once again they had been tricked. But it was what they already knew – that democracy did not work in France.

This much was confirmed for the RN in the most severe manner in the early spring of 2025 when Marine Le Pen was convicted on charges of embezzlement ('*détournement des fonds publics*') which led her to receive a four-year prison sentence – suspended and to be served out of prison, although with of course a maximum share of humiliation – and, most damagingly, being barred from running for the presidency in the 2027 elections.

It is impossible to overstate how much of a political earthquake this was in France. All of sudden, in one fell blow, the Rassemblement National had been politically decapitated. Le Pen's supporters were devastated. At the same time, there was open glee and gloating in newspapers such as *Libération* and the Communist-run *L'Humanité*, whilst the main television channel in France, TF1, wasted no time in taunting Le Pen's followers on its nightly satirical programme *Canteloup*, caricaturing them as beret-wearing, gun-carrying dim-witted rustics, '*ploucs*' totally unfitted to the modern world.

This caricature bore no relation to anyone I could see in the crowds that gathered at Place Vauban on 6 April 2025 to hear

Le Pen make her defence. Many of them were young and fashionably dressed, many too had come from all parts of France and from a variety of social classes, eager to demonstrate their support for Le Pen and to show that they would not be cowed. The crowd was estimated to be some 10,000 people, although this was dismissed in the media as untrue and RN propaganda. Le Pen's speech was short and to the point. She attacked what she saw as the hollow spectacle of French democracy and lauded the sovereignty of the people, that most cherished of French myths. This was to the now familiar crowd responses of *'On est chez nous'* and *'Vive la République, Vive la France!'* 'The country is collapsing,' she declared, her face hard and defiant, 'and the people suffer.' She went on, this time to the loudest cheers of all: 'the nation is now in rebellion!'

Her speech climaxed with 'La Marseillaise', loud and raucous, sung in broken voices loaded with fury. As Le Pen stood on the podium, against the backdrop of Dôme des Invalides, the tomb of Napoleon, with its gold-tipped roof glinting in the sun, it was hard not to think of this as an historic moment, although what it might mean was impossible to say for now. At the very least, it was yet another breaking-point in the chaotic and convulsive history of the past few decades in France.

Seen from the sweep of French history, however, the recent disturbances in France – the demonstrations of the *gilets jaunes*, the mass protests against pensions, even the riots of 2023 and Macron's gamble on the parliamentary election – seem inconsequential. There is a theory of French history which argues that the story of France, especially since the Revolution of 1789, has been made by violent transformative convulsions. The key dates are 1830, 1848, 1871, even 1968, all moments of grand drama when the very identity of France was at stake, and change was forced through pressure from the people. In contrast, the revolts of the twenty-first century seem limited in scope and ambition.

And yet they are shaping French history as much as any insurrection or revolution.

This is because they are part of a bigger, slower process which looks set to continue playing out through our own century. In the past forty years, the French Republic, the child of the great Revolution, has been slowly fractured, corroded in gradients, by social changes which directly challenge its very existence. The most significant of these changes has been the growth of many of the *banlieues* of France into something like mini-cities, with their codes, cultures and languages. They are usually at odds with mainstream France and the Republic, which in the form of the police is seen as an intrusive, oppressive presence (sometimes the word 'colonialist', with memories of the Algerian war, is used as a provocation). For all the loose language bandied about in the past few years, there is as yet no civil war in France. But there is a permanent stand-off between those who believe in France as an ideal of civilization, under the rubric 'Liberty, Equality, Fraternity', and those who have no interest in such abstractions and often violently oppose them. This is probably the deepest division in twenty-first-century French life.

For all this, one of my favourite places in the world is the *terrasse* of Café Losserand, opposite the metro station and with a wide-angle view of the crossroads of the rue Pernety and rue Raymond Losserand. At any given moment of the day, and most of the night, the scene is an exhilarating kaleidoscope of human beings of all classes and creeds, all on individual journeys you'll never know about, soundtracked by a polyphony of languages and meanings.

But this is no globalized crowd anywhere in the world. It all still feels French. You can see this, first of all, in the setting, the smells, the sounds, the architecture, the street furniture, which all tell you that you couldn't be anywhere else but France. The setting binds the passers-by together with an invisible glue, its 'Frenchness'.

Here, this is no purely abstract concept but a concrete, lived reality. One of the aspects of French life that I have always cherished is the high quality of everyday life – and here it is in the city with cafes, bakers, a butcher's, greengrocers, a bookshop, an arthouse cinema, a jazz club, pharmacies, restaurants, all within a few minutes' stroll of each other. This is one meaning, I think, of the word 'civilization' – a model of city living which prizes local experience and local needs over the forces of global capital. Most French people, of all social classes, political persuasions and racial origins, would agree that this way of living is an essential part of who they are.

My journeys through France have taught me that this way of life is harder and harder to find. Coming home to Pernety, I realized how much of French life has been degraded at the level of the street – the blank, dead quarters of Roubaix, the sinister *banlieues* of Lyon and the poorest parts of Marseille come to mind. Similarly, I have also seen first-hand how the present divisions in French society have tested and undermined the resilience of the Republic, endangering the very idea of a France based on its original Enlightenment ideals.

This does not mean, however, that France is about to die. This only happens, said the historian Fernand Braudel, when a culture is trapped and fixed, and France, he argued further, is in permanent flux – another fact which was always revealed to me on my travels. Braudel, who spent his life in pursuit of the true identity or, more poetically, the true essence of France, also wrote that 'a nation in the process of creating or recreating itself is not a simple character – it is a multitude of realities and living beings'. This is how, he concluded, French culture resists and persists, absorbing the 'dense layers of the past' into the present or, as he wrote, 'past and present locked together and forever reproducing'.[1]

From the *terrasse* of the Café Losserand in Pernety, you can see Braudel's notion come alive in the most visceral sense. The biggest mistake that historians of France can make, on the Right and the Left, says Braudel, is to conceive of France or French identity as a totality, rather than what it is in reality – a series of fragments pulled together to make a whole.

This is how French life goes on being French, with all the richness and complexity that this implies. This is also what you can still see in the ever-shifting crowds at a crossroads from a cafe table on the rue Pernety.

And this is why I can't imagine living anywhere else.

ANDREW HUSSEY
Paris
April 2025

Notes

Introduction: 'Beautiful and Brutal'

The texts consulted in this section include:

Fernand Braudel, *The Identity of France, History and Environment*, trans. Siân Reynolds (HarperCollins, London, 1989)

Louis Chevalier, *Classes laborieuses et classes dangereuses* (Tempus Perrin, Paris, 2009)

Christophe Guilluy, *No Society* (Flammarion, Paris, 2018); *Twilight of the Elites: Prosperity, the Periphery and the Future of France*, trans. Malcolm DeBoise (Yale University Press, Yale, 2019)

John Lough, *France Observed in the Seventeenth Century by British Travellers* (Oriel Press, London, 1984)

1. Christophe Guilluy, *La France péripherique: comment on a sacrifié les classes populaires* (Flammarion, Paris, 2014)
2. A full account of this interview can be found in 'The French elites against the working class', *New Statesman*, 24 July 2019
3. Alexandre Devecchio, 'Christophe Guilluy: "On nous fait craindre depuis trente ans le retour du fascisme ... C'est du théâtre"', *Le Figaro*, 21 November 2021
4. David Brooks, *Bobos in Paradise: The New Upper Class and How They Got There* (Simon and Schuster, New York, 2001)
5. Thomas Coryate, *Coryate's Crudities, Hastily Gobled Up in Five Moneths Travells in France, Savoy, Italy, Rhetia Commonly Called the Grisons Country, Helvetia, Alias Switzerland, Some Parts of High Germany and the Netherlands*, Vol. 1 (McHelose, London, 1905)

Part One: Order and Disorder

The texts consulted in this section include:

Florence Aubenas, *En France* (Editions de l'Olivier, Paris, 2014)

Richard Cobb, *A Second Identity, Essays on France and French History* (Oxford University Press, New York, 1969)

Didier Eribon, *Returning to Reims*, trans. Michael Lucy (Allen Lane, London, 2013)

François Lebrun, *Histoire d'Angers* (Privat, Paris, 1975)

Edouard Louis, *The End of Eddy*, trans. Michael Lucey (Harvill Secker, London, 2017); *Change*, trans. John Lambert (Vintage, London, 2024)

Anne Nivat, *La France de face* (Fayard, Paris, 2022)

Pilar Hélène Surgers, *Les gens du Nord et la Ch'ti-attitude* (Editions Alphee, Lille, 2008)

Michel Thibault, *Reims et ses quartiers* (Editions Sutton, Reims, 2008)

1 The Road to Roubaix

1. Effectifs de juin 2019 dans les quartiers de reconquête républicaine / Dossiers de presse / Archives Christophe Castaner / Archives ministres de l'Intérieur / Archives – Ministère de l'Intérieur
2. Rachel Binhas, 'Roubaix, La fin d'un monde', *Valeurs actuelles*, 31 March 2016
3. A slightly sneering, and indeed very Parisian 'Bobo' account of the affair can be found in 'Une banderole? Plus jamais ça!', *Libération*, 5 April 2008
4. See 'Edouard Louis, "All my writing is political – and all my life is, too"', *Guardian*, 28 January 2024
5. George Orwell, *Inside the Whale* (Penguin, London, 1994), p. 106
6. Résultats de l'élection présidentielle 2017: Roubaix (59100), Elections Actu
7. Richard Cobb, *Paris and Elsewhere* (NYRB, New York, 1998), pp. 39–47

2 The Battle of Angers

1. Arthur Young's *Travels in France During the Years 1787, 1788, 1789* (George Bell & Sons, London, 1905), p. 137
2. David Cayla, *Populism and Neo-Liberalism* (Routledge, London, 2021)
3. 'Angers. Avant la manif régionale, dialogue entre des Gilets jaunes et le député Orphelin', *Ouest-France*, 19 January 2019

3 Paris on Edge

1 '"Pour un retour de l'honneur de nos gouvernants": 20 généraux appellent Macron à défendre le patriotism', *Valeurs actuelles*, 21 April 2021
2 'Tribune des militaires: le chef d'Etat-Major juge "raisonnable" que les signataires "quittent l'institution"', *Valeurs actuelles*, 10 May 2021
3 Ariane Chemin, 'Elisabeth Lévy, causeuse de troubles', *Le Monde*, 12 December 2013
4 'Les enseignants, remparts contre l'oscurantisme', *Le Monde*, 17 October 2023
5 'Houellebecq – Onfray: la rencontre', *Front Populaire*, 29 November 2022

4 Escaping Reims

1 Didier Eribon, *Returning to Reims* (Allen Lane, London, 2009), p. 9
2 Austin K. Gray, 'Some observations on Christopher Marlowe, government agent', *PMLA*, Vol. 43, No. 3, September 1928, pp. 682–700
3 Young, *Travels in France*, p. 195

Part Two: The Unquiet Centre

The texts consulted in this section include:

Peter Hammerschmidt, *Klaus Barbie – nom du code Adler* (Les Arènes, Paris, 2016)

Dominique Le Page, *Histoire de Dijon* (PU de Rennes, Rennes, 2023)

Thierry Mantoux, *BCBG: le guide du bon chic bon genre* (France Loisirs, Paris, 1986)

Pierre Milza, *Fascisme français: passé et présent* (Flammarion, Paris, 2000)

Olivier Minot, *Fragments d'une lutte anti-fasciste* (Burn Août Editions, Lyon, 2024)

François Rebsamen, *Dijon* (Maupetit, Dijon, 2017)

Guy Renaud, *Dijon Gastronomique – d'hier et aujourd'hui* (Editions de l'Escargot Savant, Dijon, 2014)

Catherine Simon-Lélack, *Guide de Lyon des faits divers: de l'Antiquité à nos jours* (Le Cherche-Midi, Paris, 2005)

Catherine Simon, *Mangées: une histoire des mères lyonnaises* (Sabine Wespiese, Lyon, 2018)

5 Return to Dijon

1. Henry Miller, *Tropic of Cancer* (Harper, New York, 1934/2005), p. 39
2. Ibid.
3. Young, *Travels in France*, p. 218
4. John Ardagh, *France in the 1980s* (Secker and Warburg, London, 1982)
5. See Louise Lyle, Times Higher Education (THE)
6. Cobb, *Paris and Elsewhere*, p. 250
7. Michel Houellebecq, *Les particules elémentaires* (Flammarion, Paris, 1998), p. 121
8. Michel Dion, *La France profonde: entretiens sur la politique en Lorraine et en Mayenne* (Editions Sociales, Paris, 1988)
9. Henry James, *A Little Tour in France* (Penguin, London, 1985), p. 121
10. M. F. K. Fisher, *Long Ago in France* (Touchstone, New York, 1991)
11. Lawrence Clark Powell, 'Looking back at sixty: recollections of Lawrence Clark Powell, librarian, teacher, and writer', oral transcript (Los Angeles, UCLA, 1973)

6 Lyon, 'My Strange City'

1. *Causette*, September 2014
2. Mourad Benchellali, *Voyage vers l'enfer* (Laffont, Paris, 2006); *Le piège de l'aventure* (Laffont, Paris, 2016)
3. George Orwell, 'As I please', *Tribune*, 19 January 1945
4. Henri Béraud, 'Enfants de la cité des brumes', in *Lyon d'hier et toujours* (Christian de Bartillat, Lyon, 1992)
5. Ibid., pp. 272–274
6. Nizier du Puitspelu, *Le littré de la Grand'Côte* (A. Storck, Lyon, 1894), p. 51

7 Bill Buford, *Dirt: Adventures in French Cooking* (Penguin, London, 2020), p. 71
8 Young, *Travels in France*, pp. 282–285

Part Three: The South

The texts consulted in this section include:
Guide du Marseille colonial (Editions Syllepse, Paris, 2020)
Hadrien Bels, *Cinq dans tes yeux* (Pocket, Marseille, 2020)
Henri Frédéric Blanc, *Discours sur l'universalité de l'esprit marseillais* (Le Fiouoélan, Marseille, 2018)
Robert Bouvier, *Le parler Marseillais* (Lafitte, Marseille, 1986)
Fernand Braudel, *La Méditerranée* (Flammarion, Paris, 2017)
Vincent Crapanzano, *Les harkis: mémoires sans issue* (Gallimard, Paris, 2012)
Nicholas Hewitt, *Wicked City, The Many Cultures of Marseille* (Hurst, London, 2019)
Michéa Jacobi, *Marseille en toute lettres* (Editions Parenthèses, Marseille, 2013)
Jean-Michel Mension, *La tribu* (Editions Allia, Paris, 1998)
Simon Sadler, *The Situationist City* (MIT Press, Cambridge, 1998)
Ahmed Zitouni, *Manosque aller-retour* (Autre Temps, Manosque, 1998)

7 Into Provence

1 Cyril Connolly, *The Unquiet Grave* (Arrow Books, London, 1961), p. 83
2 Carol Dunlop, Julio Cortázar, *Les autonautes de la cosmoroute, ou un voyage intemporel Paris-Marseille* (Gallimard, Paris, 1983)
3 Ibid., p .199
4 Ibid., p. 225
5 Institut national de la statistique et des études économiques, 'L'essentiel sur ... les immigrés et les étrangers', https://www.insee.fr/fr/statistiques/3633212
6 Albert Camus, 'The new Mediterranean culture', in *Algerian Chronicles*, trans. Arthur Goldhammer (Harvard University Press, Harvard, 2013), p. 195
7 Ibid., p. 195

8 The Enchantment of Manosque

1. The best account of Ralph's life is to be found in his autobiography *Le consul* (Editions Allia, Paris, 1999). He also talks, often unreliably, about his life in Alan Woods, *The Map Is Not the Territory* (Manchester University Press, Manchester, 2001)
2. Edmund White, 'The Great Jean Giono,' *New York Review of Books*, 5 June 2014
3. Jean Giono, *Manosque et les plateaux* (Collection du Moulin, Manosque, 2015)
4. Ibid., p. 2
5. Déplacement de la CNIH à Manosque, Les Harkis
6. John Locke, in Lough, *France Observed in the Seventeenth Century*, p. 40
7. Young, *Travels in France*, pp. 258–278
8. Francis Hervé, *How to Enjoy Paris in 1842* (Anthem, London, 2007), p. 9
9. Prosper Mérimée, 'Lettre à Jenny Dacqui, 1834', in Michéa Jacobi, *Marseille en toutes lettres* (Parenthèses, Marseille, 2013), p. 142
10. Alexander Herzen, *My Past and Thoughts: Memoirs Vol. 3* (Chatto and Windus, London, 1924), Chap. XL

9 The 'Wicked City' of Marseille

1. Cobb, *Paris and Elsewhere*, p. 259
2. Dunlop, Cortázar, *Les autonautes de la cosmoroute*, p. 271
3. Louis Brauquier, 'La Fondation de Marseille', 1923
4. Prosper Mérimée, in Jacobi, *Marseille en toutes lettres*, p. 28
5. Philippe Pujol, *La fabrique du monstre* (Les Arènes, Paris, 2016), p. 265
6. Albert Londres, *Marseille, porte du sud* (Payot, Paris, 2023), pp. 21–22
7. William Kornblum, *Marseille, Port to Port* (Columbia University Press, New York, 2022), p. 61
8. Walter Benjamin, *Haschich à Marseille* (Fata Morgana, Paris, 2020), p. 12
9. Young, *Travels in France*, pp. 259–261

10 The View from Pernety

1 Fernand Braudel, *The Identity of France*, Vol. 1, trans. Sian Reynolds (Collins, London, 1988)

Acknowledgements

I would like to thank all those who formed part of the book one way or another. These include Mourad Benchellali, Lucas Belvaux, Geoff Bird, Professor Kenneth L. Brown, Catherine Camus, David Cayla, Jason Cowley, Jean Daniel, Emilie Dequenne, Roger Grenier, Christophe Guilluy, Michel Eltchaninoff, Jane Ferguson, Mary Fitzgerald, Les Hodge, Karen Holden, Michel Houellebecq, Ursula Kenny, Amine Kessaci, Jean-Pierre Legrand, Astrid Leplat, Elisabeth Lévy, Edouard Louis, Benoît Lupi, Louise Lyle for her wit and insight, my wise friend Guy Maruani, my cherished friend Heather Mawhinney, my oldest and dearest friends Rob and Angela Merino, Sophie Morel, Eric Pothion, Alain and Laurence Poulain, Philippe Pujol, Michel Rabain, Ralph Rumney RIP, Teresa Smith, François Thomazeau, Paul Tickell, Olivier Todd, Francis Whately and Paul Webster.

This book would not have happened without the faith in my wanderings – or 'strayings' in the Situationist language of Ralph Rumney – shown by Luke Ingram and Sarah Chalfant of the Wylie Agency. At Granta, Laura Barber again proved what an elegant and insightful editor she is. Thanks also to Jack Alexander and Kate Shearman for patient proofing.

Image credits

1. Roubaix
Le musée de la piscine © Isogood_patrick/Shutterstock

2. Angers
A new citadel © Labellepatine/Shutterstock

3. Paris
The language of war © Frederic Legrand – COMEO/Shutterstock

4. Reims
'The jewel-box of France . . . defeated, destroyed' Georges Bataille, Notre Dame de Reims, *1917* © D.Bond/Shutterstock

5. Dijon
Parc Darcy, Dijon, where I started to write about France in 1987 © Andrew Hussey

6. Lyon
Le Vieux Lyon © ColorMaker/Shutterstock

7. Provence
The author and his mates, Hyères, 1985 © Andrew Hussey

8. Manosque
Secrecy and discretion in the old streets © Andrew Hussey

9. Marseille
Entering Marseille from the sea © Sergii Figurnyi/Shutterstock

10. Pernety
Everyday life in the quartier © Andrew Hussey

Index

abayas, 63
Ackroyd, Peter, 246
Afghanistan, 59, 142, 145, 262
agoge, 139
agrégation exam, 108–9
Aix-en-Provence, 178, 200
Alamanni, Luigi, 124
Algeria, 2, 21, 43–4, 58, 63, 73, 102, 134, 234–5, 274, 277, 284
    and Albert Camus, 179–91
    and *harkis*, 218–22
    invention of Orangina, 242
    war of independence, 43, 71, 132, 182, 184, 189, 219, 259, 294
Algiers, Notre Dame d'Afrique, 234–5
Aliot, Louis, 78
Allende, Salvador, 170
al-Qaeda, 124, 142–3
Amazon, 39
Andolfatto, Dominique, 117
andouillette, 151, 279
Angers, 46–55
    gilets jaunes demonstrations, 52–5
Angry Brigade, 206
Antibes, 177
anti-republicanism, 62–3
anti-RN rap, 291–2
antisemitism, 3, 66, 146, 269, 292
Apollinaire, Guillaume, 246
Arabic, 37, 65, 180–1, 183, 187, 218, 220, 230, 235, 238, 253, 277, 284
Arabic jazz, 281
Arabs, 3, 20, 75, 127, 139, 141, 174, 180, 183–5, 238, 269, 274, 283

harkis, 218–22, 258
invasion of Provence, 195
Ardagh, John, 102–3
Aristotle, 249
Arras, 62
Ashe 22, 72
Aurès Mountains, 221
Auschwitz, 132–3
autofiction, 25–6
L'Autoroute du Soleil, 161–3, 172, 178
Avignon, 226, 229

Baader–Meinhof gang, 206
Babeuf, Gracchus, 64
Bac Nord, 65
Baines, Richard, 87
Balzac, Honoré de, 25, 66, 186
Banalystes, 211, 215
banlieues, 3, 57, 114, 130, 174, 182, 189, 236, 259, 261, 266, 283, 288–9, 292, 294–5
    Dijon, 111–15
    in films, 65, 70–1
    Manosque, 200, 219, 222–3
Banlieusards, 65
Banque de France, 54
Barbès, 274
Barbie, Klaus, 128–9, 131–3, 137
Barrès, Maurice, 79–80, 115
bastides, 194, 202
Bataclan theatre, 3, 59
Bataille, Georges, 120, 205
Baussan, Olivier, 197
BCBGs (*bon chic, bon genre*), 101–3, 121, 135
beauf, 101, 174

Beckett, Samuel, 206
Bédoin, 226
Belleville, 5
Belouizdad, Mohamed, 179
Belvaux, Lucas, 33–7
Ben Jelloun, Tahar, 127
Benchellali, Mourad, 141–5
Benjamin, Walter, 280
Béraud, Henri, 146–7, 149–50
Berber language, 277
Berger, John, 276
Bernard, Dominique, 62
Bernstein, Michèle, 198
Berrahma, Farid, 253, 267
Bertrand, Xavier, 39, 43
bicot, 283
bin Laden, Osama, 142
Binhas, Rachel, 21
Black Bloc, 1, 4, 85
Black Lives Matter, 61
Bloch, Marc, 131
Bobos (*bourgeois bohèmes*), 8–9, 60–1,
    67, 85, 102, 108
Bocuse, Paul, 152–5
le bon maître, 49
le bon ton Parisien, 116
Booba, 219
Boon, Dany, 23
Bordeaux, 4, 90
Bosco, Henri, 185
bouchon, 150–1
Boulogne Boys, 23
Bourdeaux, Marie-Christine, 201–3
Bourdieu, Pierre, 28, 83–4
Bovo, Marie, 242–3
Bowles, Paul, 127, 277
Braudel, Fernand, 10, 295–6
Breton, André, 205
Brexit, 8, 76–7
Brigade de Reconquête Républicaine, 20
Britten, Benjamin, 70
Bronx, 65
Brooks, David, 8
Brown, Kenneth L., 275–80
Bruant, Aristide, 149

Brune, Maréchal, 226
Brunhes, Jean, 10
Brussels, Jewish Museum, 38
Buford, Bill, 152–3
Burgess, Anthony, 80
Burgess, Sonny, 173
Burgundian dialect, 97
Burroughs, William, 205, 277

café à la chicorée, 22
Cage, John, 205
caïds, 253, 268
le camping, 163–6, 194
    campings libertins, 165–6
Camus, Albert, 66, 179–91
Camus, Catherine, 179, 185–9
Cannes, 172, 177
Canteloup, 292
Carbone, Paul, 250
Carte de Séjour, 174
Cash, Johnny, 173
Cassis, 234, 272
Castex, Jean, 114
Castro, Fidel, 170
Catholicism, 79, 116, 135
Causette magazine, 136
Causeur magazine, 59–60, 65
Cayla, David, 51–2, 55
Céline, Louis-Ferdinand, 38, 66,
    269
Central African Republic, 59
Cézanne, Paul, 170
ch'tis, 22–3, 29–30
Chagall, Marc, 216–17
Challe, Maurice, 58
champagne, 86
Champs-Elysées, 5
Char, René, 185
Charlie Hebdo, 3, 59, 101, 123–4, 133
Le Château d'If, 271
Chenot, Daniel, 290
Chénot, Julie, 262–3
Chez Nous, 32–3, 36
chibanis, 187, 237–8
Chile, 168, 170

Chirac, Jacques, 35
choufs, 65, 144, 261
Choukri, Mohamed, 127
le circuit Garel, 131
civil war, 2, 54–5, 58–9, 61, 142, 263, 294
  in films and books, 65–72
les classes populaires, 11
coal mining, 18
Cobb, Richard, 12, 41–2, 116, 234–5
Cocteau, Jean, 205
Colbrelli, Sonny, 43
Collard, Gilbert, 75
colons, 63
Coltrane, John, 168
Combat, 182, 186
communautarisme, 61
communism, working-class, 83
Communist Party, 7, 116
Compagnies Républicaines de Sécurité, 256
Condé, Prince of, 98
Connolly, Cyril, 163, 172
Corneille, Pierre, 101
corons, 19
Cortázar, Julio, 167–72, 194, 240
Coryate, Thomas, 12
Coulibaly, Amedy, 133
Coupe de France, 42
Covid-19 pandemic, 4, 9–11, 20, 45, 50, 55, 75, 223
Crédit Lyonnais, 125
Crete, Blanche, 135–6
Creus, Armand, 137–8
cuisine, 79, 155
  Burgundian, 99, 119
  Lyonnais, 149–55
  Marseillaise, 279
  Provençal, 200–1
la culture woke, 59

Daniel, Jean, 182–4
Darantiere, Maurice, 119
de Gaulle, Charles, 58, 132, 147, 152, 183, 212

Debord, Guy, 198, 205–7, 210–11
décalage, 115
Defferre, Gaston, 241
Deignan, Elizabeth, 43
Depardieu, Gérard, 281
Dequenne, Emilie, 32–3
Diaghilev, Sergei, 73
Dickens, Charles, 226, 281
Dijon, 93–121, 135, 238
  Cathédrale Saint-Bénigne, 120, 229
  cuisine, 99, 119
  Grand Hôtel La Cloche, 104
  La Maison Japonaise, 104–5
  Lycée Carnot, 94, 96, 116, 120
  Les Grésilles, 111–15
  university, 105–11
Dijon mustard, 165
Dion, Michel, 116
DJ Koré, 291
DJ Mehdi, 70
Douai, 87
Dubosc, Franck, 165
Dumas, Alexandre, 271
Dumont, Lionel, 38
Dunlop, Carol, 167–72, 194, 240
Durance, river, 193–5
Durand, Antoine, 139
Durrell, Lawrence, 207
Duvivier, Julien, 274

Edinburgh, Duke of, 273
Eiffel Tower, 229, 234, 236
Eliot, T. S., 119
Eltchaninoff, Michel, 78–9
Engels, Friedrich, 148
Enlightenment, 46, 64, 212–13, 295
Epernay, 87–8
Eribon, Didier, 26, 28, 82–6, 88–9
Ernaux, Annie, 25, 29
estaminets, 41
Eugénie, Empress, 235
European Parliament, 258
European Union, 67–8, 76–7, 80
Euroscepticism, 40, 77

Excelsior AC Roubaix, 42
Exmouth, Lord, 226

Fachosphère, 67
fascists, 32, 34, 43, 51, 60, 76, 80, 115, 146, 184, 291
   Lyon fascists, 133–41, 149, 244, 283
   see also neo-Nazis
Feathers, Charlie, 173
Femen movement, 80, 136
feminism, 63, 80–1, 134, 136
Fesses de Tonnerre, 104
filles de joie, 135
Finkielkraut, Alain, 60, 278
First World War, 42, 120
Fisher, Al, 118–19
Fisher, M. F. K., 12, 118–20
Fitzgerald, Mary, 276
Flaubert, Gustave, 25
FN, 8, 32–40, 43, 78, 85
   defections, 75, 77–8
   On est chez nous! slogan, 32, 80, 293
food banks, 144
Forbin, Claude, 248
Foster, Norman, 239
Foucault, Michel, 83
Fourier, Charles, 148
les français de souche, 137
la France profonde, 115–16
Franco, General Francisco, 137
François, King, 196
Franco-Prussian War, 126
Frankenheimer, John, 237
Free French Forces, 154
French Connection, The, 237, 268
French Empire, 130, 273
French Resistance, 35, 125, 128–30, 133–4, 164, 182, 185, 216, 245
French Revolution, 11–12, 48–9, 64, 87–8, 97, 156–7, 212–13, 226, 293–4
'Frenchness', 21, 64, 124, 155, 294

Front de Libération Nationale (FLN), 132, 219
Front Populaire, 69
Fuentes, Carlos, 168
Fugain, Michel, 164

galéjades, 247, 265
Gallimard, Robert, 188
Gallizio, Giuseppe Pinot, 210
Gare d'Orsay, 18
Gare de Lyon, 227–9
Gare du Nord, 3
Garel, Georges and Lili, 131
la gauche hashtag, 8
Gavras, Romain, 70–2
Gazo, 72
Genet, Jean, 128
genièvre, 22
German Occupation, 43, 128–33, 146, 185, 203–4
Gestapo, 128–9, 131, 133, 216
Ghali, Samia, 252
gilets jaunes, 3–4, 7–8, 67–8, 79, 85, 117, 293
   Angers demonstrations, 52–5
Ginsberg, Allen, 205
Giono, Jean, 203–4, 207–8, 211, 214, 220, 223, 256
Giscard d'Estaing, Valéry, 154
globalization, 4, 6, 22, 40, 51, 53, 76, 80, 115, 124, 155, 261, 268, 294–5
Goldman, Jean-Jacques, 102
Gonzalez, Bernard, 54
Gordes, 216–17
Gorges de Verdon, 195
gouaille, 60
grandes écoles, 107, 111
Great Plague, 9–10
Greene, Graham, 207
Grenier, Roger, 182–3, 185
Griffiths, Charles, 42
Gringoire, 146
Grisoni-Pirbakas, Maxette, 75
Grosso, Fabio, 283

Gruppe SPUR, 210
Guantanamo Bay, 143, 145
les gueules noires, 21
Guggenheim family, 205–6
Guillaume, le Comte d'Arles, 195
Guilluy, Christophe, 4–8, 10, 17, 52, 60, 98, 289
Guyton de Moreau, Louis-Bernard, 97

Haçienda, 198–9, 209, 212
Haenel, Adèle, 85
Hallencourt, 24, 26
Hallyday, Johnny, 11, 172
Handbook for Travellers to France, 225–7, 281
Hans le Marin, 281
Hardouin, Stéphane, 288
Haussmann, Baron, 235
Haute-Provence, 201, 203–4, 208, 214, 228
Haut-Var, 195
health service, 107
Hegel, G. W. F., 198
Héroet, Antoine, 124
Herriot, Edouard, 152
Hervé, Francis, 225
Herzen, Alexander, 227
Hidalgo, Anne, 5
Hodge, Les, 172, 174–5, 178
Hogg, James, 110
Hoggart, Richard, 28–9, 84
Hollande, François, 117
Holocaust, 78, 136
homicide *barbecue*, 253, 255–7, 267
homophobia, 24, 30
Hospices de Beaune, 229
Hotel Majestic, 73–6
Houellebecq, Michel, 67–70, 77, 79, 116, 166
Hugo, Victor, 104, 186
Hyères, 175–6, 228

identitarian politics, 138
Il Giorno, 206

immigration, 21, 38, 66, 76, 80, 85, 115, 118, 135, 141, 187, 250, 259
sans-papiers, 254
Imposters, 246
indépendants, 37
Industrial Revolution, 18, 148, 248
insécurité, 54–5, 76
ISIS, 3, 143
Islamists, 21, 38, 62, 65, 70, 81, 124, 142–3, 145, 166, 181, 264, 291
Israel, 75
Izzo, Jean-Claude, 252, 272

James, Henry, 118
Jeanbrun, Vincent, 288
Jesuits, 109
Jeunesses nationalists, 134
Joan of Arc, 135
Jorn, Asger, 210
Joyce, James, 73, 119
Juan-les-Pins, 177
Justice, 71

Kafka, Franz, 213
Kalashnikovs, 55, 113, 264
Kekra, 72
Kessaci, Amine, 253–8
Klein, Yves, 205
Kornblum, William, 276, 278
Kouachi, Saïd and Chérif, 123–4, 133

L'Echo du Centre, 245
L'Haÿ-les-Rosses, 288–9
L'Humanité, 292
L'Occitane, 197
L'Oeuvre française, 134
'La Marseillaise', 157, 293
La Marseillaise newspaper, 245, 265
La Provence, 255, 265
La République en Marche (LREM), 58, 117
La Vallée de la Chimie, 161–2, 172
La Veille, 226
La Voix du Nord, 34–5
Labé, Louise, 124

laicity, 63
Laloux, Victor, 18
Le Bien Public, 95, 113
Le Bon, Gustave, 67
Le Canard enchaîné, 101, 116
'Le Chant des *Canuts*', 149
Le Figaro, 8
Le Journal d'Abbeville, 24
Le Monde, 61, 266
Le Nouvel Observateur, 182
Le Pen, Jean-Marie, 35, 78
Le Pen, Marine, 8, 32, 35–6, 39–40, 58, 60, 73–80, 115, 136, 292–3
  'detoxifying' tactic, 78–9
  and *le peuple*, 79
  and Reims, 80–2, 85, 88, 90
  support for *gilets jaunes*, 79
'Le Réveil du Peuple', 157
Le Select cafe, 24–5, 27
'Lebanonization' of France, 278
Lebrun, Albert, 154
Lecointre, Général François, 58
Legrand, Jean-Pierre, 34, 36–40, 43
Leplat, Astrid, 34, 36, 40, 43
Les Caryatides, 134–6
Les Ch'tis d'Allah, 38
Les Inrockuptibles, 25
Les Misérables, 65
Les Patriotes, 40, 77
Les Rita Mitsouko, 102
Letellier, Jean-Paul, 228
Lévy, Elisabeth, 59–61, 64, 72, 74
Lewis, Jerry Lee, 173
LGBTQ+, 61
Libération, 292
Liberté, 245
liberticide, 63–4
Lille, 17–18, 22, 29, 31, 37–8, 52, 163, 244–5
  pigeons monument, 42
Loach, Ken, 41
Locke, John, 223–4
Londres, Albert, 273–4
Longo, Raffaele, 283
Longuet, Karl-Jean, 210

loubards, 174
Louis XIV, King, 238
Louis, Edouard, 23–30, 82, 84
Louis-Philippe I, King, 148
Lourmarin, 179, 185–9, 193
Lupi, Benoît, 215–17
Lyon, 4, 10, 12, 19, 72, 123–57, 161, 174–5, 178, 243, 295
  Basilique Notre-Dame de Fourvière, 123, 126–7, 140, 229, 234
  Centre d'Histoire de la Résistance et de la Déportation (CHRD), 129–30
  cité riots, 141–2, 146
  collaboration, 134, 136–7
  cuisine, 149–55
  fascists, 133–41, 149, 244, 283
  Fête des Lumières, 140
  flags, 139–40
  Fort Monluc prison, 130–3
  German occupation, 128–33
  Grande Synagogue, 133–4, 137
  hunger riots (1529), 139
  Jews, 129, 131–4, 136–7, 139–40, 146
  La Guillotière, 126–7, 132, 140–1, 274
  mères lyonnais, 151–2
  le parler lyonnais, 149
  révoltes des canuts, 147–9
  Sanglante semaine, 148
  traboules, 125, 147, 149
  Vieux Lyon, 124–5, 137–41, 147, 149, 283

Macron, Emmanuel, 7–8, 17, 39, 53, 62, 64, 90, 117, 270, 284
  and generals' letter, 57, 59
  and *gilets jaunes*, 3–4
  and Marine Le Pen, 35, 75, 77, 80
  Marseille initiative, 256–7
  snap election, 291–2
Mailer, Norman, 129
Mali, 59

Mairaux, Henri, 205
Mam'Ega, 260
Manosque, 193–223, 228
   harkis, 218–22
Marlowe, Christopher, 86–7, 223
Marquet, Albert, 236
Márquez, Gabriel García, 168
Mars, Coralie, 48
Marseille, 17, 19, 55, 161, 167, 169–72, 178, 228–84, 295
   Basilique Notre-Dame de la Garde, 234, 236
   Campagne Fenouil, 260
   Château de Forbin, 248
   Corniche, 9, 239, 249, 270–2, 281
   corruption, 251, 273, 280
   cuisine, 279
   European Capital of Culture, 262–4
   in films, 65, 237
   les gabians (seagulls), 240
   Gare Saint-Charles, 214, 229, 237, 264, 284
   Great Plague, 9–10
   Jews, 131
   L'Ombrière, 239
   Macron initiative, 256–7
   and Manosque, 200–2, 207–8, 216, 218–19, 221–2, 228
   Marsiens, 249–50
   Mucem, 236–7, 263
   Noailles, 231, 233, 272–5, 277, 279
   Oppidum des Baou de Saint-Marcel, 249
   Pharo Palace, 235–6, 239
   quartiers nord, 65, 232, 234, 248, 250–71, 278, 284
   le ventre de Marseille, 273
   Vieux Port, 176, 228, 233–5, 237, 239, 241–2, 245, 248–9, 251, 262, 270, 276, 282
Marseille Netflix series, 281
Marseilleveyre, 272
Marx, Karl, 148, 198, 210
Marxism, 60, 68, 83, 100, 108, 212

Massu, General Jacques, 73–4
Matruchot, Jean, 120
Mauchamp, Justine, 105–7
Maupassant, Guy de, 273
Maurras, Charles, 115
Mauthausen, 245
mauvais patriotes, 49
May 1968, 4, 28, 190, 197, 207, 210–13, 217
Mbappé, Kylian, 219
Mediterraneans journal, 276
Mélenchon, Jean-Luc, 39, 149, 292
Menton, 228–9
La Mère Bourgeois, 152
La Mère Brazier, 152
La Mère Fillioux, 152, 155
La Mère Richard, 156
Méric, Clément, 134
Mérimée, Prosper, 227, 241
Méritain, Jean, 176
Merzouk, Nahel, 289
migrants, 21, 40–1
Milice bourgeoise, 156
Milice française, 133
Miller, Henry, 93–4, 96, 118, 120
minots, 248
Le Mistral, 194
Mitchell, Eddy, 172
Mitterrand, François, 49, 60, 142, 152
Mont Blanc, 125
Mont d'Aiguines, 195
Mont d'Or, 194–5, 208, 214, 223
Montaigne, Michel de, 101
Montand, Yves, 149
Montargis, 288
Montélimar, 169, 175
Montmartre, 250
Morel, Lola, 105–6, 111
Morocco, 2, 20–1, 127
Moulin, Jean, 128–9, 131, 146
Muhammad, Prophet, 61, 124
multiculturalism, 21, 37, 69, 76, 103, 174
Muray, Philippe, 61
Murray, John, 225, 227, 281

Muslims, 20–1, 60, 63, 70, 112, 138, 142, 144, 166, 180–3, 190, 195, 221, 259, 274, 277
see also Islamists

Nairn, Ian, 290
Nantes, 47–8, 245
Naples, 176, 275–6
Napoleon Bonaparte, 162, 226, 293
Napoleon III, Emperor, 227, 235–6
Napoleonic Wars, 225
Nasser, Gamal Abdel, 184
Nazi Germany 51
Nemmouche, Mehdi, 38
neo-Nazis, 35–6, 79, 134, 173
neo-Pétainists, 136
nervis, 250
New Statesman, 75
New York Times, 21
Nicaragua, 168, 170
Nice, 172, 177–8, 200, 203, 227, 229
Nietzsche, Friedrich, 203–4
Nin, Anaïs, 96
Nobel Prize in Literature, 185, 188
Northern Soul, 244
Notre-Dame de Fidélité, 194

Obertone, Laurent, 65–8, 80
Olive, Jean-Baptiste, 228
Olympique de Marseille (OM), 241, 245–6, 248–9, 256, 282–4
Olympique Lyonnais, 282–3
Onfray, Michel, 60, 69
Orange, 226
orientalism, 278
Orphelin, Matthieu, 53
Orwell, George, 9, 38, 79, 94, 146, 268
 'How the Poor Die', 106
les oubliés, 76, 83
Ournac, Laurent, 165

pacoulins, 222
Pagnol, Marcel, 256
Palestine, 181

Pamuk, Orhan, 276
Papillons, Noirs, 246
Parcoursup, 110–11
Paris, terrorist attacks, 3, 39, 59, 98
Paris–Roubaix cycle race, 42–3
Paris Saint-Germain (PSG), 23
Parker, Charlie, 168
Parly, Florence, 58
Parti Socialiste, 35–6, 117
pataouète, 183
Paty, Samuel, 61–2, 64
Pavy, Louis-Antoine-Augustin, 234
pays réel, 115
Péguy, Charles, 79–80
Peiresc, Nicolas-Claude Fabri de, 278–9
Peisson, Edouard, 281
Pépé le Moko, 274
Percy, Thomas, 109
Périot, Jean-Gabriel, 85
'peripheral France', 6, 44, 52, 81, 223
Pernety, 45, 74, 287–96
Perreau, Louis, 105
Philippot, Florian, 40, 77
Philosophie magazine, 78
Phocaeans, 232–3, 241–2, 246, 249
Picasso, Pablo, 73
pieds-noirs, 43–4, 63, 134, 183–4, 190, 234–5
pigeons, 11, 41–2
pizzas, 176, 231–2
ploucs, 7, 32
Pompeius Trogus, 249
Popular Front, 107
Pothion, Eric, 107–8
Poulain, Alain, 62–4
Poulain, Henri, 269
Poulain, Laurence, 63–4
Powell, Lawrence Clark, 119–20
Préfet (the office), 54
Presley, Elvis, 173
Prix Goncourt, 146
proleophobie, 23
prostitutes, 93, 95, 104, 136, 251, 281
Proudhon, Pierre-Joseph, 148

Proust, Marcel, 73
Provençal dialect, revival of, 203
Provence–Alpes–Côte d'Azur
    (PACA) region, 43–4
Prud'hon, Pierre-Paul, 98
pudeur, 100–1, 135, 188–9, 214
Puitspelu, Nizier du, 151
Pujol, Philippe, 265–70, 275, 278

Rabain, Michel, 172–6
racism, 23–4, 30, 32, 39, 57, 82, 85,
    89, 103, 118, 128, 136, 173, 273
Radio Gazelle, 260
Raï music, 281
Raspail, Jean, 66
Rebeyne, 139, 149
Rebsamen, François, 117
Reconquête, 75
Red Brigades, 206
règlements de compte, 255
Reims, 80–90, 124, 136
Renaissance party, 117
Republican calendar, 148
'reurbanization', 82
Ricciotti, Rudy, 236
Rieu, Damien, 75
ringard, 243–4
Rivière, Jérôme, 75
RN, 8, 40, 43, 60, 78, 80, 83, 291–3
Robillard, Hélène, 31–3
rockabilly, 173–4, 176
Roma, 260, 290
Ronis, Willy, 216
Roubaix, 17–22, 30–4, 37–44, 46, 52,
    86, 163, 295
  Musée de la Piscine, 34–5
routes impériales, 162
routes nationales, 163
Rude, François, 104
Rumney, Ralph, 12, 197–9, 204–11,
    213–15, 217, 223, 228
Rushdie, Salman, 112

Sabiani, Simon, 250
Sade, Marquis de, 120, 212–14

Said, Edward, 278
St Bartholomew's Massacre, 87
Saint-Baume *massif*, 195
Saint-Paul-lez-Durance, 194
Saint-Tropez, 172, 177
salons de thé, 89
Santiags, 173, 176
Sarrazin, 195
Sartre, Jean-Paul, 83–4
saunerié, 196
Scève, Maurice, 124
Schiff, Sydney and Violet, 73
Schonberg, Bernard, 133
Second World War, 41, 43, 73–4, 119,
    125, 128–30, 134, 137, 153, 208
Segobrigii, 249
Serre, 240
Shakespeare, William, 87
Sidos, François, 134
Sidos, Pierre, 134, 136
Silva, Julio, 171
Simondo, Piero, 210
Situationists, 198–9, 206–12, 217
Smith, Patti, 24
le souverainisme, 69
Spirito, François, 250
Stein, Gertrude, 152
Stendhal, 147
Sterne, Laurence, *Tristram Shandy*,
    110
Stevenson, Robert Louis, 281
Stil, André and Odette, 170
Storming of the Bastille, 88
Stravinsky, Igor, 73
Suez Canal, 233
Swinburne, Algernon Charles, 109
Symeoni, Gabriele, 124

Taha, Rachid, 174
Tangier, 127–8, 277
Taubira, Christiane, 66
teachers, 61–4
tear gas, 2
TGV, 178, 229
Thatcher, Margaret, 19

Thiercelin, Jean and Raquel, 240
Thomazeau, François, 243–52, 273
Thomazeau, Marcel, 245
Todd, Olivier, 182–3
Toklas, Alice B., 152
Tolstoy, Leo, 104
Toulon, 175
Tour de France, 244
Touria, Madame, 221
Trenet, Charles, 162–3
les Trentes Glorieuses, 111, 163
Trocchi, Alexander, 205
Turgenev, Ivan, 104

unemployment, 7, 11, 23, 30, 32, 38, 82, 107, 223, 244, 259, 265
university system, 105–11
urban development, 6–7

Valeurs actuelles, 21, 34, 68, 75
　lettre des généraux, 57–9, 61
Valls, Manuel, 134
Van der Meersch, Maxence, 22
Vargas Llosa, Mario, 168
variété shows, 11
Verlaine, Paul, 80
Vetter, Gérard, 166
Veyvret, Clothilde, 135–6

Vézelay, 229
Viannay, Matthieu, 152
Vietnam War, 168, 170
villages perchés, 216
vin blanc-cassis, 120
Virgin Mary, 126, 140
Voland, Antoine, 196
Voland, Madeleine, *la pudique*, 196
Voltaire, 47
voyous, 267–8

Wagner, Richard, 273
wars of religion, 86
Waterloo, Battle of, 226
Waugh, Evelyn, 251
Wertenschlag, Richard, 133–4
White, Edmund, 204, 276
Whitman, Walt, 204, 276–7
Wilson, Tony, 199
Wolman, Gil, 210
woollen industry, 18

Young, Arthur, 12, 46–7, 87–8, 97–8, 156, 224–5, 282

Zemmour, Eric, 75–6, 78–9, 81
Zionism, 181
Zlatin, Sabine, 131